684040636734

D1635556

**Anthony Peake** studied sociology and history at the University of Warwick and completed a post-graduate management qualification at the London School of Economics and Political Science. He is a member of the Society for Psychical Research, the Scientific and Medical Network and the International Association of Near-Death Studies. A prolific author, he has written two previous titles for Watkins. His books have been translated into a number of languages including French, Russian, Spanish and Polish.

ANTHONY PEAKE

# OPENING THE DOORS OF PERCEPTION

## THE KEY TO COSMIC AWARENESS

Foreword by Whitley Strieber

WATKINS

Sharing Wisdom Since
1893

This edition first published in the UK and USA 2016 by
Watkins, an imprint of Watkins Media Limited
19 Cecil Court
London WC2N 4EZ

enquiries@watkinspublishing.com

Design and typography copyright © Watkins Media Limited 2016

Text copyright © Anthony Peake 2016

1 3 5 7 9 10 8 6 4 2

Typeset by Manisha Patel

Printed and bound in Finland

A CIP record for this book is available from the British Library

ISBN: 978-1-78028-908-3


www.watkinspublishing.com

'If the doors of perception were cleansed everything would appear to man as it is, Infinite.'

William Blake

# Contents

# FOREWORD

Anthony Peake has been on a long and captivating journey from the conclusions he drew in his first book *Is There Life After Death* to those he now draws in *Opening the Doors of Perception*.

*Is There Life After Death* proposed that the brain, at the point of dying, produced a flood of glutamate, which slowed down time perception and allowed it to carry out the life review commonly reported by those who have survived a journey to the edge of death.

However, over the subsequent years of research and writing, he has gradually come to believe that the brain is a transceiver rather than the exclusive generator of consciousness. In the current volume, he explores the possibility that consciousness not only exists outside of the brain, but that it is a universality of which the individual is a part and, holographically, the whole.

Here, Peake explores the nature of this external consciousness and our role in it, with fascinating and extremely provocative results. He references the proposal by Nick Bostrom that was put forward in his groundbreaking 2003 article in *Philosophical Quarterly* 'Are You Living in a Computer Simulation,' now known as the 'simulation argument,' and also David Chalmers' famous 'hard problem' in which he stipulates that science cannot determine how the brain could generate self-referential consciousness.

He addresses the fact that recent discoveries by a scientific group at Fermilab in Batavia, Illinois, suggest that the universe is made up of digital information – that it is, as David Bohm and others have previously speculated, a huge hologram. Other recent studies further suggest that it is a two-dimensional surface and that what we perceive as reality is that hologram, projected into three dimensions.

Beginning with the proposition that Orchestrated Objective Reduction, which argues that the brain is essentially a biological machine that filters consciousness, which originates outside of it, Peake embarks on what I see as a groundbreaking exploration of perception and its substrate, consciousness.

Peake addresses the issue of the location of consciousness by analyzing the unusual brain states that give rise to distorted – or revelatory – perceptions, ranging from migraine through autism to schizophrenia and Alzheimer's disease. These various illnesses, by the different ways they distort perception, also open a door to what is actually happening not only to those beset by them, but to all of us.

I am, for personal reasons, particularly interested in all this. In 1985 I began having what has become a lifetime of close encounter experiences. But what were they, really? What are they? Among my initial theories was that I was a victim of the seizure disorder known as temporal lobe epilepsy. Yet when I not only tested negative for this, but was found to have an unusually seizure-resistant brain, I was left at a loss.

While *Opening the Doors of Perception* does not solve the mystery of experiences such as mine, it does offer a possible direction for further study, which involves looking at the brain as a filter, and attempting to discover what it is filtering and why.

For somebody with a life experience like mine, *Opening the Doors of Perception* is a rich resource for expanding and deepening the question of what is actually happening that causes the extraordinary perceptions that have become my life experience. For example, I not only engage regularly with what appear to be aliens; like so many people who do this, I also engage with the dead.

Since my wife's passing in August 2015, this has become a profound journey, filled with complex witness to her presence involving myself and others that leave me unable to believe that some aspect of her being does not still exist.

In *Opening the Doors of Perception*, Anthony Peake points out that the belief – and it is no more than that, a belief – so general among scientists and many academics, that there can be no consciousness outside of biological structure, is an insufficiently robust explanation for who we are, where we are and what we are.

This book not only opens the doors to perception, its careful attention to scholarship and exceptional intellectual clarity throws them wide open.

—Whitley Strieber
Author of *Communion* and co-Author with Dr Jeffrey Kripal of *Super Natural: A New Vision of the Unexplained*

# INTRODUCTION

## The Doors of Perception

Weyburn is a small town in Saskatchewan, Canada. It is around 70 miles from the provincial capital, Regina, and just over 40 miles north of the USA border. With the exception of the fact that it is a major railway junction for the province, the only other fact of note about Weyburn is that it was, until 2006, the location of the Souris Valley Mental Health Hospital, an institution opened in 1921 which was, at that time, the largest building in the British Empire. At its peak it was home to around 2,500 patients. For decades it had an outstanding reputation as one of the most advanced hospitals in the world with regard to the experimental treatment of individuals with mental disabilities. This reputation attracted some of the world's top researchers in the field of mental illness. One such researcher was the British psychiatrist Humphry Osmond. In 1951, with his associate John Smythies, Osmond had moved to this isolated community with the intention of using the facilities to understand if the similarities between early-stage schizophrenia and the psychological states created by substances such as LSD (lysergic acid diethylamide) were more than a simple coincidence: could something of significance be learned from them and used in a search for a cure? Osmond was aware that he would be allowed considerable freedom to conduct experiments on human subjects under carefully controlled conditions.

Osmond and Smythies, together with a biochemist, Abram Hoffer, worked almost exclusively with alcoholics. They were all both pleased and surprised at how successful their research was. After being treated with LSD, between 40 per cent to 45 per cent of subjects had not returned to drinking after a year. The team were also delighted by the results of their work with schizophrenics. In April 1952 Osmond and Smythies published a controversial paper asserting that schizophrenia may be caused by the body creating its own hallucinogenic compounds. A hallucinogen is a chemical substance that can change how the brain functions and, in doing so, can bring about increased or decreased sensory perceptions and generate hallucinations. Osmond and Smythies advocated that in order to treat schizophrenics effectively, physicians and psychiatrists need to experience the schizophrenic world for themselves, adding that 'this is possible to do quite simply by taking mescaline'.[1]

This paper can reasonably be considered to be one of the most influential academic papers to impact on modern popular culture. Quite by chance it was to come to the attention of the USA-based British author, Aldous Huxley. Huxley had long been interested in the power of hallucinogenic substances and in 1931 had written a novel, *Brave New World*, in which the citizens of the future consume *soma*, a substance that facilitates a 'holiday' from everyday reality. At the time of writing, Huxley was somewhat negative about such substances: he had once described hallucinogenic drugs as 'treacherous and harmful ... they kill first the soul and then the body'.[2] However, in 1962 in his last novel, *Island*, he takes a totally different approach. In this book the inhabitants of the fictional island of Pala use a drug called 'moksha' for spiritual and mystical insights. Like *Brave New World's soma*, moksha was based upon a known hallucinogenic substance, mescaline. However, moksha is presented in a hugely positive light: it is a substance that facilitates enlightenment rather than one that poisons the soul. What had changed so radically Huxley's opinion of hallucinogens? The answer is a simple one: in 1931 Huxley had no personal knowledge of such substances but by 1962 he had experienced many times the particularly powerful hallucinogen referenced by Osmond and Smythies in their 1952 paper and had become convinced that this substance could facilitate the opening of human consciousness to a much wider experiential universe.

In 1937 Huxley had moved to California and become heavily involved in Eastern mysticism. In 1945 he wrote *The Perennial Philosophy*, a book that presented a series of quotations from mystics, sages and saints across the centuries, each of which suggests an inner truth within all religious and mystical traditions: a 'perennial philosophy'. In effect this 'truth' is that all consciousness is a singularity and that the reality that is presented to us by our senses is an illusion, known as *maya*. All things are simply aspects of the Divine.

It was at this time that Huxley first heard of the power of a substance called peyote, and its derivative, mescaline. His involvement with the Indian mystic school of Vedanta had changed his opinions regarding altered states of consciousness, for he now saw these to be ways of encountering the Divine within. He had also heard that mescaline created amazing hallucinations and seemed to improve a person's ability to see colours and shapes. Acutely aware that his eyesight was deteriorating, he was keen to find ways to facilitate visual experiences. But the problem was how to acquire some mescaline and how to try it under controlled and safe conditions.

This problem was solved in spring 1952 when Huxley read Osmond and Smythies' article. He contacted Osmond and asked if he could assist him in trying out mescaline. He suggested that maybe Osmond and Smythies would like to join him at the upcoming American Psychiatric Association's conference in Los Angeles in early May 1953. At that stage Huxley was attempting to procure some mescaline from a doctor friend. This proved to be unsuccessful within the timescale, so Osmond agreed to bring with him from Canada 0.4gm of the hallucinogen.[3]

Huxley had long been interested in the theories of French psychologist Henri Bergson. Bergson had suggested that the brain acts as a limiting device, taking out much of the information available to consciousness. Huxley argued that this 'filter' gives attention only to those inputs that are necessary for, as he termed it, 'biologically profitable channels'.[4] Disease, mescaline, emotional shock, aesthetic experiences and mystical enlightenment can all have the effect of inhibiting this corrective action and, again as Huxley stated, 'permitting the "other world" to rise into consciousness'. He was hopeful that his filters would be suitably inhibited.

A few days later Osmond dissolved the mescaline crystals in a glass of water and gave it to Huxley. In a letter to Harold Raymond, his editor at the publishers Chatto and Windus, written on 21 June 1953, the writer described his subsequent experience:

> It is without any question the most extraordinary and significant experience available to human beings this side of the Beatific Vision; and it opens up a host of philosophical problems, throws intense light and raises all manner of questions in the fields of aesthetics, religion, theory of knowledge ...[5]

Huxley had already started to write up his experiences in a long essay. A year later this appeared as a short book entitled *The Doors of Perception*.

The title was carefully chosen: it is taken from William Blake's poem *The Marriage of Heaven and Hell*:

> If the doors of perception were cleansed everything would appear to man as it is, Infinite.
> For man has closed himself up, till he sees all things thro' narrow chinks of his cavern.

And this is exactly what the mescaline experience did for Huxley: it cleansed the doors of perception and allowed him to experience the universe the way it really is, rather than how it is presented by the senses. In the book he creates a concept that he terms 'Mind at Large', with regard to which he acknowledges a debt to the philosopher C D Broad and, in turn, Henri Bergson. Expounding his 'theory', he writes:

> ... each one of us is potentially Mind at Large. But in so far as we are animals, our business is at all costs to survive. To make biological survival possible, Mind at Large has to be funnelled through the Reducing Valve of the brain and nervous system. What comes out at the other end is a measly trickle of the kind of consciousness which will help us to stay alive on the surface of this particular planet.[6]

This idea that the brain acts as a filter for sensory experience does not conform with the general view. We tend to assume that the brain simply presents the outside world to consciousness 'as it is'; and that what we perceive is a literal re-creation of what is 'out there'. It may come as a surprise that this viewpoint is termed 'naïve realism' by modern experts in consciousness studies. By this they are suggesting that we are fooled by the brain into believing that what we see, hear and feel is an accurate facsimile of the real universe. Neurologist Robin Carhart-Harris suggests that 'a lot of brain activity is actually dedicated to keeping the world very stable and ordinary and familiar and unsurprising'.[7] In other words, the normally-functioning brain's role is to *protect us* from the universe as it really is. Hallucinations, it seems, are glimpses of the real universe we experience when the Huxleyan 'reducing valve' is switched off, or at least turned down.

## Through a Mirror Darkly

I have called this book *Opening the Doors of Perception* because I believe that the time has come to re-evaluate the model of perception suggested by Huxley and to view it through the lens of our modern science and, more importantly, to evaluate the evidence taking into account how the web, virtual reality and holographics have changed forever the way we appreciate the external world. I hope to present a model of 'reality' that will totally support what Huxley wrote all those years ago. As with all my books. this will be a journey of mutual discovery. Along the way I will point out sights and scenes that I found of interest on my first exploration of this territory. These may seem rather random but they do have a purpose. However, as with all journeys I think it is important that we have a map of the territory so we know where we are going and why.

In my book *The Daemon* I introduced the idea that human consciousness is split into two independent foci of self-aware consciousnesses. I call these the Daemon and the Eidolon.

I subsequently proposed that Daemonic consciousness is embodied in the non-dominant hemisphere of the brain and Eidolonic consciousness in the dominant hemisphere. In this book I will be presenting a revised model: this will be introduced later. However, for clarity I plan to continue using this structure until I am ready to introduce the revised model.

Thus, effectively we have two distinct areas of awareness within the human brain. The Eidolonic perceives only the information that has been heavily censored by the Huxleyan 'reducing valve', whereas the Daemonic receives all that is available and in doing so perceives the universe as it really is, a multi-dimensional reality known for centuries by the term 'Pleroma'.

*Pleroma* is Greek for 'fullness' and has been used for at least 2,000 years to describe the universe hidden from human perception. It symbolizes a state of completeness rather than deficiency, and in this way suggests perfectly how Huxley's 'reducing valve' takes away most of the 'fullness' and in doing so allows us to focus exclusively on the immediate needs of survival.

However, the power of the 'reducing valve' can be affected by various factors, including illness and differing neurological configurations within the brain. I believe that there is a spectrum of perception that runs from 100 per cent Eidolonic to 100 per cent Daemonic and that all conscious beings sit at one point or another along this continuum. In effect, this is a reflection of just how 'open' are the doors of communication between the right and left hemispheres. In this book I will present evidence for this spectrum – which in honour of Aldous Huxley and his pioneering work I should like to term the 'Huxleyan spectrum'.

This book is presented in three sections. Part One I have called 'The Key'. This discusses evidence that there is a wider perceptual universe that is denied Eidolonic consciousness. I present circumstances in which, for a short period of time, the effects of the reducing valve can be overridden and a tiny glimpse of the Pleroma can be gained by the Eidolon. Part Two, entitled 'At the Doorway', discusses how a series of neurological conditions can facilitate longer glimpses of the Pleroma. These include classic migraine, temporal lobe epilepsy, schizophrenia, Alzheimer's disease and autism. I suggest that all these neuroatypical 'illnesses' are part of what I call the Huxleyan spectrum. Part Three is entitled 'Glimpses Through the

Doors' and, as the name implies, describes in detail the experiences of a handful of individuals who have gone through the 'entrance' and perceived the Pleroma with varying degrees of clarity. I then finish off the book by pulling together what we have learned and presenting to you a hypothetical model of what may be actually taking place.

First, I would like to expand a little on the territory. So pull on your intellectual walking boots and join me in taking our first faltering steps ...

PART ONE:

# THE KEY

# CHAPTER ONE:

# Hallucinations

What is our location? The view from the I.

The only thing I know with absolute certitude is that I am something perceiving something. There seems to be a world out there beyond my body that I can interface with by moving my body within what seems to be a consistent three-dimensional space. I also seem to move through time, which really is defined by things around me, including my body, moving from a state of order to a state of disorder. With regard to my body, this process is known as ageing; and it happens in time. Other objects and entities that exist within the three-dimensional space also seem to have this gradual deterioration. However, the parts of my body that I can see seem more part of this external world than of the internal world that involves 'me'. This inner something looks out through my eyes and in some mysterious way wills my body to take certain actions. These may involve my manipulation of my immediate environment by picking things up, moving them around, or putting them together to create new configurations of objects. I can also will my body to stand up, and by use of my legs I can move within the three dimensions of space. When I move from one location to another, my viewpoint changes and I see external objects from a different angle. This suggests to me that this outside environment has an existence independent of my perception of it. If I close my eyes and open them again, everything in my visual field is where I expect it to be. I am also aware of other beings who exist within this world. In general terms, many of them look like me. They also move around in this world and seem to perceive it in the same way that I do. They react to stimuli in the same way. I can also communicate with these other beings; and they will, if they feel so inclined, respond to me. I do this by using my lungs to expel air and make certain vocalizations. These vocalizations leave my mouth and create vibrationary waves in the air around me. These waves enter the ears of those around me and cause their eardrums to vibrate. This vibration is converted into an electric signal and sent to a part of their brains where it is perceived as a series of sounds. Without eardrums to detect them, these sounds do not exist except as air vibrations. But eardrums allow the sounds to be detected and their meaning interpreted, according to our mutual understanding of their significance. In this way I can conclude that these other beings are similar to me and that they similarly perceive the world. I can use these mutually understandable vocal sounds to share information with them regarding my perceptions.

What is the 'I' that is doing the perceiving? This seems to be the focal point of all these stimuli. Indeed, it is the receiver and processor of the information. However, this point of self-aware consciousness seems to exist in a place removed from the physical world – though by the same token I must, in some way, be created from elements within the physical world.

Our present scientific paradigm is based on a very simple but powerful philosophy: the idea that by breaking anything down to its constituent

13

elements, we can understand how it works. For example, by breaking an automobile engine down into its bits and pieces, a person with a basic understanding of engineering, chemistry and physics will be able to understand how that automobile engine can create movement and speed. A biologist with knowledge of chemistry and chemical processes can take a plant apart and understand how the plant metabolizes energy from sunlight. This process of breaking things down to understand how they function – known as materialist reductionism – is the most powerful contribution Western science has made to our understanding of the universe. Physical objects can be reduced to their constituent parts and thereby give up their secrets. This has worked well over the last three or four hundred years. However, there is one thing that is immanent in the world that defies such reductionism, and that is because it is non-material and therefore cannot lend itself to a reductionist analysis. That something is what, as I read back these words, is processing them from shapes on a page or computer screen into images and ideas. It is central to each and every one of us. It is called self-referential consciousness.

Our technology is sufficiently advanced for us to be able to monitor the brain and, in doing so, we can isolate what parts of the brain do what. Modern techniques such as PET scans, CAT scans and other sophisticated instruments can show exactly what parts of the brain light up when certain actions are considered or certain perceptions or emotions are perceived. Radical surgery and brain injuries have shown us where memory is processed (but not where it is stored) and how personality can be changed by damage to certain areas of the brain. However, all this provides us with just an overview. It does not tell us how self-referential consciousness is created. There is something in my head that looks out on the world. It has memories, hopes, fears, loves, hates, ambitions and many other traits. It is self-aware and is keen to understand itself and where it has come from. How can I 'be'?

Let us try and apply the materialist-reductionist model to the brain in an attempt to find consciousness. We need to break down the brain into its basic building blocks.

If you look at a section of brain matter, you will discover that it is composed of neurons, or nerve cells. At birth the brain contains around 100 billion of these cells. Each neuron has a cell body and tens of thousands of tiny branches called dendrites. These dendrites receive information from other neurons. Each neuron also has what is called a primary axon; this is a projection that can travel great distances across the brain. Each neuron makes contact with each other neuron at a point known as the synapse. The neurons do not actually come into contact with each other. At each synapse is a tiny gap between one neuron and its neighbour. These 'synaptic gaps' are extremely short, about 200 to 300 angstroms across (one angstrom equals one hundred millionth of a centimetre: hence we are close to the atomic scale of dimensions here). Messages are transferred across the brain via these synapses. Depending upon what you are thinking, certain synapses transfer electric current in the form of calcium ions. This is called 'firing'. Some synapses will fire and others will not. So, in a way that is rather similar to traffic lights set on either red or green, the flow of messages across your brain can be channelled in various directions.

At the end of each synapse is a receptor site. These sites are of many different types and each one is designed to work with one of a number of internally generated chemicals known as neurotransmitters. There are two types of neurotransmitter, since they can be excitatory or inhibitory. In simple terms, the excitatory variety stimulates the brain to do something and the inhibitory variety calms it down. Over 100 of these have now been identified. The major excitatory neurotransmitters are glutamate, norepinephrine and epinephrine. With regards to the inhibitory variety, gamma-aminobutyric acid (GABA) and serotonin are the major players. Those that bring about a response at the adjoining receptor site are technically known as agonists; and those that block a response are known as antagonists. Of special relevance to this book, is that there is another major neurotransmitter, which facilitates both excitatory and inhibitory responses in neighbouring receptor sites. This substance is known as dopamine.

So what have we found? An amalgamation of inanimate molecules reacting to a sea of similarly inanimate electrons: in other words, chemistry reacting with electricity. It seems that the best answer we can find is that consciousness is an 'epiphenomenon' of brain processes. It just 'kind of happens' at some point when a crucial level of complexity is reached. By the addition of one more process, one more molecule, one more electron, consciousness just pops out of nowhere. This reminds me of the cartoon by Sidney Harris in which two scientists stand in front of a blackboard. On one side of the blackboard is a mass of mathematical notation, matched by a similar mass of mathematical notation on the other side. Linking them are the words, 'Then a miracle occurs'. The older scientist points at the comment and says to the creator of the formulae: 'I think you should be more specific here in step two.'

There is a growing band of scientists who believe that the only viable explanation of how inanimate molecules and electrical impulses can be responsible for a self-referential consciousness is that the brain does not 'create' consciousness, it 'receives' it. This is analogous to a radio or TV receiver. The source of the TV programme viewed on the screen is not inside the back of the TV – in the same way that the radio announcer is not in the radio. An even better analogy is the location of the Internet. It is not located in your computer hard drive but is supplied on a need/demand basis. It exists in an informational 'field' that surrounds us. This radical model is known as 'Orchestrated Objective Reduction', and it was proposed as a specific response to a famous question raised by Australian philosopher David Chalmers.

Chalmers argued that with regard to consciousness there are two problems. The first is understanding how the brain actually works, its neurochemistry and its physiology. This is what Chalmers calls the 'soft problem'. By this he means that our present scientific paradigm has the tools to eventually crack this mystery. However, solving the soft problem will supply us only with an overview. We will be no closer to knowing how self-referential consciousness is created. The question *How can I 'be'?* confronts us still.

Chalmers calls this question the 'hard problem'. It demands answers regarding the true nature of the recipient of this brain-presented information – the entity inside the head that reacts to and evaluates these stimuli.

Arizona-based aneasthetist Professor Stuart Hameroff believes that the answer to Chalmers's 'hard problem' may be related to another neurological mystery: how do anaesthetics actually work? Although we know which particular chemicals can be used to bring about an apparent cessation of consciousness within the brain, science cannot tell us *why* this occurs. Given his profession, Hameroff had been long intrigued by this. After much research he concluded that the loss of consciousness is brought about when an anaesthetic impairs the functioning of small structures in the brain known as microtubules. These tiny rod-like assemblies act as scaffolding for the neurons, the cells that make up the brain. The number of microtubules in the human brain is truly staggering. The brain, with its approximately $10^{11}$ neurons, has $10^{18}$ microtubule units. This is 10 followed by eighteen zeros – in other words, approximately a 'quintillion' of these tiny structures can be found in the average human brain. Hameroff believed that in some way microtubules are responsible for the generation of consciousness, and that anaesthetics effectively switch them off. In the same way that switching off a TV effectively prevents it from processing the signal: switching off the microtubules prevents them from processing consciousness. If this is the case, then consciousness exists somewhere other than the brain, just as a TV signal exists outside the receiver.

Hameroff then became intrigued by the ideas of British mathematical physicist Roger Penrose. He had read Penrose's book *The Emperor's New Mind*, in which Penrose postulated that consciousness is created by processes observed in quantum physics. This was the idea Hameroff needed to make his microtubule model work. He contacted Penrose and suggested a collaboration. Penrose agreed. Two years later, in 1996, the two researchers published a paper that introduced to the world something they called 'Orchestrated Objective Reduction' (ORCH OR).[1] In this Penrose and Hameroff argued that quantum vibrational computations in microtubules were 'orchestrated' by synaptic inputs and memory data stored in the microtubules.

Not surprisingly, this theory was heavily criticized at the time, and continues to be so, by those wedded to a strongly materialist-reductionist model of reality. The very mention of 'consciousness' in connection with quantum physics brings about a shower of criticism of which the Spanish Inquisition would have been proud. But over the years there has been mounting evidence (carefully ignored by the mainstream) that ORCH-OR may be a working model that is worth further enquiry and research. The initial criticism, by Max Tegmark, was that the brain is simply too 'warm, wet and noisy' for delicate quantum processes. However, it has now been discovered that plant photosynthesis involves quantum coherence, as does the amazing ability of birds to navigate by sensing electromagnetic fields, and even, surprisingly, our sense of smell.

Another research team, at the University of Pennsylvania, have also offered an explanation for the mystery of how anaesthetics selectively erase consciousness; and, again, this involves microtubules.[2] Such research shows that there is growing evidence that looking for the location of consciousness in the brain creates, in effect, a 'hard problem', because mainstream scientists are looking in the wrong place. It is like taking apart a TV set to find the actors and the studio. However thoroughly one 'reduces' the 'material' in the TV set, taking apart its components or breaking them down to their molecular structure, the actors and studio will continue to elude detection. This is because they are not there, and never have been there.

So the 'something' doing the perceiving is not quite what it seems to be. I believe myself to be inside my head looking out at a solid, consistent world, because that is what my senses tell me. I feel that I exist a few centimetres behind my eyes and that I look out from that location. I can see my hands typing on the keyboard and I can turn to look outside the window of my study and see a typically grey English September day. But what did Huxley perceive that was so different on that late spring day in 1953? Was the far more intense world that his heightened senses presented to him a glimpse of the true nature of reality, or was it simply the chemical compound mescaline creating hallucinations?

## Hallucinations: The Facts

That we all experience two perceptual universes is fairly evident. The universe of waking experience is shared with others and takes place in a landscape that is consistent and seemingly solid. Others seem to agree with our own perceptions as to the objects within this space. The reason we believe this 'reality' to be 'real' is that others, by their own independent actions, confirm it. If I say to another person who shares my language, 'Look at that black dog next to the tree,' the person will look over and by their response or actions confirm that there is, indeed, a black dog next to a tree. I have shared the same visual experience with somebody else, and in doing so I have confirmed it as coinciding with actual fact. This makes the event veridical. It also makes it consensual, in that both myself and my associate have agreed that there is a dog standing next to a tree. A reality

19

confirmed by such a process is known as 'consensual reality'. An optical illusion, although not consistent with normal perceptual reality, can be shared by others and is therefore, by definition, 'consensual'.

Some philosophers have long argued that all sensory experience is internal: the only way to differentiate between what is accepted as 'real' and what is categorized as an hallucination and therefore 'unreal' is that, with an hallucination, only the perceiver is aware of the perception.

However, imagery that is not stimulated from external sources (not brought about by electromagnetic stimulation of the retina) causes a real problem for our present scientific model. If there is an absence of light, then how can anything be 'seen'? Where do these 'images' come from and how are they processed? Are the visuals that accompany hallucinations using the same neurological constructs as normal vision, or are they created in a totally different way?

This area of investigation has been subject to a huge amount of controversy.[34] It is my intention here to review the history of research into visual imagery and perception. In doing so I hope to present evidence that they are simply aspects of the same phenomena.

The conventional belief regarding hallucinations is that they are very different from 'normal' perceptions. Normal perceptions present to consciousness an image of external reality that is an absolute and accurate depiction of what is 'out there' in the 'real' world. Hallucinations, on the other hand, are totally brain-generated. According to the *Oxford Companion to the Mind*, a hallucination is defined as a 'sensory perception in the absence of external stimuli'.[5]

This idea that hallucinations and normal perceptions are totally different is technically known as the 'dual process model', a concept first used by psychologists Charles McCreery and Celia Green. Green and McCreery created this model simply to reject it. They suggest that all waking perceptions and hallucinations are ontologically the same experience.

Green and McCreery argue that although the hallucination itself is created by the brain, it is seen as an object in consensual space. However, if this is the case, then we are presented with a huge problem. In order for somebody to 'see' a hallucinatory object in consensual space, then the part of consensual space obscured or occluded by the hallucination must be taken out of the visual field. An unintentional example of this is given by neuroscientist V S Ramachandran with regard to a young man called 'Larry' who developed powerful hallucinations after being injured in a car accident. During one session Larry announced that he could see a vivid, three-dimensional monkey, sitting on Ramachandran's lap:

> I don't know. But it is unlikely there would be a professor here with a monkey sitting on his lap so I think there probably isn't one. But it looks extremely vivid and real ... Also there is something odd about the images – they often look too good to be true.[6]

Larry could not see the parts of Ramachandran's lap that were obscured by the hallucinatory simian. In this case Green and McCreery would argue there must be two types of hallucination being created by the patient's brain; one of addition (the monkey) and one of subtraction (the loss of visual stimulus from the neurologist's lap). The latter is technically known as a 'negative hallucination', a failure to perceive something that exists in consensual space. However, things are more complex than this. The monkey is perceived by the patient to be animated and moving around. The area of consensual space negated by the hallucinatory process needs to change to reflect the differing areas occluded by the monkey's movements. There must be a one-to-one relationship between the areas excluded and the hallucinated movements of the monkey. This mystery happens with all hallucinations involving solid objects in consensual space.

In 1975 Green and McCreery proposed a solution to such problems. They suggested that the image of consensual reality that is presented to consciousness is also a brain-generated hallucination, just as a regular hallucination is. All of what is perceived through our senses is technically a hallucination. Green and McCreery argued that as all perceptions are hallucinations, then it is not surprising that one sort of hallucination can overlap another. They called this hallucinatory spectrum the 'metachoric model of hallucinations'.[7]

They argued that the brain, based upon the perceptions processed from data gleaned from consensual reality, can create a facsimile environment identical to that consensual reality. In this way Green and McCreery can explain a series of strange perceptual hallucinations such as out-of-body experiences (OBEs), lucid dreaming and near-death experiences. In each of these cases the experiencer senses that they are outside of their body, seemingly viewing the consensual world from another location. In NDEs and OBEs it is regularly reported that the subject can see themselves and actions going on around them. In lucid dreams the person becomes self-aware while in a dream state and can interact with that Daemonic world as if it were the consensual, Eidolonic world.

Modern neurology and psychology have an explanation for these experiences. The process by which a dream overlaps into what seems like consensual reality is known as 'REM (rapid eye movement) intrusion'. This is where the person is actually asleep and dreaming but a part of the brain is still awake and processing the sights and sounds of the external world. Any dream images are then projected into the external world and seem to be part of that world. In this way, a dream can seem to be 'real'. These images are usually accompanied by a bodily paralysis, known as 'sleep paralysis' for obvious reasons. When we sleep, the body protects itself from dream-induced bodily damage by stopping the dreamer acting out any physical actions they may wish to perform in the dream state – for example, hitting out at a dream attacker. If they were to mirror this hitting out by moving their arms, they might hurt themselves – or somebody in the bed with them. By paralysing the body in this way, the brain protects it. However, if one happens to become semi-conscious in such a state the sensation of paralysis can be frightening.

Green and McCreery argue that such 'visitations' present evidence for their metachoric model. People regularly report that during some REM intrusion states and regularly in general apparition encounters, the spectral figures give off a form of light. This light illuminates the environment around the figure. Now if the figure is a brain projection into a genuine consensual environment, how can its 'light' illuminate objects in the real world? In some cases the person describes how the whole bedroom was lit up by the spectral light. This is impossible in the dual process model but entirely feasible in the metachoric model. If all the scene, background environment and spectre are part of the same 'hallucination', then such illumination is perfectly possible.

Green and McCreery's model proposes that *all* perceptions are technically 'hallucinations'. However, there is a continuum between perception at one end and hallucination at the other. In a later paper McCreery considers that out-of-body experiences are located in an intermediate position along the continuum, as they seem to contain fantasy elements that suggest a limited conscious control.[8]

I would like to suggest that the metachoric model lends itself to the idea that reality is generated by a form of simulation analogous to that of a first-person computer game and that Green and McCreery's continuum is part of this simulation. In recent years there has been a growing number of scientists who believe that the universe works on digital or holographic principles. In effect, what this means is that consensual reality itself is an illusion and everything is simply digital information. Such information could create seemingly three-dimensional realities from non-physical data. One of the first to suggest this was cosmologist Frank J Tipler in his 1994 book *The Physics of Immortality: Modern Cosmology, God and the Resurrection of the Dead*. However, it was Oxford University philosopher Nick Bostrom who really popularized the idea in a hugely influential paper published in 2003.[9] In recent years this idea has been modified and elaborated upon by quantum physicists such as Vlatko Vedral in his 2012 book *Decoding Reality*.

Associated with the idea of a facsimile reality as suggested by the metachoric model is a phenomenon known as false awakenings. One of the most famous examples of this was experienced by the renowned and notoriously sceptical philosopher Bertrand Russell. He reported that after anaesthetic he appeared to wake up hundreds of times in succession.[10]

I was personally given an amazing example of this by one of my readers, Ash Gabbidon, who emailed after a most peculiar set of events a few years ago. Ash's experience was not quite like the many awakenings of Bertrand Russell. Ash described to me how it did happen multiple times but with this difference: each time he got further into his day, only to wake up again and go through the same experience.

What differentiates the false awakening environment from the consensual world is a sense of the uncanny that seems to permeate the atmosphere. In the Type 1 version the subject seemingly wakes from sleep in the location he went to sleep in. Type 2 involves him waking up in another location.

It is important to note that false awakenings convey a feeling of total reality, in that the ongoing point of view is always as it would be in the consensual world. The person sees the facsimile through their eyes, hears it through their ears and, one assumes, feels it through their sense of touch. It has to be this way, otherwise the person would quickly realize that it was a dream. Time flow also has to follow a standard pattern. Ash Gabbidon 'woke up' at least six times and by the end of the experience he had progressed through the day until the mid-afternoon. The question that demands to be asked here is, what is it about the final waking that leads the person to believe that they are back in consensual reality? It cannot be that the waking experience appears to be shared by others in a consensual way because in all the previous false awakenings the noumenal world similarly contained other people going about their business and, presumably, acting totally normally. But the evidence that makes us believe that phenomenal reality is not a facsimile involves the self-same cues that presumably fool us in the false awakening state.

We are very aware that time can extend greatly during dream states. This is suggested from Ash's false awakenings, each one lasting a longer period of time. By a rough calculation I suspect that Ash's nested dreams accounted for around 14 hours. Even assuming a one-to-one relationship between dream time and consensual time, Ash's experience was twice as long as he would have been sleeping. However, it is reasonable to conclude, on the basis of commonplace experience, that all the false awakening dreamlets took place in a hypnopompic state of around 20 minutes or less. Therefore, if time is a totally subjective construct as far as liminal sleep states are concerned, there is no reason why a whole day, week, month, year or even a lifetime could not be subjectively experienced in such a state. For the sake of argument, let me suggest that a waking dream could last for 16 hours, a normal 'waking day'. The person then goes to sleep in the waking dream and wakes up again, seven hours later in another waking dream. A person could live a whole life in this way.

Of course, such experiences are not rare at all. Over the centuries, if not the millennia, consciousness has been able to transcend the restrictions of Huxley's reducing valve. This has been done by people simply administering any of a great number of naturally occurring substances, which have evolved along with ourselves in plants and in other animal species. These substances are known under the collective term 'hallucinogens': chemical compounds that override Huxley's reducing valve effect.

Although it may be correct to assume that consciousness may exist outside of the brain in the same way a radio signal has as its source a radio transmitter rather than the radio receiver, we still need to understand how the 'receiver' functions, because hallucinations are still modulated by that receiver. We will now turn our attention to the chemicals that bring about the sense of embodiment.

## A Neurochemical Model?

Huxley was clearly amazed by his experiences that May day in 1953. His appreciation of the true nature of reality had been changed forever. His 'doors of perception' had been opened and a new universe of experience was available to him. But what had actually happened to him? We know that he took a substance known as mescaline, but what is mescaline and how could it change his perceptions so radically?

Mescaline, as I have said, is what is known as a 'hallucinogen'. This is a substance that can change how we perceive the world. In effect, these substances create 'hallucinations'. Mescaline is one of many substances that can do this: others include LSD (lysergic acid diethylamide), psilocybin and DMT (dimethyltryptamine). The generally used term to describe these substances is 'psychedelic', coined by Huxley and Osmond after the events of May 1953. So how can a naturally occurring psychedelic bring about such dramatic subjective experiences?

It seems reasonable to imagine that hallucinogens increase brain activity, in that they are adding sensations that are not part of the external world: the brain is working harder to create these illusions. But this has been discovered not to be the case. Research by Robin Carhart-Harris and his team at Imperial College London has shown that the changes in consciousness brought about by hallucinogens involve a *decrease* in brain activity.[11] It has also been discovered that hallucinogens actually seem to make the brain work in a more organized fashion than it does during 'normal' perception. Different areas of the brain work together in a more cooperative way. In other words, the brain is made to work more efficiently when it is under the influence of hallucinogens. This is the opposite of what the general public is given to believe, by the message that hallucinogens confuse the brain and make it malfunction. So is it reasonable to conclude that a more effective brain is one that perceives hallucinations? The implications here deserve to be emphasized. Our everyday brain is not functioning at its full potential. When it does so, hallucinations occur.

In the 1950s a series of experiments took place in which human subjects had electrodes placed in their brains and then they were given hallucinogens, specifically LSD and mescaline. Clearly such experiments would be ethically unacceptable now, but they have given us some interesting information about what parts of the brain these substances influence. It was discovered that the main area is the medial temporal lobe (MTL), specifically the hippocampus, the amygdala and the septal nuclei. Phasic discharges were recorded in these areas during periods of marked hallucinosis.[12] [13] This is significant because it is known that increased medial temporal lobe activity is a major characteristic of the rapid eye movement (REM) phase of sleep and therefore, by association, dreaming. Hence there is a link between the effects of hallucinogens and the phenomenon known as REM intrusion (see pp54-56) which is thought to be responsible for hypnagogic and hypnopompic experiences, out-of-body experiences, sleep paralysis and other non-induced 'hallucinations'. We will return to the significance of these curious brain states later.

Increased hippocampal activity has recently been shown to create 'dreamy states' in subjects.[14] We also know that electrical stimulation of the medial temporal lobes can bring about complex dream-like visions to waking subjects. These sound very similar to hypnagogics and hypnopompics. In 2014 researcher P Mere and his associates experimented with direct electrical stimulation of the parahippocampus and subjects reported 'melting faces' and other complex visual hallucinations. From my own experience of hypnopompic images, melting faces is a regular theme.[15]

If the brain is actually working more efficiently during the creation of so-called hallucinations, then it is logical to conclude that perceptions without hallucinations are created by a less efficient brain. I would like to suggest that hallucinogens open up the channels of communication between Eidolonic consciousness and Daemonic consciousness: they allow the Daemon to speak directly to the Eidolon. At other times hallucinogens have created a sensation that the subject is not alone and that there is some form of presence close by. This seems to be particularly the case in relation to the powerful hallucinogen called dimethyltryptamine (DMT).

DMT, and an associate substance 5-MeO-DMT, are powerful hallucinogens that bring about profound hallucinatory experiences. New Mexico-based psychiatrist Dr Rick Strassman has long been associated with research into the true nature of this intriguing chemical. In the early 1990s Strassman was involved in an extensive US Government-funded research project into the effects of the substance. In *DMT: The Spirit Molecule*, the book Strassman wrote after the project had been completed, he suggested that it was highly likely that DMT was active in the human brain, its source being the enigmatic pineal gland. Strassman believes that the pineal gland may actually create DMT for use as an endogenous (internally generated) neurotransmitter.

In February 2009 Strassman's suspicion that DMT was a possible human neurotransmitter was confirmed. University of Wisconsin-Madison pharmacologist Arnold Ruoho had a paper published in the academic periodical *Science*. In this Ruoho described how his team had discovered that a receptor known as sigma-1 was activated by DMT.[16] We shall return to the implications of this in much greater detail later.

It has been known for some time that DMT is biosynthesized from tryptamine by the actions of the enzyme INMT (indolethylamine

N-methyltransferase). The human variety of this substance was cloned and sequenced in 1999. High levels of INMT have been found in the thyroid and adrenal gland and the lung. However, within the central nervous system small amounts have been detected in the spinal cord but none in the brain itself. If DMT is synthesized from tryptamine by the actions of INMT, then INMT must be active in the human brain. Up until 2011 no evidence of INMT had been detected there.

However, in that year researchers at the University of Wisconsin-Madison published the results of an experiment suggesting that INMT is active in the human brain. Ruoho and his associate Nicholas Cozzi questioned the effectiveness of the standard detection technique used to isolate INMT, and pointed out that it is possible that this technique simply failed to detect INMT and its respective messenger RNA molecule. They subsequently found INMT in the retinal ganglion neurons and spinal cord of a rhesus macaque monkey. Of even greater significance was that INMT was also discovered in the primate's pineal gland.[17] Subsequent research managed to isolate the gene responsible for the enzyme's presence in the retina and the pineal gland.[18]

These results stimulated the interest of another researcher, Dr Steven Barker of the Analytical Systems Laboratory at Louisiana State University. Barker, together with his associate, Dr Jimo Borjigin of the University of Michigan, had previously discovered that neuronal activity was not only detected but actually increased in the brains of recently killed rats. Barker was so intrigued by this evidence of post-mortem brain activity that he embarked upon a series of tests to see if he could isolate what particular neurotransmitters were active at the time of the rats' spike in neurological activity. If this could be shown to be a particular neurochemical, then we might be a good deal closer to understanding the near-death experience. With funding from Rick Strassman's Cottonwood Research Foundation, Barker did a series of tests on the brain material and he succeeded in finding the presence of INMT. However, in doing so he made another, unexpected, discovery: he found direct evidence of DMT within the rodents' pineal glands. The discovery was subsequently published in an article that appeared in the academic journal *Biomedical Chromatography* in December 2013.[19]

For the time being one of the most intriguing elements of the DMT experience is how it generates in many of its subjects something called the 'sensed presence'. This is a physical sensation that somebody, or something, is close by – possibly even sharing the brain of the subject. I would like to suggest that DMT facilitates a subtle communication between Eidolonic and Daemonic consciousness. The Eidolon is suddenly made aware of the presence of its hidden partner and the fact that the Daemon can, for a few fleeting moments, communicate directly with its Pleroma-embodied associate. This can manifest within Eidolonic consciousness as simply a sensation of a presence or, in periods of extreme stress or danger, as an aural 'hallucination'. Continuing with our 'doors' analogy, it is as if the Daemon is shouting through the letterbox!

In my book *The Daemon: A Guide to Your Extraordinary Secret Self* I collected many examples of seemingly impossible skills manifested by these 'voices'. I would like to give one example here, sent to me by Alan Rumney. In 1969 Rumney was a member of the Rhodesian Army dealing with an insurgency in the north of the country near Mount Darwin. This is how he described what happened to him that fateful day:

> We rounded a bend, and then it happened. A 'voice', which seemed to come from inside my head, said to the effect, and very clearly, 'This is an ambush,' which put me on high alert, and almost immediately I spotted the telltale puffs of grey smoke on the left-hand verge of the road ahead, before I heard the rifle fire, and the vehicles ahead started taking evasive

action. Immediately I swung the machinegun to the left, and as I did so I suddenly found myself pulled quite violently and inexplicably forward, and found myself hanging sideways in the V-shield webbing, with a strange sensation in my left arm and hand. Looking around, I first noticed my bloody hand, and the rather awful sight of my left thumb hanging on by a thread of flesh. There was blood oozing out of my elbow and upper arm, and then it struck me: I had been shot several times.[20]

This 'inner voice' seemed to know what was about to happen next, and when Alan failed to respond it took action in physically pushing him away from the location that the bullets were about to hit in the very near future. How could the non-dominant hemisphere of the brain access such information? These incidents, although by their nature anecdotal, challenge the idea that such voices are simply the murmurings of the mind.

It must be stressed that these 'voices' are not heard in the usual way – that is, by sound waves hitting the eardrum. Their source is far more mysterious than any modern psychiatrist would have you believe. For example, if the non-dominant hemisphere has no verbal abilities, then how can it create words and language in order to 'communicate' with its dominant partner? The voice that saved Alan's life spoke to him in grammatically correct English, stating 'This is an ambush.' Alan did not *feel* the meaning of these words, he heard them.

And we still have to overcome one amazingly simple fact about Alan's experience. How did his 'inner voice', from whatever source, know that an ambush was about to take place? Alan was certainly totally unaware of this, and without the intervention of his 'sensed presence' would have been killed. This suggests precognition.

It has been regularly reported that the Amazonian psychedelic brew known as ayahuasca can bring about precognitive and telepathic experiences. In 1905 a traveller named Rafael Zerda Bayón suggested that ayahuasca was far more than just a hallucinogenic drug. He argued that one of the two active ingredients of ayahuasca could generate telepathic communication within the visions it placed in the mind of the subject. In recognition of the discovery, Bayón proposed that this active constituent should be called *telepathine*. This name was taken up by Colombian chemist Guillermo Fischer Cárdenas when in 1923 he successfully isolated the compound. Later this highly controversial name was changed to *yagéine* and then *banisterine*.

It is evident from Alan Rumney's experience, and those of many others, that the 'sensed presence' can break through without the facilitation of hallucinogens, and research taking place in Canada over recent years has suggested that the 'letterbox' can be created by non-invasive brain stimulation and also by naturally occurring environmental factors. Individuals whose 'doors' are opened in this way I call 'accidental tourists', and it is to their experiences we now turn our attention.

# CHAPTER TWO:

# Accidental Tourists

## Michael Persinger and his 'Sensed Presence'

Michael Persinger is an American-born neuroscientist based at Laurentian University in Sudbury, Canada. He has long had an interest in the neurological source of religious and mystical experiences and over the last 30 years or so has been involved in a series of fascinating experiments.

Persinger suggests a similar spectrum to myself with regards to religious and mystical experiences. He is convinced that such experiences are created by the temporal lobes. The sense of self in relation to time and space is located in the amygdaloid and hippocampal complexes. These structures are, in turn, areas that generate anxieties and fears. The amygdala also focuses on pleasure and pain. Collectively these parts of the brain also facilitate intense feelings of significance, or meaningfulness. The temporal lobes are also known as a strong site of brain plasticity whereby the neurological structures learn and adapt in response to stimuli. Persinger argues that all people have a potential to experience transient (for a few seconds) electrical displays within the temporal lobes. These microseizures are known as temporal lobe transients, or TLTs. For a time such seizures may bring about unusual perceptions. Because of the way in which the amygdaloid and hippocampal complexes place significance or meaningfulness onto experiences, together with an underlying sensation of dread or fear, it is not surprising that such perceptions will be interpreted in a mystical and profound light. In a paper published in 1983 Persinger argued that lost memories also could be evoked in these circumstances. As we shall discover later, another Canadian-based American, neurosurgeon Wilder Penfield, had similar results in the 1930s through to the 1950s. Persinger suggested that these evoked memories may go back to infancy or even earlier, and would create the 'sensed presence' of a parent as an ever-present god-like supplier of food, warmth and tactile comfort.[1] However, the infant brain would not be able to place this presence in any cognitive understanding of the world, and therefore its origins would be a mystery.

Persinger was aware in the early 1980s that such mystic experiences had been evoked by surgical stimulation – for example by Horowitz and Adams in 1970[2] and Pierre Gloor in 1972.[3] These researchers had created out-of-the-body sensations, auditory experiences such as rushing sounds, voices, and perceptual alterations such as looking down a tunnel or seeing spinning light patterns.

Persinger calls this phenomenon 'parasitic consciousness'. In order to understand what he means by this we need to appreciate that the human brain consists of two hemispheres. They are joined together by structures known as 'commissures'. There are five of these, by far the most important being the corpus callosum: Latin for 'thick-skinned body'. As we shall discover later, if this 'bridge' between the hemispheres is cut, then effectively all communication is lost between the two hemispheres, and two personalities are created. These hemispheres are not equal, since one is far more dominant than the other. For all right-handed people and a percentage of left-handers, the dominant one is the left, with a small minority of left-handed individuals having a dominant right hemisphere. In effect, the dominant hemisphere is where we all 'live'.

Persinger suspected that the sense of the other is brought about by magnetic fields giving the dominant hemisphere an awareness of its non-dominant partner. This is brought about by electromagnetic-facilitated bursts of electrical activity in the temporal lobes. These magnetic fields are created by radio transmissions, seismic activity and even solar flares. However, as the human brain also has its own electrical components, it could create these sensations neurologically. As we shall discover, it is bursts of electrical activity in the brain that bring about epileptic seizures, so it comes as no surprise that Persinger suggested that the sensed presence was created in neurotypicals by electromagnetically facilitated microseizures focused on the temporal lobes. Persinger believed these experiments suggested that the human sense of self has two components. In 1993 he published a paper in which he described this idea as the 'vectorial hemisphericity hypothesis'.[4]

He needed to find a way to artificially bring about these microseizures, so they could be observed and measured under laboratory circumstances. With an associate, Stanley Koren, he placed a pair of solenoids inside a modified snowmobile helmet. Each solenoid was located over each temporal lobe of the wearer. In simple terms a solenoid is a thin loop of wire wrapped round a metal core. When an electric current was passed through the wire, a magnetic field is generated. In this way Persinger was able to create an artificial electromagnetic stimulation of the temporal lobes and, hopefully, reproduce the 'sensed presence' at will. He soon embarked upon a series of controlled experiments and discovered that not only was the presence successfully evoked in at least 80 per cent of the volunteers who were subject to the process, but around one per cent claimed that they sensed 'God' in the room with them. This was picked up by the mass media, and the experimental apparatus was dubbed the 'God Helmet'.

In a later study, published in 2002, Persinger described how the team had exposed 48 volunteers to the pulsed magnetic fields. These volunteers were broken down into four groups. The first group had the magnetic field applied over their right temporoparietal region, the second group experienced the same effect over their left temporoparietal region and a third group had both areas stimulated. A fourth group were told that they were going to be exposed to the field but, unbeknown to them, they were the control group and no field was applied. Two-thirds reported a sensed presence. This is an interesting result, but also of significance was the fact that a third of the control group also experienced the presence.[5]

This suggests that when sensitive to the potential for a 'sensed presence', a significant minority of people become attuned to it. Persinger believes that his experiments vindicate his vectorial hemisphericity hypothesis.

Persinger reports that many of his subjects have experienced the visual hallucinations reported by Horowitz and Adams and by Gloor. These have involved flashing lights, vortices, mandalas, tunnels and voices. One subject, who received the field over both temporal lobes, described the following:

> I felt there was a bright white light in front of me. I saw a black spot that became a kind of funnel ... I felt moving, like spinning forward through it. I began to feel the presence of people, but I could not see them.[6]

Here we have another link with Rick Strassman's research, seen in this uncannily similar description recorded by one of his DMT volunteers:

First I saw a tunnel or channel of light off to the right. I had to turn to go into it. Then the whole process repeated on the left. It was intentional that way. It was as if it had a source, further away. It got bigger farther away, like a funnel. It was bright and pulsating. There was a sound like music, like a score, but unfamiliar to me, supporting the emotional tone of the events and drawing me in. I was very small. It was very large. There were large beings in the tunnel, on the right side, next to me. I had a sense of great speed ... Things were flashing, flashing by, as if from a different perspective. It was so much more real than life.[7]

Both these experiences have powerful echoes of two other phenomena: alien abductions and the near-death experience (NDE). We shall return to these later. For now I would like to focus on the shimmering lights and vortices experienced during these states. What can they tell us about how we may access the Pleroma?

## My Friend Flicker

In his journal dated 21 December 1958 artist Brion Gysin reported a very strange effect when he was riding on a bus one evening in the south of France. The bus was driving past an avenue of trees and Gysin could see the light of the sunset through them:

Had a transcendental storm of colour visions today in a bus going down to Marseille. We ran through a long avenue of trees and I closed my eyes against the setting sun. An overwhelming flood of intensely bright patterns in supernatural colours exploded behind my eyelids.[8]

Earlier that year Gysin had met American writer William Burroughs in Paris. They struck up a friendship and collaborated on many themes central to this book. For example, for many years Burroughs had been interested in yage (ayahuasca) and was keen to explore the implications of Rafael Zerda Bayón's contention that yage facilitated telepathic and precognitive abilities.

Gysin was fascinated by the flicker incident on the bus and he discussed the experience with Burroughs. Two years later, and quite by chance, Burroughs bought a book written by the eminent Anglo-American neurophysiologist W Grey Walter. In the book, entitled *The Living Brain*, Walter described in detail his work with something known as the 'flicker effect'. Walter had done most of his research at the Maudsley Hospital in London with individuals who experienced photo-sensitive epilepsy. It had been long known that flickering light stimulated seizures, and Walter was keen to know exactly why this happened. He subsequently developed a series of tests to isolate susceptibility to these curious storms in the brain. He found that he could stimulate seizures, but he also discovered that flicker effects at specific frequencies, at between 8 and 13 cycles per second (the alpha band), brought about profoundly altered states of consciousness in his subjects – specifically, weird visual effects and an expansion of time perception. In one memorable case one of his non-epileptic subjects reported that he felt as if 'yesterday was at one side, instead of behind, and tomorrow was off the port bow'.[9]

Burroughs excitedly discussed Walter's work with Gysin. Gysin shared Burroughs's enthusiasm and believed that he could create an artificial way of reproducing the telepathic and precognitive effects of ayahuasca by using strobe lighting in the way described by Walter. He wrote to an associate, Ian Sommerville, and asked if a machine could be designed to reproduce the strobe effect at home. The two of them worked together and quickly found that by suspending a light bulb inside a metal cylinder with regular slots cut in the side and placing the whole structure on a 78rpm gramophone turntable they could reproduce an effective flicker rate. After much experimentation they hit on the perfect frequency of slits to reproduce exactly the alpha band of between 8 and 13 cycles per second described by Walter. Gysin was stunned by the power of his 'Dream Machine'.

Gysin believed that he had discovered a process by which precognition could be facilitated. In his journal he wrote that Nostradamus had used a technique whereby the great French seer would close his eyes, look at a light source and flicker his fingers in such a way as to create a dappled light effect. In this way Nostradamus was able to gain 'instruction from a higher power'.[10]

The way in which a 'higher power' can be accessed through the flicker effect stimulated Gysin and Burroughs, as we have already seen, to write extensively about what they called 'The Third Mind'. By this they meant that when two minds collaborate, a third one seems to become involved.

In this regard it is potentially significant that the term Michael Persinger initially used for the 'sensed presence' effects brought about by his God Helmet was 'temporal lobe transients'. Here we have a 'flicker effect' creating exactly the same sensation as those reported by Persinger's subjects and Strassman's DMT volunteers. Persinger's machine brought about microseizures in the temporal lobes. As we shall discover later, the flicker effect is responsible for triggering 'absence' seizures in temporal lobe epileptics; and, as again we shall discover, one of the regularly reported sensations during pre-seizure auras in cases of temporal lobe epilepsy (TLE) is a strong sensation that the subject is not one, but two, people.

The feeling of a sensed presence is one of the two major effects of stimulators such as Gysin's Dream Machine. The second effect involves increasingly complex visual hallucinations. These seem to link the natural process of viewing a flickering or stroboscopic light with the taking of hallucinogens such as mescaline, DMT and LSD. So what are these images? Are they simply brain-generated hallucinations?

## Klüver Form Constants

In 1926 German-American psychologist Heinrich Klüver was researching the effects of mescaline, with a specific focus on the nature of the visual hallucinations that this chemical compound created. As we know, this is exactly the same substance taken by Aldous Huxley, which stimulated the writing of his book *The Doors of Perception*.

Klüver noted that the hallucinations involved highly saturated colours and recurring geometric patterns. He placed these in four categories: lattices, cobwebs, tunnels and spirals. I know from personal experience that these are exactly the images created by Gysin's Dream Machine and all the similar devices that have been marketed since. As we shall discover, these images are also associated with migraine, hypnagogia, hypoglycemia and temporal lobe epilepsy and, of possible significance, the near-death experience (NDE).

Klüver noted that the forms repeat themselves over and over again, reiterating on smaller and smaller scales. He called this effect the 'geometrical ornamental structure' and noted the endless reproduction through many degrees of magnitude. This 'geometrization to infinity', as the late Oliver Sacks describes it in his book *Migraine*,[11] suggests to me a process similar to that created using a fractal geometry sequence known as the Mandelbrot set. Why should the human brain spontaneously, and for no apparent purpose, create, during a migraine aura, such a complex mathematical structure? I cannot help wondering if this is a clue to the ultimate holographic nature of reality, whereby the parts are contained in the whole and the whole found in the parts. Migraines somehow short-circuit Aldous Huxley's reducing valve and in doing so facilitate a perceptual viewpoint similar to that of Mind at Large. These migraine auras are not uncommon. For example, here is a description found on the Migraine Aura Foundation site:

> I noticed this weird thing in the corner of my right field of vision.
> Has anyone seen a Mandelbrot set? One of those fractal patterns
> that when you zoom into it is the same pattern repeating itself?
> Well that's what I saw. It lasted about 20 mins.[12]

Later, Klüver became the mentor to John Smythies on the effects of stroboscopic light on perceptions. You will recall that Smythies, with his associate Humphry Osmond at the Souris Valley Mental Health Hospital, were the researchers responsible for stimulating Aldous Huxley's interest in altered states of consciousness. It was after his work with Osmond that Smythies became really interested in the effects of stroboscopic light on human behaviour. He had noted that the visual phenomena perceived using a stroboscope were very similar, if not identical, to those experienced under the influence of mescaline. Intriguingly, his research showed that if the two were used together the visual effects were enhanced considerably. So here we have a precise linkage between artificially created hallucinations using a hallucinogen and a naturally occurring reaction to light. It seems that Gysin and his followers were really on to something. But what is it about the flicker effect that causes such reactions?

## The Huxleyan Spectrum: Through a Mirror Darkly

There are many methods by which individuals can access at least some elements of the Pleroma. As we have already discovered, this can be done by using flashing lights to create a 'flicker effect'. It can also be done by pushing to extremes through fasting or self-mortification or by the consumption of hallucinogens such as dimethyltryptamine, ayahuasca and LSD. In effect, all of these processes force the brain to increase or decrease production of certain neurotransmitters. This, in turn, seems to facilitate contact between Eidolonic and Daemonic consciousness. The contact may be either direct, in that it allows the Daemon to communicate with the Eidolon; or indirect, in that Eidolonic consciousness is allowed access to the perceptual world of Daemonic consciousness. Direct contact usually takes the form of guidance, advice or warnings. Indirect contact is far more dangerous, for without the wisdom and awareness of the Daemon an Eidolon can be easily overpowered by the sensory overload coming through from the Pleroma and can lose all grip on 'reality'. This is usually defined as insanity.

For millennia certain individuals, through personal abilities or through rigorous training, have been able to perceive the Pleroma and to learn from it. These are known as mystics, adepts or shamans. Societies have sought out such people and they have become religious or spiritual leaders.

So why is this the case? Why is it that some human beings seem to exist in both worlds, whereas the vast majority of us are trapped within Blake's 'mind-forged manacles', being given only occasional glimpses of the wider universe, possibly through mind-expanding drugs or illness?

I will argue that there is a 'spectrum' of illnesses which, for very similar reasons, allow access to the Pleroma. Certain neuro-physical and neurochemical processes open up the channels of communication between Daemonic and Eidolonic awareness.

The Huxleyan spectrum consists of a series of 'syndromes', each of which is closely related to the others. Although I have used the term 'spectrum', I am of the opinion that this is slightly misleading in that it suggests a gradation from one section to the next.

The main 'staging points', as I would like to term them, are: autism, with its related 'savant syndrome', migraine, TLE, schizophrenia and Alzheimer's disease.

Migraine melds into TLE, TLE into schizophrenia, schizophrenia into

Alzheimer's and then in a curious 'eternal recurrence' Alzheimer's and schizophrenia develops into autism. The model is more like a Venn diagram – that is, a diagram that shows all possible relations between a finite number of different sets. For example, in our model we have the set of individuals who experience migraine, another set of people who experience temporal lobe epilepsy. Each set is shown as a circle. The circles then overlap in the areas of shared factors. For example, a shared factor between migraineurs (M) and TLEs (T) is the aura. This area of overlap is called the *intersection* of M and T.

Part Two of this book will review in detail each of these 'staging points' in isolation. It will not follow the spectrum in the sense of ever-widening access to the Pleroma, but instead will be more selective. This is because, as with the Venn model, the staging points all overlap each other. Part Two will then end with an extensive discussion on how the overlapping can be shown neurologically and experientially.

PART TWO:

# AT THE DOORWAY

# CHAPTER THREE:

# Migraine

## The Doors Swing Ajar

When I was in my early 20s something very strange happened to me. I was working in my office when the tips of my fingers seemed to go numb, followed by a peculiar tingling sensation in my lips. I also felt that the top of my head was lifting off and moving upwards towards the ceiling. I then noticed that the office seemed to be getting smaller, as if I was looking at it from the wrong end of a telescope. After a few seconds the 'telescope' effect stopped, but something even more disturbing started to take place. In the corner of my vision was what looked like a disturbance in the air. It was moving around in a shimmering zigzag pattern. This was not in my eyes but out there in three-dimensional space. The zigzags had, behind them, a swirling mass of activity, as if scores of tiny snakes were winding around each other. My visual field was breaking up in front of my eyes. As the zigzags widened out from the confines of their perimeters, all I could see was pure white light. It suddenly dawned on me that I was going blind.

Within a minute or two I could only see things at the periphery of my vision: the rest was a series of zigzag shapes containing the frighteningly empty whiteness.

Fortunately, the company where I worked had a medical centre, and this was just down the corridor from me. I managed to get myself into the clinic and tried to speak to the nurse. It was really weird. My words came out in completely the wrong order, as if somebody had re-arranged them for me. The nurse seemed concerned. I say 'seemed' because I couldn't actually see her. She got me to lie down. As I did so, my vision began to come back, the white-out started to fade away. I then saw the nurse properly ... except that she looked like a painting by Picasso. Her face was made up of sharp angles, and it was as if I could see each aspect of her face even though I was looking straight at her.

'It's OK,' said my personal version of Picasso's Dora Maar. 'You are experiencing a classic migraine aura. It will fade soon.' As she said this, I had the most amazing déjà vu. I had, at some time in my past, lived that moment before. It was really peculiar. I had sensed déjà vu sensations before, but this was overwhelming and felt imbued with foreboding. Slowly the visual disturbances faded and I began to see properly again. The nurse warned me that I may need to stay in the clinic for a time, as such experiences usually foreshadow a full migraine headache.

While I was waiting for the full headache to arrive, I asked the nurse exactly what an aura was. She explained that it was still something of a mystery but that such experiences had been reported for centuries. She added that the word 'aura' is actually from ancient Greek and means 'breeze', and that it is the body's way of warning that a migraine headache is due. In my case the warning was wrong. Within 10 minutes I was back in my office feeling physically fine.

## Causes of Migraine

It may come as a surprise that an illness known to affect 12 per cent of the human population that science has yet to find a cause. It is generally thought that the pain originates from chemical activation of sensory nerves that supply the blood vessels located inside the skull.[1] These blood vessels swell and cause pressure within the skull itself. It is very unusual to find migraine in children under the age of eight. Why this is so is, again, unknown. The incidence increases again at puberty. This suggests that in the case of males it may be linked to testosterone production and in females the production of oestrogen. Various causes have been adduced, the most fascinating being that for some people migraines are triggered by flickering light, strobe lighting and fluorescent tubes. Edward Liveing described the experience of one of his patients whose migraine aura was triggered by watching falling snow. It is important here that we focus on the aura rather than the migraine, for it is within the aura state that the Pleroma is glimpsed, not during the headache. Migraine-with-aura, also known as classic migraine, is much rarer than ordinary migraine, being experienced by around one in 10 of those who suffer migraine headaches.

For those of us who do experience migraine auras, they are hypnotically fascinating. They spontaneously occur and the subject (I actually prefer the term 'observer') seems to have no control over the content of the imagery. It was a personal fascination in this phenomenon that prompted neurologist Karl Lashley to spend many years meticulously recording his own migraine auras. Lashley concluded that what was taking place was some form of progression across his primary visual cortex. This was not the prevailing wisdom of the time (the early 1940s), which linked the aura directly to the swelling of the blood vessels as discussed above. However, in 1944 a Brazilian biology PhD student based at Harvard made an amazing discovery. For his doctoral research programme Aristides Leão was investigating how epileptic seizures spread across the brain. What he actually discovered in his work with rabbits was something that is now known as cortical spreading depression (CSD).[2] CSD is a short-lasting depolarization wave that moves across the visual cortex. In effect, this is a wave of electrical silence in which the brain cells (neurons) cease firing. This wave propagation can take up to 18 minutes to move from the rear to the front of the occipital lobe. As the wave starts, it is felt as a tingling in the extremities. As the CSD makes its way through the visual cortex, there is an initial flurry of activity before the electrical current is switched off. It is this, some now believe, that causes the visual hallucinations.

A recent study has suggested that the neurotransmitter that may be responsible for CSD is glutamate. Generally glutamate is not harmful, but under certain circumstances vast amounts are generated, causing what is termed a *glutamate flood*. Glutamate is highly excitatory. When present in excess it causes neurons to die as a result of something known as excitotoxicity. This is the mechanism of neuronal cell death in hypoxia (deficiency of oxygen), ischaemia (reduction in blood supply) and, interestingly enough, epilepsy – all conditions that have been proven to lead to excessive release of glutamate.[3][4]

The researchers argue that it is this glutamate flood that generates the wave of excitement that brings about the cortical shut-off observed in CSD.[5] This is an intriguing discovery because it allows a direct link between migraine, epilepsy and near-death experiences (NDE), since the 'glutamate flood' has, as we shall discover later, also been presented as an explanation of the perceptions that accompany the NDE.

However, this discovery only manages to link a neurological event to a visual perception. It in no way explains why the images look the way they do or, more importantly, why one set of images is experienced rather than another? How does a flood of glutamate flowing through the visual cortex create anything that can be confused with objects and patterns in three-dimensional space? As we have already discovered, such images are known as Klüver's Form Constants and are not exclusive to migraine. These images are as far as my migraine-induced hallucinations have taken me. However, for others the aura imagery is far more powerful, and really cannot be explained simply as the visual cortex stimulating geometric patterns.

In 1952 American physician Dr Caro W Lippman published a paper in the *Journal of Nervous Mental Disease* entitled 'Certain hallucinations peculiar to migraine'.[6] To date this is one of the most detailed reports ever written on the differing types of migraine hallucinations.

The initial case studies presented by Lippman give examples of individuals who sense a feeling of bodily extension, particularly focused around the head and neck. This 'ballooning out', as it was described by one patient,[7] is reminiscent of the moving out of the body described by those reporting out-of-body experiences.

It has long been suggested by researchers that the author of *Alice in Wonderland*, Charles Lutwidge Dodgson, writing under the pen name Lewis Carroll, was a migraineur and that his descriptions of Alice getting larger and smaller after her encounter with the 'drink me' bottle were descriptions of his own experiences. Such perceptions of growing and shrinking have now been termed 'Alice in Wonderland syndrome'.

Of possibly even greater significance is that the sensation of falling into and then through a tunnel is reported by a number of Lippman's patients. The 'tunnel' is a regularly recorded motif in the near-death experience and, as we have already seen, is related to the Klüver's Form Constants. It is therefore no surprise to find that near-death experience motifs litter the reports collected by Lippman in his long career as a recorder of migraine 'hallucinations'.

In 1954 Lippman published another article in which he focused on another fascinating area: recurring dreams.[8] This is an experience many people have, but it seems that with migraineurs it is especially powerful and vivid. Of possible significance is that Lippman discusses the experiences of 'migrainoids' as well as 'migraineurs'. A 'migrainoid' is a person who is a direct descendant, or sibling, of migraineurs. This suggests that migraine-like symptoms are hereditary.

In the article Lippman discusses three different dream patterns, all of which are directly related to migraineurs/migrainoids and involve powerfully vivid recurring dreams, in which the experiencer returns to a location or situation that they have dreamed of many times before.

What can recurring dreams tell us about the source of the dream state? One of the ways we can tell that our waking life is 'real' is that it has a strong element of continuity. When we go to sleep, the bedroom has a certain configuration, the alarm clock is in a particular place and the book we put down before we went to sleep will stay in the same location. On awaking, everything will be, to all intents and purposes, a very close version of the external environment we saw just before we closed our eyes. This convinces us that what is 'out there' is part of a reality that continues while we are asleep. However, a recurring dream has similar attributes.

This is a very important point. As we have already discovered, the general 'explanation' of all altered states of consciousness is that they are simply brain-generated hallucinations – fantasies created by the release of certain neurochemicals (neurotransmitters) within the brain that spontaneously 'create' dreams. With regard to migraine-induced hallucinations, the major culprit seems to be the glutamate-induced cortical spreading depression (CSD). Of course, this explains nothing. If we accept that the brain itself is, in effect, an unconscious collection of cells, then how exactly does this collection of chemicals choreograph the dream narratives in all their complexity? But this is just the start of the logistical problems. We can add a further question: how does the brain facilitate the creation of a sensory 'reality' that presents itself to consciousness (or perhaps we should we say 'unconsciousness', as the observer of the stimuli is actually asleep)?

This dreamscape consists of visual images created, remember, without any external electromagnetic energy (light source) stimulating the retina; sound sources 'heard' by the observer without any sound wave distortions of the ear drum; olfactory sensations not involving the nose; and tactile sensations when nothing is being touched. This facsimile, a rendering of external reality that is so convincing that for the vast majority of people there is no realization that they are in a dream state, is magically formed out of non-physical 'material'. What decides which images are selected to populate the dreamscape? Who is the *bricoleur* who plans how the dream narrative unfolds? It is not the observer, as the observer remains exactly that, a person who perceives as a dream story unfolds in front of them. The stock answer is that it is the 'unconscious' that does this. If this is the case, then the unconscious mind is independent of the everyday 'conscious' mind. Not only that but it must have some degree of self-awareness in order to create the dream narrative in the way it does.

The dream-like quality of many migraine auras suggests that there must be a link between REM intrusion states and the migraine aura, leading me to conclude that migraine may give a small glimpse of what is behind Huxley's 'doors'. Sometimes this involves hallucinations but other times it is just a feeling that the universe is far more than whatever is presented to us by our senses.

## Migraine and REM Intrusion

A much-reported altered state is the out-of-body experience (OBE). Many of these are experienced late at night and seem to be related to the hypnagogic and/or hypnopompic states. At the start of their OBE, many subjects have reported a curious vibrationary state accompanied by humming or hissing. We know that tinnitus is related to a low-level form of epilepsy or a symptom of migraine, so this may be significant. Furthermore, there are reports of migraineurs waking up with the feeling that an earthquake is taking place.

Pioneering migraine researcher Dr Caro W Lippman termed these effects 'space-motion hallucinations'.[9] In his article he specifically points out that these occur 'during the period of relaxation preceding sleep'.[10] One woman reported to Lippman that she experienced powerful shaking in which, as she described it, a huge earthquake shock sets 'the room, the bed, and me, shaking violently'. This continues for about 30 seconds and then 'fades to a vibration'. She commented that the feeling of movement is very real, and yet she knows that the room is not moving. As she describes it, 'the draperies and the chandelier remain stationary'. I cannot help commenting that the world has certainly changed since this report was made: I suspect that there are few of us with chandeliers in our bedrooms. So real was the sensation that she took to hanging a stocking over the back of a chair next to the bed. She knew that if the stocking was not swaying, it was a hallucination. Of possible significance is that on occasions she also had the sensation during the day when she was relaxing. This happened to her two or three times a week. Another of Lippman's respondents, Miss W A, described in detail her 'space-motion' migraines:

> Once or twice when I went to bed very tired, just before falling to sleep, I would suddenly find myself rushing through space. Not the body, necessarily, but the part that feels motion. It's the feeling you get when you sit in a speeding car and close your eyes.[11]

I am struck by this, as I have spoken to a few individuals who have taken DMT, either in the form of ayahuasca or in a purer form. They described to me almost identical sensations. I have received similar reports from individuals who have had out-of-body experiences (OBEs). But the real parallel here is the 'tunnel' sensation described by NDErs. Does the evidence point to all four being aspects of the same experience? Could it be that endogenous DMT may be responsible for the migraine and NDE perceptions?

That migraine auras can be part of the hypnopompic state was suggested by a paper published by migraine aura expert Klaus Podoll. In this he described how one of his subjects, while in a liminal dreaming state, perceived migraine aura-type visuals as part of the brain-generated hypnopompic hallucinations. On waking, the aura imagery carried through from the dream and imposed itself into the subject's waking perceptions.[12] Some researchers have suggested that migraine can be directly linked to another fascinating altered state of consciousness known as 'lucid dreaming'. This was brought to public attention by the movie *Inception*. Most of us, when dreaming, are totally unware that we are dreaming. However odd the dream circumstances become, we simply accept what is taking place. However, some individuals, by chance or by training, become aware that they are in a dream state, and in doing so can impose their will on the dream. Psychologist Harvey Irwin has shown that migraineurs are significantly more likely to experience lucidity in dream states than neurotypicals.[13] Irwin has even suggested that a migraine attack may be responsible for triggering the lucidity.

If migraine does stimulate REM intrusion, then it is reasonable to expect reports of Persinger's 'sensed presence' during migraine aura states. I am delighted to report that these are common. For example, author/migraineur Richard Grossinger states that during a migraine aura he feels that he is more than one person, or has 'access to separate minds'. In their research Podoll and Robinson have noted that the migraine aura in some creates a sensation of a 'presence' that is not that of the experiencer.

## TLE and Migraine: Are They Linked?

If my idea of a continuum is correct, then there should be clear neurological, neurochemical, physiological and psychological links between migraine and temporal lobe epilepsy. In this section I will review the evidence for such a belief.

That there is a link between the two 'disorders' has long been suspected. In 1875 John Hughlings Jackson, the founding father of epilepsy research, stated: 'I have seen cases intermediate in type between migraine, epileptiform seizures, and epilepsy proper.'[14]

In 1898 in an editorial in the *Journal of the American Medical Association* it was argued that there was a great need to find a 'plausible explanation of the long-recognized affinities of migraine and epilepsy'.[15]

Seven years later, on 8 December 1906, and in possible response to this request, Sir William Richard Gowers, one of the pioneers of modern neurology, gave a talk at the National Hospital for the Paralysed and Epileptic in London. Gowers commented that migraine and epilepsy often occurred together in the same patient.

The similarities between the two have also, over the years, caused a degree of difficulty in general diagnosis, and there is a strong 'comorbidity' (simultaneous occurence), for research has shown that if a person has one disorder then they are more than twice as likely to have the other.[16] Researcher Fred Andermann, in his introduction to the book *Migraine and Epilepsy*, suggested that there are three possible explanations for the comorbidity. The first is that both are fairly common illnesses so that by a simple application of statistical probability there will be an overlap. His second suggestion was that one illness leads to the other; and his third was that there is a shared genetic or physiological basis.[17] In 1987 Andermann reinforced his hypothesis with a survey in which he discovered that the overlap between the two conditions fell in a range between 1 per cent and 17 per cent with a median of 5.9 per cent.[18]

In 1993 Marks and Ehrenberg found that 79 of 395 patients with epilepsy also experienced migraine. This calculates as 20 per cent.[19] A year later, in 1994, researchers Ottman and Lipton interviewed 1,948 adults with epilepsy and 1,411 of their parents and siblings. In this regard epilepsy was defined as a lifetime history of two or more unprovoked seizures. For a headache to be defined a migraine it needed to have two or more of the following symptoms: unilateral pain, throbbing pain, visual aura or nausea. Thus, the symptoms included those of migraine with aura (classic migraine) and migraine without aura, and migrainoid aura without headache. They discovered that 40 per cent of epileptics experienced migraine. Their statistics indicated that the incidence of migraine is 2.4 times higher in persons with epilepsy than persons without epilepsy. They concluded that migraine and epilepsy were 'strongly associated, independent of seizure type, etiology, age at onset, or family history of epilepsy'.[20]

In 2005 another study by Velioglu and Ozmenoglu found that among 412 adults with epilepsy 14 per cent experienced migraine.[21] A year later a retrospective study of Icelandic children between the ages of 5 to 15 showed that there was a four times higher chance of an epileptic child having migraine than a non-epileptic child.[22]

So does the empirical research have experiential support? This does seem to be the case. During the recovery period after a seizure, around 40 per cent of those experiencing partial epilepsy report a post-seizure (postictal) headache and 26 per cent of these patients described symptoms that would be considered, after applying the criteria of the International Headache Society, to be migraine.[23] Intriguingly, migraine-like postictal headache occurred significantly more often in cases of temporal lobe epilepsy and occipital lobe epilepsy than in cases of frontal lobe epilepsy.[24]

Of possible significance is a variation of epilepsy known as Gaustaut syndrome. This is a comparatively rare form of late-onset epilepsy that involves partial seizures with visual symptoms.[25] Post-seizure, a significant number of patients reported migraine-like headaches.

In 1960 William G Lennox and his daughter Margaret A Lennox suggested a condition that they termed 'migralepsy'. This has now been officially recognized and is included in the classification scheme of the International Headache Society, who in their handbook code migralepsy as IHS-7.6, ICD10/G44.82. In the article on their website they list the forms of epilepsy that seem to have a high incidence of migraine. These are benign occipital epilepsy, benign rolandic epilepsy and corticoreticular epilepsy with absence seizures.

In 2008 a team of French researchers reported the case of a young patient who suffered both migraine and epilepsy and experienced auras relating to both conditions. The patient desribed how his auras started off with primitive visual hallucinations, which then developed into coloured figures. At this point the classic epilepsy-aura element of fear took over. This suggested to the researchers a continuum between migraine aura and epileptic seizure with regard to this patient. They took this as strong supporting evidence for the idea that migralepsy is a trigger mechanism for epileptic seizures, and that migralepsy is similarly part of a spectrum in which migraine and epilepsy are related elements.[26]

A couple of recent reports have re-ignited the debate regarding the relationship between epilepsy and migraine. In 2013 a study that took place at Columbia University Medical Center in New York under the supervision of Dr Melodie Winawer set out to discover if migraine-epilepsy comorbidity was genetically based. Winawer and her associates analysed data collected from participants in the Epilepsy Phenome-Genome Project. Known as the EPGP, this is a genetic study of epilepsy patients and families from 27 clinical centres in the US, Canada, Argentina, Australia and New Zealand. The results showed that study participants with epilepsy who had three or more additional close relatives with a history of seizure disorder were more than twice as likely to experience migraine auras than patients from families with fewer individuals who had had seizures. This suggests that there is a gene, or genes, that cause both epilepsy and migraine.

A second study, the results of which were published in 2014, discovered yet another link between migraine and epilepsy.[27] The team led by Steven J Schiff, Brush Chair Professor of Engineering and director of the Penn State Center for Neural Engineering, was keen to understand why it was that epileptic seizures are marked by electrical hyperactivity but migraine auras are marked by a silencing of electrical activity in part of the brain. This would suggest very different neurological causes and yet, as we have seen, the two conditions create very similar hallucinations.

I think that the association between migraine and epilepsy has been demonstrated. However, epilepsy, specifically the variety focused on the temporal lobes, carries us much further along the Huxleyan spectrum and allows the Pleroma to leak through even more to consensual reality. It is to this world of overlap that we now take our enquiry.

# CHAPTER FOUR:

# Temporal Lobe Epilepsy

## Neurological Aspects: What Is Temporal Lobe Epilepsy?

> I had experiences like yogism [...] Once I saw an aura of a dog
> [...] I had visions of unity [...] Time has come to mean nothing to
> me [...] I slip out of its meshes like a sardine through a herring
> net. I had the feeling that I was split into two or more.[1]

Above is a series of quotes taken from the autobiography of a little-known but highly regarded Welsh novelist-poet, Margiad Evans. She is describing as best she can the experiences that took over her life from May 1950 until her death in 1959 at the tragically young age of 50. For those nine years she found herself regularly falling into another form of existence, realizing that her body was simply 'a curtain: or as Blake said, a shady grove'.[2] What brought about these extreme perceptions was the next location on the Huxleyan spectrum: temporal lobe epilepsy (TLE).

The first thing that has to be understood is that epilepsy is a symptom, not a disease. It has been shrouded in superstition ever since it first appeared, when it was assumed to be evidence of demonic possession. It was first described as a medical disorder by Hippocrates (460–370 BCE), who even noted that damage to one side of the head could lead to seizures that affected the opposite side. It has been attributed to St Paul, Julius Caesar, Napoleon and many other historical figures, but in fact anyone can have an epileptic fit. It is simply a period of disorganized activity in the brain and can be brought on by a head injury, electric shock, drugs asphyxia or even a severe bout of flu. These fits, which involve muscle spasms and convulsions and lead to unconsciousness, are not merely *like* epilepsy: they are epilepsy. There is the possibility that in its wider manifestation epilepsy may be a psychosomatic reaction to threat or danger. This suggestion takes epilepsy out of the area of brain damage and neural disorder and makes it a behaviour pattern that can be produced in any normal brain and might, in certain situations, have survival value.

Somewhere in the region of 6 to 7 per cent of the population will suffer at least one seizure in their lives, 4 per cent are prone to recurrent seizures, and around 1 per cent have active epilepsy. These figures are surprisingly high and show that a fair minority of neurotypicals may experience these transcendental effects at some time in their lives. However, it seems that such glimpses of the Pleroma as described by Margiad Evans are specifically created by epilepsy that has as its source a part of the brain known as the temporal lobes. Please note that although I will henceforth refer to the temporal lobes in the singular I am, in effect, referring to the right- and left- hemisphere temporal lobes, unless I specifically state otherwise.

The temporal lobe is the part of the brain that deals with sensory input and attempts to make sense of what is received. It also contains two very important structures: the hippocampus and the amygdala. The hippocampus processes long-term memory and spatial awareness and the amygdala has similar responsibilities regarding memory and emotions.

There are two types of TLE. One, which is much more common, has as its source the hippocampus and amygdala, while a second, rarer category arises in the outer surface of the temporal lobe. The former is known as Mesial TLE (MTLE) and the latter variety is called Lateral TLE (LTLE).

Both share a pre-seizure sensation known as a 'simple partial seizure', popularly termed the 'aura'. In an aura state the subject does not lose consciousness but does, as Margiad Evans so eloquently described, slip out of normal reality like a 'sardine through a herring net'.[3]

Evans makes an interesting reference to extreme religiosity in connection with the TLE state. She argues that such perceptions of the numinous and 'profound excursions into infinity' tend to result in a profound belief in the mystical and the noetic brought about through the most profound means – namely, personal experience. Evans had had early warning throughout her life that epilepsy was just below the surface. In her autobiography *A Ray of Darkness* she describes how, on occasion, she would perceive 'moments of separation from my consciousness – moments when I was quite literally conscious and unconscious at the same time'.[4] She also incorporated into her novels incidents in which her characters experience aura-like sensations. For example, in her 1934 novel *Turf or Stone* one character describes how 'something like a telephone rings in my head, and then my neck goes numb [...] When I was a child I thought the ringing was meant for a warning, and I used to say, out loud, "Thank you, thank you ... message received."'[5]

Throughout *A Ray of Darkness* Evans describes ongoing sensations that she is not one, but two, people. She came to dread a state that she termed 'double bodiedness'.[6] Later she asks, 'If I were two people, who were they?'[7] It seems that her TLE was allowing her access to another, hidden part of her own psyche. With regard to this sensation of another presence, religiosity and a ringing sound, consider the following passage:

> I could hear a bell ringing mournfully in the distance and I
> was convinced that somebody was standing beside me. I could
> almost glimpse his face out of the corner of my eye. An aged,
> senile mask with empty eyes.[8]

The similarities are uncanny. These words were written by another TLE experiencer, the author and ex-nun Karen Armstrong, and are taken from her fascinating and incredibly honest autobiography, *The Spiral Staircase*.

In this book Armstrong describes a series of very similar incidents to those related by Margiad Evans in *A Ray of Darkness*. She explains how, from her teenage years onwards, she was afflicted with a series of mysterious blackouts. She knew when the blackouts were about to take place, because she would smell a disgusting odour like that of rotten eggs. However, after leaving the convent and becoming a student at Oxford University, Armstrong's 'blackouts' took a sinister turn. She had been up most of the previous night writing an essay and she was working hard to complete it alone in her room. Her nose was invaded by the familiar stench but this time she did not slip into unconsciousness. It is then that she encountered the sound of a ringing bell and her semi-hidden partner.

The incidents described by both Evans and Armstrong have powerful parallels in the cases studied by Michael Persinger, as discussed earlier. You may recall that Persinger and his team designed a helmet that generated an electromagnetic field with the intention of seeing if altered states of consciousness could be reproduced in volunteers. The helmet was placed on the volunteers, so that a weak magnetic field could be generated next to the temporal lobes. Many of the subjects reported a sensation identical to that described by Armstrong and Evans; and, just like the two TLE authors, Persinger's subjects believed their experiences to be very real. For Armstrong it is as though 'a comforting veil of illusion has been ripped away and you see the world without form, without significance, purposeless, blind, trivial, spiteful and ugly to the core.'[9]

Armstrong, like Evans, was to discover the real cause of these 'revelations' many years later. After she had left Oxford, she moved to London and took up a lecturing position at Bedford College in Regent's Park. One evening in February 1976 she was making her daily commute back to her flat in Finchley. She entered Baker Street tube station and was on her way through the ticket barrier when the familiar acrid smell appeared:

> But just after I had gone through the ticket barrier it hit me: the smell, the acrid taste, the flickering quality of the light and the terror [...] my thought processes splintered and the fluorescent station lights began to flash violently with a ferocity that was almost blinding.[10]

Michael Persinger would, I am sure, see parallels between the tube station incident and the mystical aspects of his research. The stimulus was not an electromagnetic field but a flickering light. However, I would argue that it was the flickering lights in the tube station together with the electromagnetic fields generated by electric cables used by the trains that brought about her aura state. This curious mixture of circumstances, together with her neurological susceptibility, flung open her 'doors of perception' and for a few seconds she was perceiving elements of the Pleroma.

Karen Armstrong was found in an unconscious state at the station and taken to the Middlesex Hospital. It was here that she was informed that she had had an epileptic seizure. After subsequent neurological tests it was confirmed that her epilepsy was focused on her temporal lobes. This had probably been caused by slight brain damage at birth when, for a very short period of time, she had been deprived of oxygen. She now knew the reasons for her strange hallucinations and could find ways to deal with them.

Karen Armstrong and Margiad Evans are but two of scores of writers, poets and other creative individuals who have manifested many elements of what was initially known as the 'interictal personality' (that is, the everyday personality manifest between seizure episodes). This includes hyper-religiosity, depression, mania, hyper-morality, a compulsion to write things down in detail and at great length (hypergraphia) and a sense of presence. These effects are now grouped together under the more accurate term of Waxman-Geschwind syndrome, which has become closely linked with temporal lobe epilepsy (TLE).

## Photosensitivity and Epilepsy

One of the factors that stimulated Karen Armstrong's slipping into an aura state followed by a full seizure was a flickering light. As we have already seen in relation to the work of Brion Gysin, this is a very common cause of seizures. For example, in June 2007 a video entitled *Everyone's 2012* was broadcast on UK television. Part of the promotional material for the London 2012 Olympics, this consisted of a series of brightly coloured, flashing zigzags following people competing in various sports across London. The video reached a crescendo with a diver jumping off a high board. As he plummeted towards the surface of the water, it exploded into a succession of flashes, stripes and changing colours.[11] After the video was shown, at least 30 people from across the country had reported that the flashing images brought about epileptic seizures. It was immediately withdrawn.

This is not the first time a UK TV broadcast had caused problems. In 1993 there was an advert for a snack known as Pot Noodle. This showed a news presenter sitting in front of a background of reversing patterns and flashes. These were not in colour but black and white. The ad caused three seizures the first time it was shown. However, the largest effect of this kind was produced when 685 people were admitted to hospital in Japan in December 1997 after the cartoon *Pokémon* was shown on Japanese TV. Of these it was confirmed that 560 had experienced seizures.

According to the UK charity Epilepsy Action, around 23,000 people in the UK are susceptible to what is known as photosensitive epilepsy. The syndrome is also twice as common in females as males. In relation to the central theme of this book, it is significant that, although the majority, when exposed to flickering or stroboscopic light, experience generalized convulsions, a smaller but significant number experience visual auras. It is also noteworthy that 76 per cent of those affected in the Japanese *Pokémon* incident had no previous history of epilepsy.

Most photosensitive epileptics are sensitive to images that flicker at 3 to 30 flashes per second. Frequency of flashing is measured in Hertz, an expression of the number of flashes per second. Around 15 per cent of patients show sensitivity at 60Hz. Subsequent investigations regarding the 1997 Japan incident concluded that the major cause of the seizures was a series of red flashes broadcast at 12Hz.

On the website epilepsy.com, a TLEr describes what they feel after they have had an absence seizure:

> I get the strangest feeling, most of it can't be put into words. The whole world suddenly seems more real at first. It's as though everything becomes crystal clear. Then I feel as if I'm here but not here, kind of like being in a dream. It's as if I've lived through this exact moment many times before. I hear what people say, but they don't make sense. I know not to talk during the episode, since I just say foolish things. Sometimes I think I'm talking but later people tell me that I didn't say anything. The whole thing lasts a minute or two.

This has powerful echoes of the descriptions of TLE-aura states by Margiad Evans and Karen Armstrong. These are terrifying excursions into a universe in which nothing can be taken for granted. It is a world in which other entities are encountered, beings that are sometimes seen and often heard. It also is a place where the future may be perceived in precognitions.

## TLE Auras and Precognition

One of the most frustrating elements of my research for this book was the way in which academics are happy to follow up on elements of what I term the Huxleyan spectrum but fail to follow up on fascinating cases and to draw the most obvious conclusions from them. One paper that illustrates this point is 'Prescience as an Aura of Temporal Lobe Epilepsy' by R Mark Sadler and Susan Rahey of the QEII Health Sciences Centre in Halifax, Nova Scotia. This was published in the academic journal *Epilepsia* in 2004. I was excited on discovering this paper, as I anticipated it being a review of a handful of cases and an attempt to explain exactly what is taking place when a TLE experiencer states that their aura state involves precognition – a perception of events that have yet to happen. The researchers were careful to explain their terminology: 'precognition' is defined as 'antecedent cognition of knowledge' and 'prescience' as 'knowledge of events before they happen'.

The researchers isolated three patients of the QEII Health Sciences Centre who had reported prescience as part of their TLE aura state. Each one presented a fascinating example of how TLE seems to facilitate an ability to see the future. I think it is important to note that two of the three individuals actually believe that their perceptions are 'prescient' as defined by Sadler and Rahey. One can but assume that these beliefs are based upon actual reinforcing experiences. If, as suggested by the respective definitions ('precognition' and 'prescience'), such perceptions were 'illusory', then the patients would always have observed that their pre-perceived future events did not come to pass. It seems totally irrational to continue to believe you are precognitive when all the evidence points to the contrary. However, they do believe this, and it is reasonable to conclude that these beliefs are based on observed and confirmed facts. Here 'patient 1' describes her experiences, followed by a specific example:

> They start with a rising feeling in my stomach and a feeling of déjà vu, by which I mean that it feels like all of this has happened before. At the same time I have a different feeling that I know what is going to happen next. For example, one day I was talking to a customer in my store, and had the profound sense that I knew what he was going to say next. On other occasions, I have looked at a customer just as the seizure is starting, and I have a feeling that I know which compact disc he is going to go over and pick up.

So we have the gustatory aura, followed by a feeling of déjà vu. This is a fairly standard aura state and is not unusual. Patient 1 then feels she knows what the customer is about to do. It seems, as the paper states, that around 30 seconds after these perceptions she has a 'loss of contact' with her environment and is amnesiac for the next five minutes. I suspect that 30 seconds is sufficient time for her to observe if the customer does fulfil the prediction. However, it seems that the researchers did not bother to ask her whether the 'illusory feeling' is actually confirmed or not. In my humble opinion this is *the* most important part of the research. But the paper remains silent on the matter. Whether they did ask the patient this crucial question, or whether she shared this information voluntarily, is simply not recorded. I suspect that the logic being applied here is simple. Precognition and prescience suggest that the future can be seen before it happens; but according to our present scientific paradigm this is impossible; therefore to pursue such a line of enquiry is unscientific and a waste of time. Fortunately, in 1900 Max Planck did not follow a similar line of logic when confronted with the ultraviolet catastrophe, and similarly Einstein believed that good science involved following up any line of enquiry with regard to the mysterious photoelectric effect. In taking these approaches Planck and Einstein facilitated the birth of a new paradigm of science.

The second patient gives a similar example of prescience that had been experienced over a period of years:

> In the past a wave would sweep over me, and I had the distinct sensation that I knew what was going to happen in my immediate environment. Over the years this sensation has changed; I have déjà vu experiences that occur together with a feeling that I know what movements my body will make before it actually moves; it is like I know that my arm will move before it does.

Knowing what is about to happen suggests pre-knowledge of future events, as if this life has been lived before. Such a belief is, it seems, part of the TLE experience.

In 2003 an article was published in the academic journal *Psychopathology*. Written by two members of the Department of Psychology at Kyoto University Medical School, Toshiya Murai and Kenjiro Kukao. The article describes how, in 1997, a 23-year-old male temporal lobe epileptic reported to his physicians that he was living his life between the ages of 21 and 25 over and over again. Such was his frustration at his *Groundhog Day* nightmare that he had repeatedly tried to commit suicide. It will be recalled that in the *Groundhog Day* movie the central character, Conners, attempts a series of multiple suicide attempts to facilitate escape from this 'eternal return'.

If this was an isolated case it could be written off as an interesting but unique example of a peculiar hallucination. However, it is not unique. Three years before, in 2000, another Japanese academic paper had reported a similar case involving a young woman who was suffering from temporal lobe epilepsy caused by meningitis. She reported that she was perceiving powerful precognitive déjà vécu sensations that were convincing her that 'the happenings here are exactly the same as those which I dreamed before'.[12] This woman said that she was experiencing these 'delusions' several times a day. Yet again the subjective evaluation of what was taking place is totally ignored, because the authors are sure that what she was reporting was a 'delusion'. Again, testing her belief against the reality of what happened would surely have been a way of proving to her that she was imagining her precognitive abilities.

The woman's experience is an example of what Swiss-based American Jungian analyst Dr Arthur Funkhouser calls the 'dream theory of déjà vu'.[13] Funkhouser argues that most déjà sensations are memories of recent dreams and that the dreams themselves are precognitive. Is it possible that temporal lobe epilepsy can facilitate the remembering of these dreams, something usually denied to neurotypicals by the Huxleyian filtering facilities of the brain? Interestingly enough, one of the 'mainstream' psychologists studying the déjà phenomenon, Alan Brown, has also suggested that dreams may be the explanation for the déjà experience.[14] Like Funkhouser, Brown suggests that the present experience is confused with a similar dream scenario that has been forgotten. How a similar dream sequence perceived earlier in time is not a precognition I am not entirely sure, but the present scientific paradigm demands that precognition is impossible. But then again another impossibility as far as the previous paradigm was concerned was how light waves travelled from the sun to the Earth without any medium to wave within. When science was forced to face up to overwhelming evidence that the lumniferous ether did not exist, a new solution had to be found (light was particulate) and a new paradigm was ushered in by a certain Albert Einstein.

The researchers noted that the 'paramnesia' suffered by their patient was a classic symptom of temporal lobe epilepsy. However, this is another example of 'labelling'. By giving something an impressive name, preferably Latin- or Greek-based (in this case the Greek *para*, meaning 'contrary to' and *mnesia*, meaning 'memory'). Naming it appears to 'explain' it, whereas in fact all that has happened is that it has been given a somewhat pejorative label that reinforces the idea that it is a false illusion.[15]

The subject, known as S N, believed that he had lived this period of his life five or six times. Here S N describes what had been happening:

> Up until the age of 25, my life was unremarkable. I was employed, and often enjoyed going for drives or to karaoke with my friends on weekends. I cannot remember the details. At the age of 25 I married a girl from Hiroshima, and lived safely. Nothing particular happened after my marriage. However, soon after, I noticed that I was again 21 years old and unmarried ... Then I lived again between the ages of 21 to 25. Once again I held the same job, and again at the age of 25, I married the same girl. This endless cycle has already repeated itself five or six times. Now I am sure I will continue forever. I attempted suicide to escape from this endless repetition.[16]

In 1985 Dr Pethö Bertalan of the Society of Research of Endogenous Psychoses in Budapest had reported a case of a 25-year-old woman who also believed that she had lived her life before. This 'delusion' had continued for 12 years. Bertalan proposed that as the woman had shown no signs of schizophrenia this was a totally new syndrome. He termed it 'chronophrenia'.[17] The woman, known as 'Barbara', had an interesting neurological history. Bertalan describes it thus:

> 'Barbara's' deep-down conviction of 'reduplication' resisted heavy doses of neuroleptics and even 10 sessions of ECT (electro-shock therapy). A couple of hospitalizations (the first one at age 25, the second following the death of her father) helped her stabilize herself to the point that she was able to graduate from the university, marry, have a daughter and hold down a demanding job. She no longer manifested psychotic symptoms and was able to lead a normal life (while continuing to be convinced that she was reliving everything).[18]

Barbara also believed that she was telepathic. She heard an 'inner voice' that involved itself in her life. However, it is her opinions regarding the permeability of her own future, one that she had, according to her own beliefs, lived before, that most intrigued Bertalan. Here he describes one particular discussion:

> On another occasion, when it was mentioned that she might possibly go to see the 1976 Olympic Games, in reply to my question about whether the future had already happened to her, she replied: 'Yes, but the question is, on what level; I have experienced not one future but several different ones. It could happen that I will go to the '76 Olympics – I have a memory of it. But I also have a memory that I won't go [to] the '76 Olympics so that that memory won't come back to me.'[19]

Barbara also offered an interesting analogy to describe her attitude to time. She likened the link between the old and the new world of memory to an accordion. 'What has to disappear from public awareness,' she said, 'closes up like the two sides of an accordion, then the time interval or years or other historical period is repeated when the sides of the accordion open up again.'[20]

This observation is hugely perceptive. Modern science sees time and space as aspects of the same thing. Time is space and space is time. It was Albert Einstein, developing the ideas of his teacher Hermann Minkowski, who first suggested that space and time should be defined in a new term, 'spacetime'. Space became the fourth dimension, joining height, width and breadth to the dimensions in which we exist. Spacetime viewed from a location outside of the five dimensions, in effect a sixth dimension, would present itself in a way similar to that attempted in the 2014 movie *Interstellar*. From this viewpoint, spacetime could be seen as a closed-up accordion as described by Bertalan's patient. Could this be a partial explanation of precognition? Well, it certainly may explain some of the experiences of our next subject, Myron Conan Dyal.

## Myron Conan Dyal: The Man on the Border

Myron Conan Dyal is an artist based in Chatsworth, California. He is also a temporal lobe epilepsy experiencer and has been most of his life. Myron contacted me many years ago, soon after the publication of my first book in the USA. For me, Myron is the classic example of exactly what it is like to have your consciousness in both worlds, Consensual Reality and the Pleroma. I will now take the opportunity to give examples, taken from Myron's autobiography, *The Boy Nobody Wanted* – sadly still unpublished.

Myron was born into a God-fearing Christian family in Inglewood, California. At four years old he fell into a deep coma and was fully unconscious for a month. When he came to, his memories had been wiped clean. It was as if he had been reborn.

The actual cause of the coma was never ascertained, but it was suspected to be epilepsy. However, what was not in doubt was that from then on, young Myron experienced the most powerful hypnagogic and hypnopompic 'hallucinations'. Between his dream world and the world of 'waking life' there was a very thin veil. Myron's encounters echo strongly the examples given by Michael J Hallowell in his 2007 book *Invizikids*. In this fascinating review of 'imaginary friends' Hallowell argues that these entities are not elements of a child's imagination but have an independence that suggests sentience and personal motivation. Taking the view that this is a much-neglected area of research, Hallowell suggests that much could be gained by understanding their true nature and significance. He calls them quasi-corporal companions (QCCs).[21] It seems reasonable to place Myron's childhood companions within Hallowell's category of QCCs. We shall return to this important phenomenon later, looking at it in greater detail. Myron regularly encountered what he describes as the 'red-eyed creatures'. These initially manifested at night when he was about to go to sleep, a classic REM-intrusion scenario, but soon he was encountering them during the day. He describes them as 'dark hooded beings'. This image is almost a Jungian archetype: it has been reported for centuries and across many cultures. I am also reminded here of DMT encounters, NDEs and even alien abductions. It is interesting to observe that one of these 'beings' seems to make a particular effort to communicate with him. According to shamanic belief, this is his 'spirit guide'. This particular entity communicated with him using a form of telepathy. It is no accident that these communications usually ended with Myron having a seizure. This suggests that the 'encounters' were directly related to his aura state and it was while this window on the Pleroma was open that the entities could communicate directly with his mind.

While in his seizure state, he would visit what he called his 'High Place'. This seems to be an alternative level of reality and is strikingly similar to the place visited by individuals during near-death experiences, shamanic travelling and DMT trips. One of the consistent themes of such experiences is flying on the back of a huge winged creature, usually a bird or a butterfly. This is how Myron describes his experience:

> I found myself reclining on the black wings of a gigantic crow gracefully gliding through a beautiful patch of clouds. The cool wind delightfully stroked my face as we soared majestically across the tops of the black mountains surrounding us on all sides. Below us, the valleys and darkened canyons were covered with a red-tinted fog.

It seems that one of the entities had a particular role, and that was to protect the young Myron. For example, when he was quite young he was about to cross a road but out of nowhere a voice shouted to him, 'Stop!' This was clearly not sufficient. The next thing he knew there was the sense of somebody seizing his shoulder and pulling him back. At the same time a car sped around the corner right through the spot where he would have been had he continued walking. The voice, and subsequent physical intervention, had saved his life.[22] This has uncanny parallels with the Alan Rumney incident discussed earlier in this book (p30).

The young Myron also seemed to experience out-of-the-body states, and these suggest that his consciousness was able to leave his body and travel within the Pleroma. There is an argument that OBEs are a form of disassociation and that they express a need to escape from unpleasant circumstances being experienced at that time. However, all Myron's OBE incidents take place when he is in a neutral or even calm mental state. For example, he describes how, in May 1957, he had been enjoying a wonderful afternoon playing in stacks of newly cut grass near his home. He describes how nice the smell was and how happy he felt as he made his way home bathed in the light of the setting sun. It seems that for Myron light,

77

particularly sunlight reflecting off objects at a certain angle, stimulates seizures. Myron describes how he starts to feel very strange and then he suddenly finds himself surrounded by a golden aura. Looking up, he sees a 'host of beings' approaching him from what seems miles away. He is then hit by what he describes as a 'ball of fire', and the impact sends him flying through the air. The ball of light disappears with a hissing sound and he finds himself in the middle of a vast desert plain with a line of hills in the distance. He then notes that surrounding him is a group of beings wearing white robes tied with golden ropes around their waists: he calls these beings 'The Elders'. One of them announces to him, 'Welcome to Zelcon,' and then holds Myron's hand. As he does so, the scene fades and Myron finds himself coming to in a gutter.

I am intrigued by the reference to a 'golden aura'. DMT psychonauts call this the 'chrysanthemum', and it is regularly encountered in DMT trips. As we shall later discover (p199), NDE experiencer Eben Alexander also perceived this phenomenon.

For a few years Myron lived comparatively seizure-free and had no reportable unusual experiences. However, in 1962 things were to change. Owing to a series of unfortunate events Myron was in a deep period of depression, and in June of that year he finds himself considering suicide when standing high above a reservoir at the summit of Ridge Drive. However, he is saved from these negative thoughts by another seizure. Again conscious of being in his 'other world', he sees a huge bird approaching him. The bird lands next to him, folds its wings and looks at him. Looking into the bird's eyes, he feels that they are portals into his own future. In these eyes he sees a 'great room filled with paintings and sculpture and books and the sound of music'. In the room he sees a man seated at a large desk and writing in a black book. Myron cannot see his face, as the man has his back to him. The man then turns around as if sensing that he is being observed. Myron writes:

> Somehow I knew, intuitively or at an even deeper level, that this was me, later in life, filling his/my journal with his/my most intimate thoughts, things he/I would not even come near to wanting to share with others until his/my later years, and even then with much trepidation and hesitancy. The hair was gray, the face expressive of memories, too painful to be spoken, almost too much so to be committed to writing.[23]

The young Myron hoped that the works of art in the room were his own; however, as he had no training or aptitude in this field, he was sure they would not be. This 'future vision' has proven to be totally correct, in that Myron is now a very successful artist and specializes in painting and sculpture. The question is, did this vision make him follow this life course or was it a genuine precognition? He has confirmed to me through a personal communication that what he saw back in 1962 is his present studio and that the person he saw is, indeed, how he looks now.

In February 1975 the Pleroma erupted back into Myron's life in the most amazing fashion. In that month Myron was having difficulty with a particular piece of music that he had been asked to compose for a local theatre group's production of Shakespeare's *The Tempest*. He got up early one morning and, in an attempt to clear his mind, went for a walk in the local park in El Segundo. Through the early morning mist he could see the old Spanish-style water fountain. Feeling the need for refreshment, he took some water from the fountain and splashed it on his face. He looked around at the trees surrounding him. Amid the eddies of Californian sea mist curling around the tree trunks his attention was drawn to a movement. Much to his amazement, out of the swirls came a small figure wearing a blue blazer and carrying a silver pocket watch. It was a white rabbit. Myron blinked and on opening his eyes again saw that the rabbit had gone but had been replaced by a small leprechaun-type creature with a long white beard and a long-stemmed pipe. Then he noticed more of these creatures: 'Leprechauns, elves, white unicorns, all of them classical symbols of the elusive Trickster figure of folklore. Their numbers began to overwhelm my eyesight; I feared sensory overload.'[24] He staggered back and fell against the fountain. On recovering from the fall, he realized that the creatures had disappeared.

This hallucination did not involve Myron being transported to another place: the images imposed themselves within the three-dimensional space of the park of El Segundo; they were in his version of 'consensual space'. The original image of the white rabbit was created by Lewis Carroll, a migraineur. To me this suggests that Carroll used the archetypes welling up from his unconscious and facilitated by his migraine auras. Indeed, white rabbits also feature in many accounts of alien abductions and UFO sightings. Robert Anton Wilson has written about these connections, even suggesting that they constitute a whole branch of UFO study he called 'lepufology'. Rabbits and hares feature regularly in the phenomenon known as QCC, which I have already mentioned (and will explore further later, in Chapter 7). The motif is used to great effect in the movie *Donnie Darko*, in which a large rabbit-like creature symbolizes what I would term the 'Daemon' with regard to the mental state of the eponymous hero.

I have noted that on many occasions Myron's seizures are stimulated by sunlight, usually the rising or setting sun. In fact, it was the light of the setting sun that stimulated one of his most amazing experiences. He is watching the sun set at a location he calls the 'Place of the Four Stars' on Stony Point. He senses a movement in his peripheral vision. On focusing on a black figure in the undergrowth, he realizes, to his amazement, that he is looking at a minotaur, a creature from mythology that is half man, half bull. He fights this creature, kills and dismembers it, and then cooks and devours it. Later, he is taken from this same place by the Ferryman to Hades and encounters a creature like the Devil. They reminded me of the shamanic rite of passage in which an animal is dismembered and eaten. Myron has never been sure of the provenance of these experiences. He writes:

> I was never able to determine definitively if my experiences on the mountain were seizure-induced dreams, psychologically based hallucinations, the influence of the old Indian spiritual forces, genuine journeys through inner worlds, or what. There was always an element to these episodes that never quite added up to a completely understandable picture, the actual, final source of my visions being as elusive as the dreamscapes themselves.[25]

After this series of strange lucid dreams experienced on Stony Point, Myron eventually encounters the entity he knows as Charon. On 16 October 1978 Charon appears in front of him and makes the following curious statement: 'What is the essence of your nature is that one and one seldom equals two.' Charon then explains that Myron is able to exist in two worlds, this one and the world he encounters in his seizure state.

The shaman's journey also involves personal dismemberment as part of the initiation. Such beliefs have come about over millennia and have been recounted by countless initiates. In traditional societies shamans are usually selected because of their seemingly bizarre behaviour, and many are epileptics. In his seminal book on the subject, *Shamanism: Archaic Techniques of Ecstasy*, Mircea Eliade states that 'the only difference between a shaman and an epileptic is that the latter cannot deliberately enter into a trance'.[26] The shaman enters a state of catalepsy in order to begin his, or her, journey into the Pleroma. Of course, in order to be able to go 'shamanic journeying', a novice has to be assisted in one way or another. Unplanned seizures is usually the starting point; and once the novice enters this state, 'spirit guides' will be encountered and these will impart techniques by which the state can be entered at will. Of course, assistance can also be gained by the use of entheogens such as ayahuasca, peyote, mescaline or DMT.

Myron needed none of these in order to cross the threshold. His undiagnosed epilepsy did this for him, and once he was in the 'upper world' his spirit guide, in the guise of Charon, was ready to help. However, according to the teachings of many indigenous cultures, in order to become a shaman the initiate has to take a journey to the 'lower world'. Is this what Myron encountered when he visited Hades? The dismemberment episodes he describes are totally in keeping with the well-trodden shamanic path. Compare Myron's experiences with this description of a typical shamanic initiation by Eliade:

> The content of these first ecstatic experiences, although comparatively rich, always includes one or more of the following themes: dismemberment of the body, followed by a renewal of the internal organs or viscera; ascent to the sky and dialogue with the gods or spirits; descent to the underworld and conversations with spirits and the souls of dead shamans.[27]

Here is Myron's description of what happens to him on one of his 'journeys' when he encounters awful creatures that remind him of huge black wolves. They attack him as a pack:

> Then I was overwhelmed by them, consumed. Skin hung from me in tatters, my bones were snapped between their powerful jaws, my skull caved in, my eyes were their appetizer, my heart their entrée. It was the episode with the black minotaur but in reverse. This time, I was being eaten. They chewed great gouts

82

of flesh out of me, then with quick jerks of their massive canine
heads they threw them into the night. Finally, I was no more.[28]

This dismemberment theme is also found in reports by DMT and ayahuasca
users, and also individuals who claim to have been abducted by UFOs.

The dismemberment is followed by the resurrection of the shaman and
an encounter with the divine self, the other that is hidden. This is exactly
what happens to Myron. As soon as the horror of attack is over, Charon
appears to him in the guise of a tall old man with a white beard, dressed
in a white robe.

Since that time Charon has been a central part of Myron's life. His
'illness' has now been diagnosed as temporal lobe epilepsy. In my opinion,
Myron's epilepsy is of a particular sort, something known as SLPE
(schizophrenia-like psychosis of epilepsy), a form of epilepsy in which the
Pleroma is only a stone's throw away and the doors of perception are wide
open.

## Temporal Lobe Epilepsy and Schizophrenia

In the late 1970s neurologists and psychiatrists started using a new term to
describe the type of hallucinogenic epilepsy that we have been describing in
this chapter. As with all modern terminology, it was known by an acronym,
SLPE. This has never been accepted as a distinct diagnosis, as this would
suggest a clinical condition similar to schizophrenia but not identical to
it. However, it is generally believed that this is an effective diagnosis of
symptoms found in epileptics that are also present in idiopathic forms of
schizophrenia. The word 'idiopathic' sounds very precise and authoritative,
but it actually means a disease or illness to which there is no known
medical cause. In effect, this is an admission by the professionals that
they have no idea what the actual cause of the illness is. So schizophrenic
behaviours that have no known cause are labelled 'idiopathic'.

In general terms, SLPE is a form of temporal lobe epilepsy that has many features of schizophrenia. A series of tests reported on in 2000 showed that patients with SLPE had almost identical neurophysiological profiles to patients diagnosed with schizophrenia.[29] From this it was concluded that there is, in effect, no distinction between the two conditions.

The relationship between epilepsy and schizophrenia has been of interest to neurologists and psychiatrists for many years. As far back as 1910 Emile Kraepelin noted that 18 per cent of his schizophrenic patients experienced epileptic phenomena such as petit mal absences and full seizures.[30] Nine years later, in his hugely influential treatise on dementia praecox, Kraepelin wrote that 'as in dementia praecox epileptiform seizures occur, the malady may be taken for epilepsy.'[31] Many years later, in 1952, it was noted that the medial temporal lobe may be the area where pathologies may be shared between the two conditions.[32]

It has long been noted that there are strong similarities between hallucinations in temporal lobe epilepsy and those experienced in schizophrenia. These seem to be linked to the limbic structures. In 1991 Simon Crowe and Miriam Kuttner published the results of research investigating this link. They reported that the TLErs in their study featured more marked positive schizophrenic symptoms, particularly hallucinations and bizarre behaviour, than the non-TLE group, and that the TLErs show relatively fewer negative schizophrenic features than the schizophrenia-only group.

Denis Hill, a psychiatrist at the Maudsley Hospital in London in the early 1950s researched the unusual frequency of epileptic wave forms in the electroencephalographs (EEGs) of schizophrenics.[33] Up to 25 per cent of younger individuals showed such traces, and they were particularly noticeable in those who suffered from catatonic schizophrenia. He was particularly interested in the resemblance of the chronic paranoid-hallucinatory states experienced by temporal lobe epileptics to those experienced by schizophrenics. He specifically noted the level of auditory hallucinations and the perception that there was another presence that was attempting to influence and control the subject's thoughts. This suggests that in these liminal areas between TLE and schizophrenia, the 'sensed presence' facilitated by Michael Persinger breaks through without the need for a 'God Helmet'.

In 1963 psychiatrist Eliot Slater and two associates studied 69 patients from the Maudsley Hospital and the National Hospital, both in London (36 male, 33 female). All of them were confirmed epileptics who had subsequently developed an illness that resembled schizophrenia. More than two-thirds of the chosen patients experienced epilepsy focused on the temporal lobes. These patients were monitored over a 10-year period. The mean age of onset of schizophrenia was 30 after a mean duration of epilepsy of 14 years. Note that the actual range for onset was from 12 to 59. This suggests that schizophrenia does not start until the early teens at the earliest. In almost every case the delusions were of a religious or mystical nature. This suggests Waxman-Geschwind syndrome. The hallucinations were categorized as: 46 per cent auditory; 16 per cent visual with complex and often mystical themes. The mystical visual hallucinations were usually accompanied by auditory hallucinations as well. All the hallucinations were identical to the types reported in schizophrenia.[34]

So is it reasonable to conclude that TLE merges into schizophrenia in a way that is similar to migraine merging into temporal lobe epilepsy? The evidence does seem to suggest this. In which case, is it that the mystery causes of these seemingly related 'illnesses' might be understood better if we realized that we are looking in the wrong places and that a wider explanation is needed? With this in mind, we will now move from the overlap area of SLPE to full-blown schizophrenia which is when the doors are flung open and the Pleroma is experienced in its entirety.

# CHAPTER FIVE:

# Schizophrenia

## The Doors Swung Open

We have seen how migraine opens up the 'doors of perception' slightly, but only during the aura states preceding a classic migraine. The opening becomes wider for those who experience temporal lobe epilepsy. Again these glimpses are of a short duration and are related to an aura state. However, there is another group of individuals, those who can be found at the extreme end of my Huxleyan spectrum, who receive the full force of the universe as it really is: the Pleroma blasts through their meagre defences. These people experience what modern neurology hubristically calls schizophrenia.

In the early 1980s the American periodical *Schizophrenia Bulletin* published a request that individuals suffering schizophrenic episodes should write in and describe their experiences. In a 1984 edition some of these responses were published.[1] Some were surprisingly positive. For example:

> Should I let anyone know that there are moments, just
> moments, in the schizophrenia that are 'special'? When I
> feel I am traveling to someplace I can't go normally? Where
> there is an awareness, a different sort of vision allowed me?
> Moments which I can't make myself believe are just symptoms
> of craziness and nothing more.[2]

This is not what the layperson would expect from a schizophrenic.
However, experiencers of this peculiar 'illness' have no doubts about its
conflicting nature. Later in the 1984 edition another correspondent, a
37-year-old female artist attempts to describe the sensory overdrive that
she experiences when in such 'altered states':

> What's so special? Well, the times when colors appear brighter,
> alluring almost, and my attention is drawn to the shadows, the
> lights, the intricate patterns and textures, the bold outlines of
> objects around me. It's as if all things have more of an existence
> than I do, that I have gone around the corner of humanity to
> witness another world where my seeing, hearing and touching
> are intensified, and everything is wonder.[3]

A few years earlier another young woman attempts to explain what may
be taking place at such times. She believes that her 'doors of perception'
had been flung wide open at the onset of her schizophrenia-facilitated
experiences, making her suddenly able to perceive 'reality' in all its
terrifying power. Over many years of such experiences she had come to a
profound conclusion:

> Each of us is capable of coping with a large number of stimuli,
> invading our being through any one of the senses. We could

hear every sound within earshot and see every object, line and colour within the field of vision, and so on. It's obvious that we would be incapable of carrying on any of our daily activities if even one-hundredth of all the available stimuli invaded us at once. So the mind must have a filter which functions without our conscious thought, sorting stimuli and allowing only those which are relevant to the situation in hand to disturb consciousness.[4]

In a similar way physicist Raynor Johnson created this wonderful analogy to describe what it is like to have the 'doors' open fully:

We are each rather like a prisoner in a round tower permitted to look out through five slits in the wall at the landscape outside. It is presumptuous to suppose that we can perceive the whole of the landscape through these slits – although I think there is good evidence that the prisoner can sometimes have a glimpse out the top![5]

The aura 'breeze' that is experienced by migraineurs and temporal lobe epileptics is as nothing to the hurricane that is schizophrenia. Schizophrenics are within the storm at all times. The doors are not opened, they are blown off, leaving the schizophrenic Eidolon faced directly with the awe-inspiring power of the Pleroma as perceived by the Daemon. With no protection from the hurricane's forces, the schizophrenic recedes into behaviours that seem, to neurotypicals, to be totally irrational and insane.

The story of schizophrenia as a psychiatric illness began in the early 20th century when Emil Kraepelin, a German psychiatrist, proposed that most mental illnesses could be categorized as one or other of two major disorders: manic-depressive insanity and dementia praecox.

Kraepelin believed that all forms of mental illness that showed signs of improvement over time should be defined as manic-depressive insanity. These illnesses may involve hospitalization, but given systematic care and professional assistance the prognosis is promising. He had no such optimism for dementia praecox. He considered this to be a progressive illness that started in adolescence or early adulthood and followed an inexorable downhill course. Recovery, if it ever occurred, was usually short-term, and afterwards the patient would continue their decline. Note the use of the word 'dementia'. It was argued that schizophrenia, as it was later to be defined by Eugen Bleuler, was simply a form of dementia that is experienced by the young.

Schizophrenia is a surprisingly common 'illness'. Across the world it affects, at any one time, around 1 per cent of the population. It occurs in all cultures and across all geographic areas. This suggests some very intriguing implications with regard to its causes and its function.

If genetically transmitted, it must have 'evolved' using classic evolutionary (that is, Darwinian) processes. If this is the case, then why has such a debilitating and socially problematic condition not been eradicated from the gene pool? If the role of Darwinian selection is to create efficiency through adaption to social and environmental conditions, why is it that schizophrenia did not disappear millennia ago? For example, it is known that schizophrenia normally manifests itself around the time of maximum sexual proclivity – the time when seeking out and finding a mate is at its most important. Schizophrenics are known for being loners, and would clearly not be an ideal target for those seeking out (overtly or unconsciously) the best possible gene carrier for the next generation. It is reasonable to conclude that such individuals would be actively ignored. But this has clearly not been the case.

The dispersal of human populations across the globe has taken approximately 100,000 years. The consistency of the incidence of schizophrenia across geographically spread populations suggests that the illness existed within the human gene pool at that time. So across countless generations the schizophrenic gene has managed to carry through. This can only be because those showing schizophrenic tendencies managed to reproduce and ensure that the gene continued to the next generation – time and time again. So there has to be some kind of evolutionary purpose for what seems a totally debilitating illness. What can this be?

## Schizophrenia and Perception

Experimental psychologist Charles McCreery, whose work with Celia Green we have already discussed in detail, has suggested that schizophrenic perceptions may be brought about by a phenomenon known as 'micro-sleeps'. Curiously enough, these are brought about by hyperarousal rather than under-arousal.[6]

To appreciate why this is so strange we need to understand how brain cells (neurons) communicate. We have already discovered how neurochemicals modulate the messages being sent from neuron to neuron. But within each neuron itself the actual message is transferred using electrical impulses. In effect, millions of neurons working together create waves of electrical activity that move across the brain. These 'brain waves' can be measured using devices such as an EEG. It has been discovered that there are four different types of brain waves. These are identified by a particular Greek letter. Beta brain waves, in terms of the Hertz scale used to describe such frequencies, have a frequency of 13 to 60 Hz; they are found in people who are consciously alert. The frequency rises as the person becomes agitated or afraid. Alpha waves, with a frequency of 7 to 13 Hz, occur in someone who is relaxed but aware of what is going on around them. Theta waves, at 4 to 7 Hz, occur when the person is asleep and dreaming. Anything lower than 4 Hz is called the Delta state and is found in individuals who are in a very deep sleep and therefore unconscious.

It has long been noted that levels of brain activity related to dreams and schizophrenic states, specifically those involving psychotic behaviours, are similar. When we dream, we enter a very curious world in which events and circumstances are beyond our control. We are acted upon rather than taking action. Dreams also seem to have an air of significance that is absent in the non-dream state. In dreams we also take for granted seemingly impossible situations. We suddenly can fly, or we are somebody famous. In most cases, such impossible circumstances do not lead us to realize that we are dreaming: we simply accept the situation. All these circumstances are experienced by schizophrenics within consensual reality.

McCreery argues that schizophrenics, when experiencing a psychotic state, are actually asleep. In effect, perceptions encountered within the Pleroma carry over into consensual reality.

When neurotypicals dream, they usually enter a state characterized by something known as 'rapid eye movement' (REM). This is reflected in Beta brainwave activity, reflective of a fully wakened state. However, studies have shown that schizophrenic patients, when in psychotic states, do not show the REM activity that is characteristic of dreaming.[7] McCreery suggests that the reason for this is that schizophrenics are in a state of high arousal when they micro-sleep, rather than the low arousal associated with sleep states in neurotypicals. He cites the work of psychiatrist Ian Oswald, who considered that sleep was a 'provoked reaction', as exemplified by soldiers who have fallen asleep while waiting to go into battle. It is regularly recorded that in times of extreme stress individuals experience out-of-the-body states. The standard explanation for such events is that they demonstrate depersonalization, whereby the experiencer is trying to mentally escape from a dangerous, painful or unpleasant situation. This makes a degree of sense but totally fails to explain the regularly recorded veridical aspects of such experiences, and is not consistent with examples taking place during childbirth where the expectant mother has every incentive to remain, as it were, embodied.

In a series of experiments Oswald was able to evoke sleep onset by administering painful electric shocks at 10-second intervals to the wrist or ankle of the subject.[8] With this in mind, McCreery suggests that the relationship between sleep and high arousal – in effect, mania – should not be considered as linear, as it normally is, but instead as circular.

Imagine this to be like a clock face. At the 12 o'clock point we find the normal waking state. Increasing arousal is monitored by a movement following the arc of the clock face from 12 o'clock down through the 3 o'clock point and ending up at the 6 o'clock point in a fully aroused state of consciousness. Conversely, increasing drowsiness can be shown by an anti-clockwise movement from the normal waking state at 12 o'clock to drowsy at around 9 o'clock and fully asleep at 6 o'clock. From this it will be noted that both increasing and decreasing arousal meet at the same point, where sleep and high arousal share the same state.

McCreery gives us an example of how high and low arousal states are related by citing catatonia, a condition observed regularly in schizophrenia. Catatonia involves the schizophrenic adopting a position of immobility for extended periods of time. Much to the surprise of researchers, individuals in this state could be brought out of it by the administration of amobarbitol, a sedative. This makes no sense if catatonia is a state of low arousal: to give a catatonic person a sedative should place them in an even deeper state of arousal, not wake them up from it. McCreery cites the work of Stevens and Darbyshire, who concluded from their research that the 'psychic state in catatonic schizophrenia can be one described as great excitement'.[9]

It has been discovered that one of the EEG markers of schizophrenia is a lack of alpha rhythms within the brain. Alpha rhythms are large, slow waves of electrical activity that are registered by an EEG and are associated with a state of total rest. They disappear as soon as the subject starts to think about anything or experiences pain. These waves are usually centred on the occipital lobes. They are particularly active during REM sleep. Conversely beta waves are suggestive of a full waking state. Some studies have shown that delta rhythms show higher than average levels of activity in fully awake schizophrenics. These are extremely slow waves with a frequency of less than four pulses per second. In neurotypicals this is associated with very deep sleep states in which REM activity ceases altogether. McCreery considers this to be strong evidence that, even though seemingly awake, schizophrenics are, in fact, in a deep sleep state.

I would like to add that in my opinion it is in such states of high arousal that the doors of perception are flung open for schizophrenics. The delta activity allows the Pleroma to leak over into waking life and causes massive cognitive confusion. As we have already discovered, McCreery and his associate Celia Green have proposed a mechanism by which one reality can overlay another, and in doing so they suggest an explanation for many altered states of consciousness such as the out-of-body experience and the near-death experience.

McCreery's model does seem to offer an explanation as to how schizophrenics' 'hallucinations' seem to be a regular part of their waking life. Schizophrenics are continually in a state of semi-sleep and at any moment can fall into a very deep sleep state whereby the images usually associated with dreaming break through to manifest in the everyday world.

Of course, a central feature of schizophrenia is a subject we have touched with regard to various other elements of the Huxleyan spectrum: namely, the hearing of voices. This is probably the dominant factor in the general public's image of schizophrenia. The voices are usually not supportive of subjects and, in some cases, incite them to terrible acts. It is as if the schizophrenic's reducing engine has wound down too far and all kinds of negative impulses seep through. There is a total loss of control, and the person is simply overpowered by the sensory inputs.

What is taking place in the schizophrenic state with regard to clearly

93

destructive voices is, I admit, a major issue regarding the Huxleyan spectrum. If these 'voices' are simply those of the Daemon, why do they sometimes seem to do harm to an already confused and defenceless Eidolon? A partial answer may be that the wavelength of signal being received may be much broader, allowing other elements of the Pleroma in some way to tune in. What these are is open to conjecture, but history is full of examples of demonic possession and attacks from other negative forces. This may or may not be the explanation, but it is an area of important research that needs to be pursued.

However, as we have seen, the majority of voices, even in schizophrenia, are in general supportive or, at worst, indifferent. Even so, it must be accepted that, in general, schizophrenia is a far from pleasant experience. Indeed, one of the associations made by the original researchers into the condition, Kraepelin and Bleuler, may be of huge significance in this regard. This is to do with how schizophrenia mirrors another very upsetting and disturbing illness, at least to those who have to witness it: the illness we call dementia or, as it is now becoming known, Alzheimer's disease.

## Schizophrenia and Alzheimer's: A hidden relationship?

On 9 December 2014 a paper was published in the prestigious *Proceedings of the National Academy of Sciences* (PNAS) journal.[10] It linked an illness that seems to occur early in life with one that seems to occur late in life. A team at Oxford University led by Gwenaëlle Douaud examined the brains of 484 subjects ranging in age from eight to 85 using magnetic resonance imaging (MRI) scans. They were looking to discover how the human brain changes over time. It seems that the areas that develop latest deteriorate earliest. In other words, as we get older our brain seems to go backwards in time. For example, high-level processing of visual, auditory and sensory information do not fully develop until late adolescence or early adulthood. However, as we age, these are the first faculties to deteriorate. They are particularly susceptible to the damage brought about by schizophrenia and Alzheimer's disease.

This may be of huge significance with regard to the central thesis of this book. For many years the similarities between schizophrenia and dementia have been noted by neurologists, psychiatrists and psychologists. Indeed, as we have already seen, schizophrenia was originally called dementia praecox, which is Latin for 'premature dementia' or 'precocious madness'. It was noted by Kraepelin that this early-onset form of dementia manifested in the early teens, usually around puberty.

Douaud and her team discovered that the lateral part of the primary motor cortex and a small section of the lingual gyrus were areas that showed the delayed development and the earliest deterioration. These areas are known to be the ones most affected by schizophrenia and Alzheimer's, specifically in the bottom of the folds on the surface of the brain in that area. It is exactly here, as we shall discover later, that higher levels of a protein called ß-amyloid (beta amyloid) have been discovered in individuals suffering from Alzheimer's.

In effect this discovery reinvigorates a long-neglected scientific idea known as 'retrogenesis' which was popular in the 1880s; in simple terms, this proposed that mental abilities decline with age in the same way that they develop with age and through evolution. It may be significant that chimpanzees and our other close primate relatives do not have the neural centre identified in the study. This gives them a seeming immunity to naturally occurring schizophrenia and Alzheimer's. In turn this suggests that these two diseases may be what makes us human. We will be discussing some controversial observations later regarding this intriguing concept.

Birth and death are the two states that bracket our lives. One thrusts us crying into consensual reality from the Pleroma and the other ushers us back there at the end of life. If we are lucky and manage to avoid dying in accidents, by illness or by the hands of our fellow human beings, we will eventually shuffle off this mortal coil with the assistance of Alzheimer's disease. Indeed, as our medical technology manages to control the major killing diseases of the past, enabling us to live longer, more and more of us will succumb to this disease. It relates directly to an ageing brain and, it is reaching epidemic proportions, particularly in the developed world. It has been calculated that every 67 seconds somebody in the United States develops the disease. Worldwide around 35.6 million people have the disease, and by 2050 this number is expected to have tripled. It mirrors a related epidemic, on which we will focus later.

So why does an illness that differentiates us from all other animals work as the last resort in making sure that we move on, stepping aside for the younger generation? Let us now spend some time looking more closely at this condition that many of us will one day face.

# CHAPTER SIX

# Alzheimer's Disease

## Introduction: My Mother's Experience

About 10 years ago I received a phone call from my elderly mother. At that time she was in her early 80s. As a bit of background, 15 years before she had lost her left eye after being diagnosed with malignant melanoma. She had accommodated this disability very well. She had lost her perception of depth but otherwise she was fine. Sadly, a few months before the phone call she had discovered that she had glaucoma in her remaining eye. This was not good news as she lived alone, my father having died in the late 1980s. However, she had re-kindled a friendship with my father's sister, and regularly my aunt stayed at my mother's house in Bromborough Pool Village on the Wirral peninsula, in northwest England.

In the phone call my mother described how she and my aunt had been walking into the village. My aunt had stopped for a second to catch her breath and my mother stopped with her. As she did so, she noticed something odd in the sky over 'Prices', a local factory site, now abandoned.

She described it to me as a circle of smoke with a more solid disc-shaped object in the middle. The object had two flashing coloured lights on it. She watched in amazement as the smoke ring began to spin and then, in a moment, the whole thing just disappeared. She felt that whatever it was had, for a few seconds, been here, and then returned to wherever it came from. Unfortunately, my aunt has even worse eyesight and saw nothing.

My mother was keen to have my opinion on what she had seen. Although she knew about UFOs from my own interest in the subject, she had never read anything about them. I agreed that what she had seen was odd and suggested that maybe it was related to her deteriorating eyesight, possibly a 'floater' on the surface of her eye.

A few days later she rang me again, early one morning. Whereas she had been very calm and matter-of-fact with regards to her 'sighting', her mood was totally different this time. She was clearly very upset, and not a little frightened. Since my father's death she had lived alone and coped very well. Clearly, something had occurred to disturb her feelings of safety. After I managed to calm her down, she explained that she had woken in the early hours of that morning. Her bedroom was illuminated from a streetlight outside her window. Something had disturbed her. She looked around the room and noticed that the bedroom door was slightly ajar. She thought this strange, as usually she shut it. As she looked at the door, she noticed a movement. It was a set of long, thin fingers coming around the side of the door. These were followed by a large head which poked itself into the room. The creature looked around and then spotted her in the bed. This obviously disturbed it, and it dodged back behind the door. My mother was, as she described it to me, petrified with fear. She could not move. She was trapped in this state for a fair amount of time and then eventually drifted off to sleep.

After she woke up, the previous night's visitation was still on her mind. She rushed downstairs and rang me. I asked her what her nocturnal visitor looked like. She said that it had been the height of a small child with a huge, bulbous head. It had really long fingers and spindly arms. However, what really disturbed her was that it had huge black, insect-like eyes. She also added that it seemed to have no nose, just two slot-like nostrils. She asked me what on earth it was.

I attempted to calm her down by explaining that it was simply a very vivid dream. This seemed to calm her down. As she lived alone, the last thing I wanted to do was give her additional cause for concern. Thankfully, the 'entity' never returned, at least not in that particular guise. But I was very much intrigued.

As I have mentioned, my mother has no knowledge of UFO lore. That she had described in perfect detail a classic 'grey' had, quite frankly, scared the hell out of me. She has always been a somewhat grounded individual. She does not believe in ghosts or aliens. Indeed, when I was younger she slightly mocked my interest in 'such nonsense'. So how did her unconscious create such an image? But more importantly, was this associated in some way with the UFO incident of a few days before? I was keen to not have her link these things at all, and never discussed the subject with her again.

Three years ago I posted a description of this incident on my Facebook Wall. I quickly received a response from a friend named Morrigan Howkins. Morrigan explained that on the very day that my mother had seen the UFO, Morrigan had seen the same object from a mile or so in the opposite direction. She was in a taxi with a friend, and both the taxi driver and the friend saw it too.

For me this changed what my mother had seen from a hallucination to something far more intriguing. Either this 'hallucination' was a 'collective' one facilitated by mass hysteria, or it was a real object in the sky. As Morrigan, her friend and the taxi driver have never met my mother – and they were about a mile away from her at the time – I think that a collective delusion brought about by infectious mass hysteria is not in any way an adequate explanation.

If the UFO sighting was an external event, what does this tell us about the subsequent 'visitation'? Were the two events related or was this a simple coincidence? Subsequent developments after the sighting and nocturnal encounter make this even more intriguing.

Soon after my mother's encounter with the 'entity' in her bedroom, she started to report strange things happening at home or when she was out shopping. She told me that there was an 'elderly man' in her house. She saw him regularly and he always smiled at her. I asked her if it was a neighbour popping in to see her. She replied that this was not the case. What surprised me was her lack of concern regarding this apparition. This was puzzling, but what took place next helped me to explain the mystery. One day, again in passing, she mentioned to me that the 'little children' had been in the house earlier that day. I asked her who the children were. She replied that they were the same children that regularly brushed past her in the street when she was shopping. She explained that they were very friendly and chatted among themselves and sometimes sang songs. I asked her how they got in the house. She replied, 'They are always here.'

I realized what was going on. In my research into visual hallucinations I had encountered something known as 'Charles Bonnet syndrome' (CBS). In this, elderly individuals with failing sight report seeing small people, non-existent animals and other bizarre things. These are seen in consensual space and seem to have their own motivations and agendas. We will return to this later. What concerned me was that my mother had been showing increased confusion and memory loss, together with irrational habitual behaviours. As CBS is also associated with the early stages of dementia and Alzheimer's disease, I was keen to have a formal diagnosis. A few days later I took her to see her physician. To my surprise the doctor had never heard of CBS but at my suggestion she agreed that we should test my mother for Alzheimer's. Over a period of months my mother's condition deteriorated and a formal diagnosis of dementia with Lewy Bodies (DLB) was made. On researching this, I was not surprised to discover that CBS is a symptom of early-stage DLB. My mother's 'alien' encounter and the subsequent visual perceptions of little children were symptoms of the developing condition.

My mother is far from alone in exhibiting this very mysterious 'syndrome' – it is mysterious in that psychiatry and neurology are very good at describing the effects of the 'illness' but not so effective at explaining why such images spontaneously occur and how they seem to have an independence from the observer. My mother didn't 'create' the 'grey' in her bedroom. It, or some external force with its own motivations, decided to appear in her life at that stage. So is the explanation that CBS images are simply 'hallucinations' in any way adequate or, more importantly, convincing?

## Charles Bonnet Syndrome

Charles Bonnet syndrome (CBS) is named after the physician who first described it, Charles Bonnet (1720–1773). Bonnet was a fascinating individual. He was the first person to observe 'parthenogenesis', whereby an unfertilized egg can produce an embryo. However, his somewhat limited fame lies in the 'syndrome' named after him. His grandfather, Charles Lullin, had been suffering from cataracts, and at the age of 72 underwent an operation to have them removed. At that time this was a very hazardous thing to do. However, Charles survived. But 11 years later something strange happened: he began to have really powerful hallucinations. He saw people and animals moving within the tapestries that adorned the walls of his house. He also had incidents of macropsia and micropsia (whereby objects appear larger or smaller than they really are) and objects appearing and disappearing within his visual field. Bonnet was fascinated by all this and recorded what his grandfather reported.

But there is an even more intriguing link to be made here. My mother has experienced migraine and migraine auras since teenage years. There is a form of migraine known as 'migraine with brainstem aura' (MBA), also known as basilar migraine or Bickerstaff's syndrome.[1] The condition is known to first manifest in young women who then continue with it well into late middle age. This is exactly when the illness first affected my mother. The hallucinations associated with the aura states of basilar migraine are generated in the brain stem and the occipital lobes. The brain stem is one of the most primitive parts of the brain. In turn the occipital lobe is the location of the primary visual cortex and is closely linked neurochemically and neuroelectrically to the retina. Damage to the occipital lobes is known to cause vision problems and hallucinations. Significantly, it is known that occipital lobe epileptic seizures are triggered by light flicker, strobe lights and flash photography. These are technically known as photo-sensitivity seizures. So what does modern science make of this very strange experience?

## Under the Easter Bonnet

The neuroscientist V S Ramachandran and the late psychiatrist Oliver Sacks have both been fascinated by the effects of CBS. In his book *Hallucinations* Sacks describes how one elderly woman reported seeing two miniature policemen guiding a miniature criminal to a similarly tiny police van. Now for me, and for those who experience these hallucinations, there is one huge question that the standard 'hallucination' explanation fails to address: that is, why does the brain create such bizarre yet vivid images?

Another patient, of Ramachandran's, saw children in her left visual field – strange enough in itself but what is stranger is that she also reported hearing their laughter. This is exactly how my mother described her encounters with 'the children'. By the time this patient turned to the direction of the laughter, the children had disappeared. Ramachandran puts together a case for explaining these effects as visual hallucinations, but here we have an auditory hallucination accompanying the visual images. If CBS is simply the brain confabulating visual images to accommodate the loss of vision, then why does the auditory cortex also become involved, creating sounds that reinforce what is being 'seen'? The visual pathways of the brain are totally different from the auditory pathways.

That children feature regularly in these hallucinations is intriguing. I suspect that what is really being seen is 'small people', not specifically children. These entities have been reported throughout the centuries as the 'little people', the 'fey', or the 'Secret Commonwealth'. Interestingly enough, Ramachandran ventures a similar conclusion, although he links it to the perception of ghosts and UFO sightings rather than 'fairies'. As I have already mentioned, the first clue to my mother's sadly undiagnosed CBS was a UFO sighting, followed by the ghost of an elderly man in her house. She also saw the children and a classic 'grey'. Of possible significance here is that she subsequently developed Alzheimer's disease and was a life-long migraineur. How many boxes need to be ticked? Of course, her experiences were all subjectively reported. My question is, in what other way could her experiences have been reported? Hallucinations, by their very definition, are private, internal experiences.

In another particularly interesting case, an elderly man reported into his local hospital, explaining that for the previous 10 days he had been perceiving a series of complex hallucinations in his right visual field. The hallucinations usually lasted for a few seconds at a time. They each consisted of a cat or small dog, and they were totally realistic. Each animal was static and looking up at him. He realized that if he quickly moved his eye, the animal disappeared; but a slow movement of the eye did not affect it.

I am reminded of how similar these effects are to hypnagogic or hypnopompic images, and I suspect that there may be a link between the two, maybe facilitated by a form of REM intrusion. What is particularly interesting about this comment is that both authors independently acknowledge that the hallucinations have a seeming outward and autonomous existence. In other words, the hallucinations seem to be independent of the observer. It is usually stressed by academic researchers that the perceiver of such hallucinations at no time believes that the entities he or she sees are actually real. I wonder how this is. If the hallucination has a seemingly three-dimensional solidity, is located in three-dimensional space and shows self-motivated actions, then why does the observer not conclude that it is a genuine element of consensual reality? After all, all the above, when perceived under 'normal' perceptual conditions, will be accepted as proof that what is being seen is actually real. From this I can only conclude that the non-reality of a perception is confirmed when it is known that others do not perceive it. Of course, this then places the experience firmly within the general definition of a hallucination as a perception of something that does not exist in the external (phenomenal) world. In simple terms, if nobody else sees it, it is counted as a hallucination.

## Neurological Explanations of Charles Bonnet Syndrome

I am intrigued as to how mainstream science explains this incredible phenomenon. In a web search I came across an article that originally appeared in the magazine *Health and Ageing* in April 1998. This is an attempt by its authors (Dr Stephen J Doyle, an ophthalmologist at Manchester Royal Eye Hospital, and journalist Maggie Harrison) to describe what is happening to laypersons who suddenly find that the 'doors of perception' are opening and all kinds of weird and wonderful entities are sharing their consensual space. They comment:

> Why these hallucinations should occur is not known, but the best
> explanation so far is that of the 'dual-input model'. According
> to this paradigm, both external sensory input and internal

memory input contribute to image formation and a sustained level of sensory input is required to inhibit the emergence of pre-formed images from within the brain. If sensory input falls below a given threshold, a release of previously recorded perceptions into awareness may occur.[2]

Note here that the authors fall back on the 'dual-input model', the very same theory dismissed so effectively by Green and McCreery. But does this 'explanation' of CBS in which 'internal memory input(s)' contribute to the images perceived actually hold water? One of the major mysteries of CBS is that people 'see' images of places they have never been to or people they never met. These are clearly *not* memories. For example, Oliver Sacks's patient Rosalie saw 'people walking up and down in Eastern dress' and later experienced an incident in which the wall of her room became a huge gate in which scores of elaborately clad people milled through into her reality.[3] For Rosalie these people seemed absolutely real.'[4]

There is another form of CBS that involves what I suspect is a variation on hypnagogic or hypnopompic imagery, which occurs on the borderline of waking and sleeping. These images present scenery and events that seem very mundane and therefore have a feeling of reality.

Ivy L, another CBS patient of Oliver Sacks, and one who also suffered from macular degeneration, described how, as a passenger in a car, she would close her eyes and in her mind's eye would see a facsimile of the passing scenes as they may have been had her eyes been open. Curiously the hallucination never involved her perceiving people or other vehicles.[5]

Please bear in mind that these images are not in any way 'willed' by the observer, they are seemingly independent and have within them scenes that have their own inner consistency and an air of total normality. Ivy closes her eyes and the images appear. However, she still believes them to be hallucinations.

Not so another of Sacks's patients, identified as 'Janet B'. Janet was a great lover of reading and, because of her declining vision, had taken to listening to audiobooks. On occasions she would find that she was not alone in listening to the narrative. She would be joined by a group of unknown individuals who would pay great attention to what was being read out loud. These people never responded to Janet's questions to them and seemed unaware of her presence. Initially Janet considered her associates to be hallucinations. As her dementia worsened she began to insist that they were real.[6]

Here we have a woman who initially believes that what she is perceiving is a hallucination, but as time goes on and she has the time to evaluate the situation she comes to the conclusion that the hallucination is actually real. Sacks is more than happy to agree with a patient when they acknowledge that the hallucinations are mind-created and unreal, but when the very same patient, after due consideration, revises that position, he or she is thought to be in a delusional state. In my opinion, the images seen by Janet B suggest to me that she may have been 'remote viewing' a scene in a book group? The overall description suggests that she is an invisible 'observer' of a real event that is taking place elsewhere. I am intrigued as to why a brain-generated hallucination creates an image in which the people in the image do not acknowledge the observer.

Sacks recognizes that CBS hallucinations involve extremely vivid coloration and detail. This is exactly how DMT users describe the world they enter when they take the hallucinogen. He then goes on to describe the more common CBS hallucinations as involving physical shapes such as squares, checkerboards, rhomboids, quadrangles or else honeycomb patterns, phosphenes or clouds of colour.[7]

You will recall that these are exactly the image types known as Klüver's Form Constants, and they facilitate a direct link with migraine auras, as do the involvement of phosphenes. Surely such similarities suggest a common cause?

In my opinion a big mystery, and one that suggests that CBS is far more than simply a set of subjective hallucinations, is the simple fact that certain themes can be found in many of the reports of its occurence. For example, my mother had no knowledge of CBS and yet she reported regularly to me 'the children'. In his book *Hallucinations* Oliver Sacks describes a patient of his known as Marlon who, like my mother, saw children and little people.[8] However, as his CBS developed, Marlon begin to believe that the beings he saw in his hallucinatory state were actually real. Sacks is always keen to stress that CBS experiences can be differentiated from other kinds of hallucination by the subject's knowledge that what they are seeing is not real. He attempts to explain this by proposing that at night a person's abilities to differentiate reality from illusion is lost. With regard to Marlon, he comments that 'late in the day his insights break down.'

Might I suggest an alternative explanation here? Individuals with CBS are approaching the end of their lives. They are going back to a state of awareness that they had in infancy and early childhood. Their 'doors of perception' are opening again and they can access elements of the Pleroma. Infancy and old age are the liminal places where consciousness is emerging from, or going back to, the Pleroma. This also happens when death approaches at any age.

Of possible significance in my mother's case is that her diagnosis is 'dementia with Lewy Bodies'. Lewy Bodies, which are made up of proteins, collect in the brain stem, basal ganglia and sometimes in the visual association cortex. This suggests that they may facilitate hallucinations. Sacks associates this condition with Parkinson's disease but it is clear that it is also related to standard dementia. He considers that the main difference between Lewy Body hallucinations and those defined as CBS is that the former are complex and multi-sensory, in that sound and smell are also involved, in contrast to the CBS type which is exclusively visual.

Indeed, they are so vivid that, in Sacks's words, they may lead to 'delusions' that they are real.

Dementia with Lewy Bodies (DLB) is one of a group of diseases known under the umbrella term 'sporadic dementia of Alzheimer's type' (SDAT). The main difference between standard Alzheimer's and DLB is that DLB sufferers regularly experience CBS, whereas classic Alzheimer's do not. However, these two conditions are closely related and are frequently misdiagnosed. In my opinion, DLB opens the 'doors of perception' slightly wider than Alzheimer's, but in the final analysis they bring about the same outcome: a gradual moving out of this reality into another one. It is to this mini-spectrum of age-related illnesses that we now turn our attention in greater detail.

## Alzheimer's and Related Liminalities

It has been calculated that every 71 seconds somebody in the world will be diagnosed with SDAT. It has been shown that SDAT is associated with microtubular dysfunction and is characterized by the appearance of specific cytoskeletal cellular abnormalities, including neurofibrillary tangles and senile plaques. The areas affected by Alzheimer's are the hippocampus, the limbic system and the cortex. But with regard to our enquiry, the most important discovery regarding SDAT is that it is directly caused by the destruction of microtubules.

As you will recall, Roger Penrose and Stuart Hameroff believed that the microtubules – thin molecular tubes – are crucial for the processing of consciousness. They carry proteins along neuron branches within the brain; they also act as a scaffolding for cells. They are a component of the cytoskeleton and can grow as long as 50 micrometres. However, they are very narrow. The outer diameter is about 24 nanometres, the inner diameter about 12 nanometres. Penrose and Hameroff have suggested that consciousness is created by these structures, so any damage to them will affect the way in which the brain can receive its signals. I know that I have used this analogy several times but it is repeating the point: just as a radio receiver does not contain the musicians, announcers and studio, so it is that the brain itself does not need to *contain* consciousness. If the radio is damaged or destroyed, the broadcast may become garbled, disjointed; if it ceases to function altogether, the signal is lost. As far as the listener is concerned, the radio has died. But, to reiterate, the studio continues to exist.

In effect, the microtubules are the equivalents of a radio receiver. If they are damaged, the signal becomes similarly garbled and will, as the damage worsens, seem to die. Consciousness cannot get through and the brain gradually reverts back to its autonomic functions. As we know, a body does not need a self-aware consciousness to function. People in persistent vegetative states continue to live and can do for years as long as they are supplied with food and water.

There is growing evidence from SDAT research that Penrose and Hameroff are correct. In a healthy brain the microtubules are kept healthy by a protein known as the tubulin-associated unit (TAU). In a normal brain tau proteins interact with tubulin to stabilize the microtubules; also, when replacements are needed, they stimulate the tubulin to assemble itself into new microtubule structures. When Alzheimer's takes over in the brain, the tau ceases to function and aggregates into structures known as amyloid fibrils. These are, in effect, tangles of tau proteins. On their own, tau proteins are easily dissolved. However, once in a fibril they are far more resistant to degradation. These then congregate together and in so doing disrupt the way in which signals cross the brain from neuron to neuron. They literally clog up the brain.

Another series of experiments have also lent indirect support to the microtubule model of Penrose and Hameroff. Scientists have managed to re-create similar symptoms in rodents to those observed in SDAT patients by administering a drug called colchicine.[9] When introduced to the brain, colchicine binds to tubulin and brings about a very similar level of microtubule destabilization as the amyloid fibrils. This again results in massive cell death.[10]

As mentioned earlier, one of the most significant recent discoveries with regard to the overall thesis presented in this book is the fact that a high level of ß-amyloid (beta amyloid) has been found in the lateral part of the primary motor cortex and small part of the lingual gyrus.[11] This is exactly the area where cell death has been recorded in schizophrenics as well as those suffering from Alzheimer's. This suggests a significant link between the two illnesses, one of which manifests fairly early in life and one that appears towards the end.[12]

## Alzheimer's and Déjà Vu

If Alzheimer's disease facilitates the opening of the 'doors of perception' towards the end of life, then there must be evidence of precognitive sensations, telepathy and episodes of altered states of consciousness (ASCs). As we have already discovered, Alzheimer's does facilitate unusual ASCs, including the odd hallucinations that go under the label of CBS.

One such phenomenon that suggests that short-term precognition is possible is déjà vu. As we have already seen, this experience is regularly described by individuals who suffer from migraine, temporal lobe epilepsy and schizophrenia. In fact, déjà vu experiences are considered by medical professionals to be one of the symptoms of all three conditions. Therefore it should come as no surprise to discover that déjà vu is also associated with Alzheimer's disease.

In July 2006 an article appeared in the *New York Times*. Under a striking title, 'Déjà Vu, Again and Again', the narrative cited the case of a 77-year-old woman called Pat Shapiro who lived with her husband Don in Dover, Massachusetts. In December 2005 Pat was sitting in a car with her daughter Susan outside a store when her attention was drawn to a woman and her baby getting into a car nearby. She said to her daughter, 'I saw her last time I was here. The baby did exactly the same thing'. Pat noticed another woman smoking and chatting on a cell phone wearing a scarf, and again she knew that she had seen exactly this set of circumstances before, at some undefined time in her past. When they got home, Pat admitted to Susan that these strange sensations happened regularly to her.

The accepted scientific definition of déjà vu, put forward in 1983 by a Seattle-based psychiatrist, Vernon Neppe, is: 'any subjectively inappropriate impression of familiarity of the present experience with an undefined past'. However, it is important to note that Pat was actually experiencing an associated experience on the déjà spectrum, something known as 'déjà vécu' (already lived), a term first used by Swiss-based physicist-therapist Dr Arthur Funkhouser. Déjà vu literally translates as 'already seen', and although Pat was 'seeing' the circumstances again, she was also 're-living' them.

In December 2000 Chris Moulin, now of the University of Leeds, was working at a memory clinic in Bath. A local doctor sent him a referral letter regarding an 80-year-old retired engineer who had recently developed powerful and ongoing déjà vu sensations. Moulin visited the man, now referred to as A K P, at his home. A K P's wife had become very frustrated by the way her husband announced, with absolute certitude, that he knew what was going to happen next when they were watching TV programmes.[13]

The scientific literature has regularly recorded an increase in déjà vu sensations in elderly individuals who are manifesting memory issues. For example, in 2001 a paper was published describing how an 87-year-old woman reported that she was continuously re-living the past; and most of her daily experiences were ones she had lived through before. Similarly, in the mid-1990s Harvard psychologist Daniel Schacter published a paper describing the ongoing déjà vu sensations of a man in his mid-60s.

Moulin requested that the Bath clinic send him any cases that might be similar to that of A K P. In early 2001 he received details about a 70-year-old woman, subsequently identified as M A. Her déjà vu sensations were so powerful that she had even stopped playing tennis, because she knew the outcome of every rally.

What is also significant about these late-onset 'persistent déjà vécu' experiences, as Moulin describes them, is that the subjects genuinely believe that they know what is about to happen next. This is different from most déjà vu experiences. These are simply vague recognitions, nothing more. However, there is nothing vague about these persistent déjà vécu cases. They are interpreted by the subjects as genuine, and powerful, precognitions. As usual science is very good at giving impressive-sounding names to such conditions and then, as if by magic, the nomenclature becomes the explanation. In this case, if you genuinely believe that you are experiencing short-term precognitions you are 'suffering' from a neurological condition called 'anosagnosia', making you an anosagnosiac. So what is the evidence that this is a condition that has its roots in neurochemistry or brain physiology? Well, none actually. It is simply a label that is used to describe people who are 'unaware of their condition'. That is, they are unaware that they are unaware of their condition – this could end up being an infinite regress.

In my opinion, the real cause of this 'condition' is related to what is taking place in the brains of some elderly individuals. They are in the early stages of Alzheimer's disease, which may, as we shall discover later, facilitate communication with alternative areas of information, extra-sensory information. Subsequent brain scans of A K P and M A showed abnormal levels of cell death in their temporal lobes. So here we have another link within the Huxleyan spectrum. We know that TLErs regularly report déjà vu sensations as part of their aura state, and there is also powerful evidence that the temporal lobes are involved in similar déjà sensations perceived by migraineurs. Indeed, in a later paper Moulin, and his associates Akira O'Connor and Gillian Cohen, stated that patient A K P's experiences resulted from 'cell death in his brain as part of a dementing process'.[14]

Moulin has now researched scores of cases of déjà vécu in the elderly. He believes that the phenomenon may be very common but that most people are too nervous to mention it to the doctors in case they are considered crazy.

What can we make of these 'precognitive' abilities? Are they simply delusions created by a demented mind, or are they clues we are missing with regard to the true nature of reality? For example, let us just assume for a moment that these individuals are actually perceiving the future. If this is true, what possible mechanism could explain this? Well, there is one, and that is that they are 'remembering' the circumstances from another time in their past. They are 're-living' a set of circumstances, and in doing so they recognize certain things which in turn stimulate the memories. Actually, Moulin is being very perceptive in his choice of terminology, even if, as I suspect, it conveys a meaning that was not intended. In his paper he calls such Alzheimer-related precognitions 'persistent déjà vécu' – already lived, rather than déjà vu, which is already seen. Evidence for such an opinion may be found in the intriguing Alzheimer's-related concept of 'retrogenesis'.

## Retrogenesis

In 2008 director David Fincher released a movie, entitled *The Curious Case of Benjamin Button* and starring Brad Pitt, loosely based on a 1922 short story written by F Scott Fitzgerald. The story line has 'Benjamin' born in November 1918 with the appearance and physical maladies of an elderly man. As time passes, Benjamin becomes younger, and it is clear that he is living his life in reverse. In the final sections of the movie, he reverts back to childhood and then infancy. Much to the surprise of his social workers, the ever-younger Benjamin starts showing signs of Alzheimer's and dies as an infant of 84 years of age. Time reversal has been a popular theme in movies and novels over the years. Philip K Dick used it as a central theme in his novel *Counter-Clock World*, as did Brian Aldiss in another novel, *Cryptozoic!* Interestingly, both came out in 1967, showing that sometimes ideas spontaneously occur independently at the same time. However, in the Aldiss and Dick novels everybody is affected by the time reversal, and therefore the contrast is not as marked as it is in the F Scott Fitzgerald short story and the Fincher movie.

In the Aldiss novel it is discovered that although we perceive time to be flowing forward, it is in fact going backwards. Our mind creates the illusion of the past-to-future flow, whereas in reality future is becoming past. Of course, these stories are just clever fictions written to entertain. However, Alzheimer's and dementia may be evidence that life is, in a very particular way, a circle.

In a paper published in 1984, researcher Barry Reisberg resurrected the term 'retrogenesis' in specific relation to Alzheimer's. By this he meant that Alzheimer's is a reversal of the developmental processes that take place during infancy and childhood. In effect, the Alzheimer's patient is going backwards in time and approaching birth from another direction.[15] He noted an almost perfect reversal or mirroring in the development of an infant and the decline of a dementia patient, specifically in the areas of cognition, coordination, language, feeding and behaviour. In response to Reisberg's retrogenesis hypothesis a new process of caring for Alzheimer's patients has been devised in which the mother-infant relationship is applied by the carer to the patient, and this has proven to be very successful. However, the overall dynamic is, again, a reversal, as there is no hope of improvement for the patient, just an ongoing deterioration followed by death. It was this aspect that was so touchingly depicted in the Fincher movie.

115

Of interest here is that an infant has no concept of ego. Their world is simply an extension of themselves. They are 'at one' with the universe. Retrogenesis suggests that this 'at-one-ment' is also active in the final stages of Alzheimer's. The patient has no sense of self and their senses are open to everything. I would argue that this is, in effect, another 'opening of the doors of perception' – that in the final stages of life the Huxleyan 'reducing valve' no longer functions and the Pleroma is perceived. Indeed, in many ways Alzheimer's is like a passive form of schizophrenia whereby the subject is trapped in a less and less mobile body and can no longer communicate fully the experiences they are having.

But for me what is most curious is that the decline of dementia does not stop at the point of birth with regard to the mirroring effect of infancy. It continues reflecting a reversal of the embryo's development in the womb. The person becomes silent and unmoving and starts to echo the fetal position of hands and legs curled in and the back bent forward. This seems to be a journey back to source.

And then what? Could it be that the process starts again and the person starts to move forwards again in time? If this is the case, there should be evidence of this as the development of the embryo within the womb is mirrored in the progressive behavioural changes of the Alzheimer's patient. Are there any clues to Alzheimer's-like behaviours in the developing embryo and the infant?

It is reasonable to assume that if a person manages to survive all life's dangers and fatal diseases, then their natural span is brought to an end by Alzheimer's. This is reflected in the simple fact that as medicine has become more effective in its saving of lives, Alzheimer's is on the increase. This seems to be the way in which the brain 'switches off' its abilities to interface with consensual reality and at the same time nullifies the effectiveness of the Huxleyan 'reducing valve'. In doing so the dying person reverts back to childhood, infancy and then to an embryo stage. I believe that evidence of this can be shown in the way in which elderly individuals experience 'hallucinations' that mirror similar 'hallucinations' experienced in childhood, specifically the similarities between Charles Bonnet syndrome and Michael J Hallowell's concept of 'quasi-corporal companions' (QCCs) that we encountered earlier with regard to the experiences of TLEr Myron Dyal.

I was fascinated to discover that in an article in the UK magazine *Fortean Times*, from 2009, which featured a series of examples of Hallowell's QCCs, there was one in which a respondent called Paul Murphy described how, when he was four, his QCC, called 'Cal-Cal', informed his four-year-old companion that his parents would get divorced. Two days later Paul's father left home and his parents did, indeed, get subsequently divorced. This is an example of precognition. In another case, described by Paul Dale, there are strong elements of Charles Bonnet syndrome. The five-year-old Dale had two QCCs, Gumby and Bongabeers. Both were a couple of feet tall. Gumby dressed in a green suit and Bongabeers wore a beige jumper and brown breeches.

Such entities have been reported for centuries. French UFO researcher Jacques Vallée has long argued that these creatures are real in that they inhabit alternative dimensions and, on occasion, can break through into this world through human perceptions. A similar position was taken by American UFO researcher John Keel whose book *Project Trojan Horse* is a classic of this interpretation of the UFO/abduction phenomenon. Vallée's book *Passport to Magonia* suggests that these beings have been visiting us for centuries, if not millennia. Magonia is where one of the medieval 'elementals' said he lived. Is Magonia just another word for the Pleroma, and are the 'doors' more open between Magonia and our world for the very elderly and the very young, or is it a specific area of the Pleroma from which self-motivated entities can gain access to our reality? Is this the real source of 'greys' and other 'elementals'? This would certainly explain my mother's experience.

Such perceptions are hugely supportive of Reisberg's retrogenesis model, as are 2014 findings of Gwenaëlle Douaud, discussed previously (p94). You will recall that Douaud's research showed that the areas of the brain that develop earliest in childhood deteriorate latest in old age, and vice versa.[16] I cited this research in support of a linkage between schizophrenia and Alzheimer's. However, Douaud's findings can also link these two elements of my Huxleyan spectrum with a third and, in many ways, the most intriguing element, autism and its associated conditions, Asperger's syndrome and savant syndrome.

# CHAPTER SEVEN:

# Autism

## The History of Autism

In October 1938 a boy, now known to history as 'Donald T', was brought to Baltimore's Harriet Lane Home for Invalid Children by his concerned parents. Donald had been born after a full-term pregnancy at a birth weight of seven pounds (3.175kg). He developed quickly and was walking after 13 months. However, it was his mental abilities that intrigued his parents. At 12 months old he was able to pick up tunes and songs and would subsequently be heard humming them to himself. By the age of two years he had developed an unusual memory and could recite short poems with ease. However, as the years progressed these 'abilities' seemed to develop to such an extent that he began to behave strangely. His parents became so concerned that just after Donald's fifth birthday they took him to the Harriet Lane clinic, where he was taken on as a patient by Leo Kanner.

Donald's condition fascinated Kanner, who, in 1943, published a paper on it in the academic journal *Nervous Child*. Kanner used the term 'early infantile autism' to describe the syndrome.

In this paper Kanner described a series of characteristics that typified autism. These included 'extreme autistic aloneness', an 'anxiously obsessive desire for the preservation of sameness', an 'excellent rote memory', oversensitivity to stimuli and 'delayed echolalia'. The first characteristic echoes Bleuler's use of the Greek *autós*. We shall look at the others in detail later.

Over the years Kanner was to return many times to these characteristics, and in 1956 he decided that it was only the first two that were key elements of autism, the others simply being a consequence of them.[1]

Less than a year after Kanner's 1943 paper, Hans Asperger entered the arena with a paper on something he termed 'autistic psychopathy' in childhood.[2] That it was over 50 years before this paper was translated into English, by Uta Frith, may be taken as evidence that the English-speaking world was not especially interested in typologies outside all-encompassing schizophrenia.

## Diagnosis

It is now believed that autism is a spectrum rather than a single syndrome; and there are even discussions as to whether autism can be considered a syndrome at all. However, research by Lorna Wing and Judith Gould in 1979 proved that it does qualify. In order for a 'syndrome' to be recognized, there has to be a pattern of symptoms that cluster together. Wing and Gould decided that the accepted symptoms of autism were social impairment, verbal and non-verbal language impairment and repetitive/stereotyped activities.

This pioneering work gave rise to the concept of the triad of impairments, a diagnostic tool still used by specialists in the field. As it was subsequently recognized to be a spectrum disorder, it became generally known as 'autism spectrum disorder' (ASD).

It has been observed that ASD is four times as common in boys as girls. Why this is so is very unclear, but it may be related to testosterone release in the womb during gestation.

It may be significant that the actual causes of ASD remain mysterious. In general it is recognized that the possible causes are divided into two typologies: primary ASD (also known as idiopathic ASD) and secondary ASD. The former term is used when no underlying factors can be identified to explain why ASD has developed; the latter when there is an identified underlying medical condition or environmental factor thought to have increased the risk. Not surprisingly about 90 per cent of cases of ASD are primary (unknown cause), while about 10 per cent are secondary (assumed cause). You will recall from what I have written about the supposed 'causes' of schizophrenia that 'idiopathic' actually means 'we don't have a clue' – yet again we see the subtle tactic of using an impressive-sounding medical term to subtly deflect us from the truth. Labelling is being used to serve an orthodox agenda, as with that wonderfully flexible word 'hallucinations'.

## Autism and the Doors of Perception

One autism expert who does not shy away from the mysteries of this condition is Dr Olga Bogdashina. Her book, *Autism at the Edges of the Known World*, presents a reasoned argument that those experiencing autism are actually perceiving the world in a different way from those of us labelled as 'neurotypical'.

From the earliest days of research into autism it has been recognized that autistics have particular sensory sensitivities. Both Kanner[3] and Asperger[4] made reference to the unusual way that their patients reacted to extreme sensory inputs such as sight, taste and smell. This suggested to both researchers that the symptoms of autism were defence mechanisms against these perceived sensory assaults.

However, it was later noted by Lorna Wing that sometimes these responses suggested that synaesthesia was involved. She noted that some autistic children would place their hands over their ears to cut out a blinding light or would close their eyes when hearing what they experienced as loud noises. We will return to this confusion of the senses later, as it has also been reported in schizophrenia, migraine and temporal lobe epilepsy.

Sadly, as we have described, the materialist-reductionist paradigm has a strong hold on most areas of psychology and psychiatry. In effect, any unusual response, suggesting that autistics are accessing areas of the sensory universe denied to neurotypicals, has been soundly ignored. This has been frustrating for some higher-functioning autistics who have described in books and articles how they actually perceive the universe. One such author is Temple Grandin, whose fascinating experiences and refreshingly open-minded approach to her condition we shall return to later. Grandin described her annoyance in typically blunt style: 'So many professionals and non-professionals have ignored sensory issues because some people just can't imagine that an alternate sensory reality exists if they have not experienced it personally.'[5]

The suggestion that autistic children receive a wider range of sensory information than 'normal' children was first proposed by researchers Bergman and Escalona in 1949.[6] They argued that in order to deal with this, the child develops a series of defence mechanisms, and that these mechanisms are the traits associated with the condition. In 1961 Mildred Creak added 'unusual perceptual experiences' in her list of core experiences associated with autism. Creak actually considered these experiences to be associated with schizophrenia.[7] In fact, although they did not focus directly on the importance of these reactions, both Kanner and Asperger had described them in earlier papers.

However, it was the ground-breaking work of Lorna Wing in the early 1970s that really focused on these, as she termed them, 'paradoxical' responses to external sensory stimuli.[8] A few years later, in 1974, Carl

Delcato argued the anxieties brought about by these unusual inputs create the characteristic compulsive behaviours and communication difficulties regularly observed in autistic individuals.[9]

In October 2015 newspapers around the world picked up on the case of a young Australian woman called Rebecca Sharrock. Rebecca claims to remember everything that has happened to her since she was 12 days old. She not only remembers the incidents, she effectively re-lives them: she feels all the associated emotions and physical pain. Fascinatingly, she also remembers almost every dream she has ever had. Significantly, Rebecca has been diagnosed as autistic. So why has this young woman such a powerful memory? Is it to do with her autism or is there something more? Rebecca has been diagnosed with a condition known as 'highly superior autobiographical memory' (HSAM), which technically is termed 'hyperthymestic syndrome'. We will be returning later to review this in greater detail.

It is evident that autistic brains work very differently from 'neurotypical' ones. In many ways this is a hugely debilitating condition, and yet it could also be said to offer a powerfully rich inner world of sensory overload. We need to understand what makes autistic brains so 'special'. According to Bogdashina, the responsibility lies with structures known as 'minicolumns'.

By definition, minicolumns are the smallest units in the brain capable of processing information. They are vertical columns of glutamergic acid and gamma-aminobutyric acid. Studies have shown that these structures are different in autistic individuals than in neurotypicals: they are smaller and more numerous.[10] Moreover, and even more importantly, in the non-autistic brain neocortex information is transmitted through the core of the minicolumn, which means that the signal cannot activate its neighbours. This is not the case with regard to the smaller autistic minicolumns: stimuli overflow into neighbouring units. One of the researchers in this field, Manuel F Casanova, likens this to a shower curtain. When working properly, the inhibitory fibres that surround the minicolumns act like a shower curtain keeping the shower water from flooding out into the shower room. In autism the 'water is all over the floor'.[11]

This 'amplifier effect', which brings about a hyper-excitability, may be responsible for the opening of the 'doors of perception', at least in autistics. It has been discovered that the growth rate of the cerebral cortex and consequent brain volume in autistic children is greater than in non-autistics of the same age.[12][13] Autopsies have shown that the greater volume is made up of minicolumns in the cerebral cortex.[14]

It has been discovered that by exposing the brains of rats to a substance called valporic acid (VPA), the major symptoms of autism can be reproduced. Work by Henry and Kamila Markram with VPA in rats have lent support to the hyper-excitability proposition. The Markrams discovered similarities between the brains of VPA rats and autistic humans, particularly in the incidence of minicolumns. They discovered that a VPA rat has up to 50 per cent more connections than a normal rat. In effect, the minicolumns have a higher than normal capacity for processing information. Imagine a TV tuned to maximum in terms of volume, colour saturation and number of channels that can be received at any one time. This is what it is like to be autistic.

Bogdashina has called this sensory overload 'gestalt perception'.[15] The Markrams give it a more prosaic but nevertheless very accurate name: the 'Intense World syndrome'. In effect, individuals experiencing autism are being bombarded with information – that is, sensory overload. Not only that, but they also *remember* too much.

In order to deal with this gestalt perception, autistics learn techniques to cut out certain sensory streams. But in doing so they have to withdraw into themselves. They manage to 'absent' themselves, leaving the perceptions to another part of their being. In many ways this is like a form of disassociation. Autistic writer Donna Williams has called this the 'preconscious system' or 'unknown knowing'.[16]

When in this 'unknown knowing' state, the autistic person is free to interface more closely with the external environment. They seem to be able to expand their senses to envelop people, animals and objects around them, as if they were tuning into some form of holistic field. Williams explains:

> I could resonate with the cat and spend hours lying in front of
> it, making no physical contact with it. I could resonate with the
> tree in the park and feel myself merge with its size, its stability,
> its calm and its flow.[17]

This way of tuning in to a holographic informational field reminds me of the 'oceanic experience' described by mystics through the centuries. For example, philosopher Pyotr Ouspensky, sailing across the Sea of Marmora in 1908, felt that he had 'entered into the waves, and with them rushed with a howl at the ship. And in that instant I became all. The waves – they were myself: the far violet mountains, the wind, the clouds hurrying from the north, the great steamship, heeling and rushing irresistibly forward – all were myself.'[18]

Others have described curiously similar sensations during near-death experiences (NDEs). For example, William Murtha, dying of hypothermia in the waters of the English Channel, describes how his 'emotions were being drawn away from my surroundings':

> I started to notice how I was continuing to expand to fill every
> space, until there was no separation between me and everything
> else. I encompassed – no, became – everything and everyone.[19]

But going beyond such experiences, there is something uncanny about how those experiencing autism 'resonate' – something that modern science is keen to ignore. They seem to develop a form of telepathy. In the following example, notice how the subject describes their experience without imposing a materialist-reductionist interpretation:

> When I was younger I heard lots of noises in my head, spoken things and unspoken things. Tell me you can hear people think. I wish I didn't. If there is a medication that will kill peoples' thoughts I will try and take it.[20]

Here is an individual quite clearly stating that they experienced a form of telepathy when younger, which seems to have been lost in later life. Sadly, I have no information about the age of this person. It would be of interest to know if the loss of telepathic ability took place at puberty.

Donna Williams is someone who clearly showed signs of hypersensitivity. Here she describes how colours became far more than a simple visual stimulus. I am intrigued that she calls these periods of heightened awareness a 'buzz state':

> [The] street lights were yellow with a hint of pink but in a buzz state they were an intoxicating iridescent-like pink-yellow. My mind dived deeper and deeper into the colour, trying to feel its nature, and became it as I progressively lost sense in its overwhelming presence. Each of the colours resonated different feelings within me and it was like they played me as a chord, where other colours played one note at a time.[21]

Here we have a mixing of colour and a suggestion of music. It seems as if Donna was perceiving the at-one-ment described by mystics. Here again we have somebody describing an inner depth to reality in which all things 'resonate' with all other things. In quantum physics this is known as 'entanglement'; it is also a facility of holograms. Is it this underlying holographic information field that Donna and her associates sense when they are in their 'buzz states'?

## Intense World Syndrome

In his book *The Autism Prophecies* author William Stillman describes a survey he did with his fellow autistics. One specific question was, 'Have you ever sensed a divine presence close to you?' This is a fascinating question because any response can be linked directly to the 'sensed presence' work of Michael Persinger and Michael J Hallowell on quasi-corporal companions (QCCs). I was not at all surprised to discover that a series of intriguing responses was collected. One was from 'Angie Carlotta'. Her description has many parallels with reports by DMT experiencers on their encounters with 'alien entities'. Angie describes how when she was under 10 years old she awoke in the middle of the night and sat up in bed:

> By the doorway I observed four bodies of light. They were
> 'talking' to each other. There were no wings or clothes on them;
> they did not look like ghosts or past people, they were just that
> – light in the form of bodies with faces.[22]

Note that this was a young child whose programming would have prompted her to see classic 'angels' with wings. But this is specifically what she did *not* see. It is also significant that she 'woke up' in the middle of the night. This suggests a classic REM intrusion scenario. I am led to think that whatever facilitates autistic perceptions in the brain is directly related to all the other scenarios we have discussed whereby the Pleroma is accessed. For example, I will later present evidence that, owing to lack of myelination of the corpus callosum, young children have little inter-hemispherical communication and accordingly have a consciousness located in the non-dominant hemisphere of the brain.[23] I am suggesting that in children autism widens the already ajar doors of perception to such an extent that a schizophrenia-like state is encountered. This is why Bleuler and Kraepelin used the term 'dementia praecox' to describe both childhood autism and schizophrenia.

One of the most common behaviours of autistics is repetitive movements such as rocking, twirling, hand flapping and vocalizing. Very similar processes are used by mystics, shamans and those in religious orders to access higher states of consciousness – think of the repetitive nature of Gregorian chanting, the structured prayers in the rosary, the use of prayer wheels, the spinning of Sufis and the hand clapping of charismatic Christians. The technical term for such actions is 'self-stimulatory behaviour or 'stimming'. The movement can be in the body itself or in the spinning of objects such as a wheel.

In his book *Autism and Asperger Syndrome: The Facts* British autism specialist Simon Baron-Cohen describes how one of his patients, Jamie, would rock backwards and forwards in a chair until, in Baron-Cohen's words, he would enter a 'trance-like state'.[24] The rocking behaviour had ceased by the time Jamie had reached adolescence but other behavioural tics had carried forward from his childhood. One involved 'flapping a piece of string in front of his eyes'.[25] Now, I have witnessed similar behaviours with children and teenagers at a special school where I worked recently. I would like to be controversial and suggest that flapping long thin objects like a piece of string or waggling one's fingers in front of one's eyes shows the child attempting to reproduce the flicker effect we discussed earlier with regard to the work of Brion Gysin. I noted that the children would do this while looking towards a bright background, never an area of darkness. Later in his book, when systematizing the behaviours observed in classic autism, Baron-Cohen writes that one of these could be 'flicking a straw at high speed in peripheral vision'. Is this not another attempt at bringing about an altered state by the flicker effect? I would also suggest that stimulation of the peripheral vision areas is important. It is known that by using our peripheral vision we stimulate an area of the eye known as the parafovea, rather than the fovea itself. It is the fovea that sends visual information to the conscious, thinking part of the brain. However, most of the visual information that hits the parafovea is subliminal: it is not processed by the conscious mind but is available to the unconscious mind, in my terminology the Daemon. Using peripheral vision to enter a trance state has, again, been used by shamans for millennia. In recent years this has been updated by practitioners of Neuro Linguistic Programming (NLP) who train people to use their peripheral vision as a quick way to enter a light trance.

One writer who is fascinated by these alternative approaches to autism is the American autistic-experiencer Dr Temple Grandin, whose work we shall now consider.

## Temple Grandin and Autistic Perceptions

Grandin is interested in how autistics perceive the world differently from neurotypicals. In her book *The Autistic Brain* she makes the very reasonable point that we all use five ways of understanding what the external world is: our senses. But the brain *interprets* the inputs of those senses to create an internal facsimile of the phenomenal world. This is not a one-to-one reproduction but something that is *created*, using information that has been gleaned over a lifetime. In an edition of the BBC 4 radio programme *In Our Time* perception scientist Richard L Gregory gives a compelling account of the creation of an inner percept using visual stimuli. He describes how the receptor neurons in the retina convert a tiny, inverted, postage stamp-sized image into electrical signals that are then sent to the darkest place in the brain (the visual cortex in the occipital lobe) where they are re-assembled into an illuminated, bright, three-dimensional, enveloping facsimile of the external world. But the source data, the postage stamp area of photon-stimulated chemicals, is nothing like the image the brain creates. And there is more. The brain takes similar encoded information from the ears, pressure signals from the skin and olfactory signals from the nose to create a singular perception of being 'in the world'. But 'we' are not in that world at all: it is an illusion. We are locked away deep in the brain, the ghost-like 'observer' of this illusion. And there is more still. As Gregory points out in the broadcast, each segment of the source data (sight, sound, touch and smell) is processed in a radically different part of the brain. But we sense it all happening *now*. Although Gregory does not name it as such, this is a reference to the 'binding problem'.[26] The mystery is a simple one – but unfortunately there is no simple explanation within our modern understanding of brain processes. Different parts of the brain are responsible for processing different sensory inputs. Some parts attend to vision, some to hearing, some to touch. And even within a specific sensory system, let us say vision, there are parts that process colours, parts that process orientations, and parts whose role is to focus on angles. All these locations are spread across the brain and not in immediate communication with each other; some are nearer to their informational source than others. How this all comes together so that the perceiver has a unified and seemingly immediate perception of the world is one of the great unsolved mysteries of neuroscience. Of course, we can add to this the mystery of where exactly in the brain is the location of the perceiver. Is the perceiver in one single place, the place where it all 'comes together', or are perceptions distributed across the whole brain in a form of a cloud or field?

In her book Grandin asks this seemingly simple question about perception:

> What if you're receiving the same sensory information as everybody else, but your brain is receiving it differently? Then

> your experience of the world will be radically different from
> everyone else's, maybe even painfully so. In that case you would
> literally be living in an alternate reality – an alternate sensory
> reality.[27]

Her final statement here turns a simple observation into something of profound significance. As she says, the perceived universe of autistics is an 'alternate sensory reality'.

Grandin is disappointed that other academics show no real interest in the 'sensory overload' of autistics. She points out that in a 1,400-page book on autism, in 2011, the only chapter that referenced sensory issues was the one she contributed.[28] She believes this is due to the stranglehold that behaviourism still has on neurology and psychology, with the consequence that to even suggest that sensory problems are real flies in the face of an entrenched belief system. She pointedly observes: 'They call themselves strict behaviourists. I call them biology deniers.' The truth, she suggests, is that sensory conditions are central to understanding the behaviour of her fellow autistics. Some crave loud noises or deep pressure, which is why they clap, rock, twirl and shout. But as I have suggested, there is more to this: I believe these behaviours to be attempts to bring about altered sensory states, in the same way that a flicker effect, created by moving the fingers in front of the eyes, brings about such a state.

Modern science, represented by Grandin's much-disliked behaviourists, has a real issue with the subjective reports of autism experiencers. Grandin finds this approach totally *un*scientific. She argues that one can only know what is going on in the mind of any other human being by asking them. This also involves asking what they are experiencing and have experienced. The subjects themselves are the best source of information in this regard. She writes:

> Researchers routinely disparage self-reports, saying they're
> not open to scientific verification because they are subjective;
> but that's the point. Objective observation of behaviours can
> provide important information. But the person suffering from
> sensory overload is the only one who can tell us what it's really
> like.[29]

This will always be a problem for this kind of research, particularly if the experiences reported present information counter to the present scientific paradigm.

I am not part of this conspiracy. For me, what autistics can tell us about their world is of profound importance. In view of this, we will now focus on what it is like to be autistic by experiencing the world through the eyes and ears of a couple of famous exemplars: Tito Rajarshi Mukhopadhyay and Carly Fleischmann.

## Autism: The View from Inside

Tito Rajarshi Mukhopadhyay was born in India in 1989 and moved to Austin, Texas, with his mother, Soma Gopal, at the age of 13. Up until the age of three he showed evidence of severe retardation. He showed no signs of communication nor any language abilities. He was diagnosed as having an extreme form of 'locked-in syndrome'. However, his mother, a chemist, noticed that he regularly stared at calendars. Soma designed a numbered and lettered board that allowed him to communicate. From four years old he was able to describe his world. Later his mother tied a pen to his hand, which allowed him to write. He described how he felt himself to be two areas of perception. He called these his 'acting' self and his 'thinking' self. This has echoes of my Daemon hypothesis as introduced in my book *The Daemon: A Guide to Your Extraordinary Secret Self*.[30] To recap, I suggest there that all human beings have two centres of consciousness.

On the one hand, there is the 'everyday' person that calls itself 'me' or 'I', which I call the *Eidolon*. On the other, there is the entity that seems to be our internal guiding spirit, a sentience that seems to have far greater knowledge than the in-the-world Eidolon: this I call the *Daemon*. The existence of the Daemon has been proposed by mystical and religious groups for millennia. It has gone by many terms including the *ka* (ancient Egyptian), *urvan* (ancient Persia), Hun (Chinese), *thymos* (ancient Greek), *biomgbo* (Kalabari), *genius* (ancient Rome), *Ruach* (Kabbalah), *nafs* (Sufism) and *aumakua* (Polynesian Huna). In this book I have added to this model by suggesting that the Daemon is located in the Pleroma and guides its Eidolon through the pitfalls and dangers encountered as a player guides an onscreen avatar in a first-person role-playing computer game.

I would propose that Tito's 'thinking self' is a Daemon that, because it shares Tito's consciousness with a very low-functioning Eidolon (his 'acting self'), has taken a greater degree of control. For me this is evidenced by Grandin's description of a meeting she had with Tito in a medical library in San Francisco. Tito was able to respond to her questions with the help of a keyboard. After each response he got up and ran around the library, waving his arms about. She realized that the 'spinning, flailing, flapping boy' is what the outside world sees of who Tito is. This is Tito's 'acting self' as viewed with objective dispassion by his 'thinking self'.[31] In his book *How Can I Talk if My Lips Don't Move: Inside My Autistic Mind* he describes how his 'acting self' is 'weird and full of actions'. He always refers to the 'acting self' in the third person. This is clearly the 'thinking self' again observing the actions of the 'acting self' with no empathy. He describes how his 'thinking self' is 'filled with learnings and feeling an embodied entity that understands very well what is being said to it.[32]

After describing her meeting with Tito, Grandin comments that this idea of the 'two selves' has validity with regard to autism. She writes that the notion is 'reinforced' in the writings of Carly Fleischmann.[33] Fleischmann's life experiences, like Tito's, may be able to tell us much about the inner workings of the brain – all brains. Carly was, for the first 10 years of her life, a seemingly non-verbal child with deep autism. When she was old enough, she was supplied with a touch keyboard with pictures on the keys. In this way Carly could, by pressing a particular image, prompt a recorded voice to reproduce the sound of that word. The keyboard did have an alphabet function but this was not used – and given that it seemed redundant, her therapist thought about deleting it to free up memory space.

On the very day that this deletion was considered, Carly turned up for her lessons. She was in a particularly restless mood that day. The reason for this was soon to become apparent. One of the therapists, with a degree of irritation, asked her 'What do you want?' Whereupon Carly grabbed the keyboard and typed in H-E-L-P-T-E-E-T-H-H-U-R-T. The voice transcoder then vocalized what Carly had typed. The staff were stunned. This again was the 'thinking self' taking control. Like Tito, Carly also had an 'acting self' that rocked, screamed and was very destructive – again suggesting a bicameralism of consciousness.

This 'bicameralism' is a reflection of how the brain is structured. As we saw earlier, we all have two cerebral hemispheres, joined by a bridge of around 200 million nerve fibres called the corpus callosum. Under certain circumstances the effectiveness of communication across this bridge is disrupted. When this happens, we become not one but two separate areas of consciousness. As all of us are 'located' within the dominant hemisphere (usually the left), we are never consciously aware of our silent partner. In the mid-1960s a series of operations took place known as corpus callosotomies. These involved the cutting of the corpus callosum in an attempt to cure intractable epilepsy. The main surgeons in this pioneering work were Philip Vogel and Joseph Bogen. Later, neurobiologist Roger Sperry and psychologist Michael Gazzaniga became involved in evaluating how these operations affected the subjects. It was discovered that although each hemisphere was still able to learn after the split brain operation, one hemisphere had no idea about what the other hemisphere had experienced or learned. In effect, they had created two people, sometimes with very different personalities and motivations. In 1976 Sperry, who received the Nobel Prize in 1981 for his work in this field, wrote: 'In these and many other respects, the split-brain animal and man behave as if each of the separated hemispheres had a mind of its own.'[34]

Taking the cases of Carly and Tito together, we have astounding subjective evidence of my Daemon-Eidolon dyad and how this duality comes to the fore as we move along the Huxleyan spectrum. We know that in the early days of study autism and schizophrenia were considered to be the same condition. The last 50 years or so have seen a sharp demarcation made between the two. However, the reported autistic perceptions of Persinger's 'sensed presence' suggest that autism and schizophrenia have areas of commonality. It may come as no surprise that modern neurological research is reaching similar conclusions.

## Autism and Schizophrenia: Yet Another Link?

For many years one of the major question regarding schizophrenia has been whether it is inherited or acquired. This is a classic nature vs nurture debate. Research has shown that if both biological parents have schizophrenia, there is a 40 per cent chance that their children will inherit the illness. By contrast, there is a 1 per cent chance of a child with non-schizophrenic parents developing the illness.

This suggests a genetic link, but as of today no one gene has been found to be responsible. There seems to be no difference between men and women in this regard. It is unusual for a person to be diagnosed with schizophrenia under the age of 18. This is not because schizophrenia does not occur in younger people, it is simply that it is called something different: 'childhood-onset schizophrenia' (COS). This is extremely rare, with a recent statistic telling us that for children under 12 years old the incidence is 'less than one-sixtieth as common as the adult-onset type'.[35] This suggests that there is a one in 6,000 chance of a child being diagnosed with COS.

According to the Mayo Clinic website, the earliest indicators of COS are language delays, late walking and abnormal motor behaviours such as rocking and hand flapping.[36] However, the major diagnosis is the persistence of our good old friend hallucinations, together with delusions. If either of these two persists for longer than six months, then the child is diagnosed as having schizophrenia.[37] If the child is under seven years old the hallucinations and delusions can continue for far longer and no diagnosis of schizophrenia will be made.[38] This probably explains why there are so few youngsters with schizophrenia. Diagnosis is made by observation and questioning rather than by any objective physiological testing.

So, by definition a child under the age of seven will not have schizophrenia, however extreme that child's hallucinations and delusions may be. So if a child does show these behaviours and reports hearing voices and experiencing hallucinations, the question arises, what is wrong with them? It seems that the automatic diagnosis will be autism.[39]

I find this extremely interesting. We know that very young children have very active imaginations. Indeed, many have imaginary friends that persist throughout infancy.

As we have already discussed, researcher Michael J Hallowell has argued that these 'quasi-corporal companions' (QCCs), as he terms them, are far more than simple hallucinations. Hallowell cites recent research from the USA suggesting that up to 65 per cent of children up to the age of seven have QCCs.[40] This rather invalidates the argument that such encounters are the creations of a lonely, isolated, child. It is also of interest that, although many QCCs manifest as children of a similar age to the experiencer, a surprising number are perceived as elves, pixies or gnomes.

Hallowell terms these 'elementals'.[41] I find it intriguing, and potentially significant, that these QCCs seem to have similarities with Charles Bonnet syndrome hallucinations. I shall return to this connection later.

Young children normally live in a rich imaginary world in which fantasy and reality seem to overlap. They may also fixate on curious delusions about themselves, their friends, their toys and their family members. If the rules were changed (they are just rules) and schizophrenia could be diagnosed for the under-sixes, I suspect that the vast majority of infants would be diagnosed as schizophrenic.

Autism, however, can be diagnosed by the age of three. So between the ages of three and seven a schizophrenic infant would be automatically considered to be suffering from autism. Is it then the case that on their seventh birthday autistic children showing the abnormal behaviours of rocking and hand flapping are automatically diagnosed as schizophrenics? Or do they, as I suspect, continue with the autism diagnosis?

Over recent years there has been an epidemic of autism. According to a 2007 article in *Scientific American*, one in 166 children in the USA suffer from autism. For decades this had been around one in 2,500. In the 10-year period between 1993 and 2003 the US Department of Education recorded a 657 per cent increase in the nationwide incidence of the condition.[42] On 27 March 2014 the Centers for Disease Control and Prevention (CDC) released new data showing that one in 68 children now have autism spectrum disorder (ASD). These figures break down as one in 42 boys and one in 189 girls.[43] A similar increase has been reported across the globe.

There is clearly something of significance taking place within the world's population – or is it simply that we are now far more attentive to what children are telling us about their world – a world that many of us have lost but can dimly recall. Is early childhood and infancy yet another place where the Huxleyan spectrum can be found within neurotypicals?

However, there is another element of autism that suggests that the world that autistics live in is far richer and more complex than anything neurotypicals can imagine. It seems that certain autistics can use their glimpses through the Huxleyan doors to do astounding things. These individuals are known as savants, and for me these incredibly talented members of the human race stand as testament to the power of my Huxleyan spectrum. It is to them we now turn in our enquiry into the borderlands of human experience.

# CHAPTER EIGHT:

# Savant Syndrome

## The Social Isolation Model

It was Edward Sequin who first suggested that social isolation and sensory deprivation may be responsible for the development of savantism in those on the autistic spectrum. In 1971 Edward Hoffman argued that being in solitary confinement creates a need to keep the mind active by thinking about mathematical or logical problems.[1] In these circumstances, individuals may spontaneously discover shortcuts or note mathematical sequences that can facilitate fast calculations. This may be the case with regards to neurotypicals who have already been taught mathematical processes, but it is difficult to understand how individuals who have spent all their lives in isolation are able subliminally to know how to do even basic calculations. For example, how can social isolation facilitate what is known as 'lightning calculator' skills? It is regularly witnessed that certain autistic children can, on being given a date in the past or future, immediately give the day that date fell or falls on. It has long been suggested that they use some firm of calculating trick or that they have memorized universal calendars. However, if savant syndrome is related to social isolation, how can they know about these 'tricks'. In fact, the suggestion is that they come up with them spontaneously.

To be autistic, by definition, is to be 'neurologically atypical'. Something is going on in the brains of individuals who show autistic behaviours that is different from how the brains of the larger population work. There is growing evidence that this is to do with the way the cells of the brain communicate. The connectivity may be either greater or lesser than that found in 'neurologically typical' individuals.

This neurological atypicality can manifest itself as generalized impairments with regard to social abilities in most autistic individuals, but in some the connectivities can facilitate skills that manifest as astounding mathematical, artistic, musical and/or recall abilities that are far in excess of the neurotypical.

How can this be? One proposed explanation is that some savant skills can be explained by eidetic imagery. This is where a strong after-image is left in the visionary field after something has been observed, in a way that is reminiscent of photographic memory.

Although this is a reasonable explanation, it still suggests an uncanny skill that many academics believe does not exist. A report in the *American Journal of Mental Deficiency* published in November 1965 described the case of a 16-year-old girl who had powerful calendar calculating abilities. As she had been born blind with retrolental fibroplasia, photographic memory was impossible for her. However, in support of the sensory isolation hypothesis, it may be of significance that she and her twin sister were virtually ignored by their parents for the first three years of their lives.[2]

Another explanation, but one firmly rejected by most scientists, is that there is a form of extrasensory perception taking place. This would explain why the savants themselves are at a loss to explain where the information comes from. Time and time again we hear of autistics stating that the information just appears in their mind and that they simply repeat the answers parrot-fashion. One independently-minded researcher in this field is Bernard Rimland, who simply reports things as they are and only then attempts explanations, however unconventional or 'unscientific'. In a paper published in 1978 he reported that around 10 per cent of his sample of 5,400 autistic children showed skills and abilities that could not be explained using our modern scientific model.[3] One particular case, directly cited by savant syndrome expert Dr Darold Treffert in his book *Extraordinary People*, is very difficult to dismiss, although it has to be stated that it is a parent-reported case and may have been embroidered. A blind musical savant called Ellen announced to her parents, one week before Christmas, what she would receive as gifts on Christmas Day. She had been given no clues by her parents, and as she was blind it is scarcely conceivable that she had discovered the hiding place of the gifts and taken a 'peek'.[4]

Rimland terms this ability 'high-fidelity attention'. He argues that this is a reflection of just how intense the sensory world is for most autistics and can be related to the 'intense world' model of Henry and Kamila Markram as discussed earlier. We neurotypical people can choose to what degree we focus on things, whereas autistic children cannot.

However, if my Huxleyan spectrum hypothesis is correct, then under certain circumstances a neurotypical individual should also be able to access savant-like skills. The 'information field' exists external to each individual consciousness and as such should be open to access. In the late 1970s an intriguing case was reported by Rimland and was subsequently published in *Psychology Today*. At that time a set of twins called George and Charles had received a fair degree of media coverage. Both were severely autistic and, not surprisingly, showed the much-noted 'calendar calculator' skills. As part of a TV documentary on savants, members of the Psychiatry Department of the University of Oklahoma had visited New York to interview the twins. It was suggested that one of the graduate students, Benj Langdon, should see if he could find ways to reproduce the calendar skills. Langdon spent days memorizing a table of dates and a series of complex calculations. After spending a considerable amount of time and effort, he was able to do the calculations but was unable to match the speed of the twins. Then suddenly something quite surprising happened. Langdon found that he *could* match the twins' speed of calculation. His brain had somehow automated the processes. He found that calendar calculating had become second nature to him.[5]

This suggests that savant skills are not unique to autistics, and that we all have these skills in a latent form, but it does seem that it is in autistics that they are most highly developed. Research has shown that savant syndrome occurs in far greater numbers in those diagnosed with autism than in any other neurological group. Of even greater significance is that individuals who are neurotypical but have savant tendencies also tend to show behaviours that are related to autism.

Savant skills are not related to IQ: artistic savants usually score below average on IQ tests. Artistic savants do not paint in abstract expressionist styles, nor do they write novels or delve into philosophy. Theirs is a skill based upon the typical non-reflective tendencies of those found on the autistic spectrum.

It seems that savant skills can be generated in neurotypical individuals if the left frontal temporal lobe (LATL) is suppressed. A team led by Allan Snyder at the Centre for the Mind at the University of Sydney, Australia, used this process to reproduce a brain state similar to that experienced by autistic individuals. This is brought about by repetitive transcranial magnetic stimulation (RTMS) pulses. The method was particularly effective in terms of drawing, proofreading and numerical abilities. This suggests that savant syndrome is facilitated by something unusual taking place in the left hemisphere, which is, for most people, the dominant hemisphere.

It suggests that if the left hemisphere of 'normal' people is manipulated, savant skills can be created.[6]

## The Work of Darold A Treffert

In his fascinating and highly influential book *Extraordinary People: Understanding Savant Syndrome*, psychiatrist Darold A Treffert gives us a mixture of personal anecdotes and hard science, presenting a 'state of the art' position with regard to savant syndrome as it was in the late 1980s.[7]

In July 1959 Treffert joined the Winnebago State Hospital near Oshkosh, Wisconsin, as the new director of psychiatry for a small children's unit within the hospital. It was here that he noticed how certain children had amazing abilities. Most of these subjects had been diagnosed with early infantile autism (EIA), as defined by Leo Kanner in 1944. These accounted for around a third of the children. The second third had been diagnosed with 'childhood schizophrenia'. Unlike those with EIA, this group had been born normal, their illness becoming apparent only as they got older. The final group were children whose brains had been damaged by illness or accident. As we have already seen, Rimland presented data suggesting that around 10 per cent of EIAs show savant-like tendencies.

In 1964 Treffert became superintendent of the whole Winnebago facility and in 1979 he left to set up a private practice in Fond du Lac, alongside his work as executive director of a local health care centre. While at his Fond du Lac practice he began using sodium amytal to enhance memory recall with some of his adult patients. He became fascinated as to how this chemical could facilitate powerful and detailed memory recollections, some involving long-lost memories recalled in precise detail.

This is not as crazy as it seems. As we have already seen, in the 1930s through to the 1950s Canadian-based American neurosurgeon Wilder Penfield did a series of experimental operations on the brains of conscious patients. An unintentional, and totally unexpected, outcome of these operations was that Penfield discovered that long-forgotten memories could be evoked by stimulating the surface of the brain with an electrode pen. These were more than memories: the patients reported that they were literally re-living part of their past. In his book *Mystery of the Mind*, published just before his death, Penfield was quite categorical about the nature of these recollections. He believed them to be actual memory traces that were being automatically called forth from the unconscious.[8] It was not as if the patients decided to remember a particular event: they had no control over what the memory was or at what point it started or ended.

In 1970 psychologist Albert C Cain published a case report that reinforces the Penfield 'total recall' model with regard to savants. In this report Cain discusses the case of his patient 'Millie'. Millie suffered from early infantile autism (EIA). This was first described by Kanner himself in 1944[9] and is typified by the infant's extreme isolation from others and a profound resistance to any form of change. Millie was typical in that she rarely communicated with others. Her language skills were very restricted. However, this did not affect her specific memory skills:

> She repeats verbatim (typically not upon request) lengthy conversations or radio or TV material, often heard years before. She accurately reads and reproduces (including the spelling) virtually any word she has seen even once, including words many years beyond her age level, and quickly corrects others' misspellings of such words. She writes backward almost as readily as she writes forward.[10]

Although Millie's sense of social isolation must have been overwhelming to her, the social world of autistics who also suffer from blindness must involve a feeling of even more total isolation. For such individuals the only stimulus from the outside world will be sound and touch. But as with many areas of sensory deprivation, the remaining senses seem to take on a compensatory role.

An intriguing example from Treffert's research is the case of 'Ellen', a talented musical savant with extreme autism. Treffert describes how she has her own internal clock which allows her to know the exact time. Ellen is blind and has never used any form of time gauge such as a Braille clock. This ability spontaneously appeared when Ellen was eight years old. At that time Ellen had a great fear of the telephone. To overcome this her mother had her listen to the talking clock facility. What happened next was, it must be said, quite uncanny:

> After listening for less than 10 minutes Ellen returned to her room where she mimicked what she had just heard. She correctly continued on, after the last minute-and-second reading of the hour, to the next hour: when she came to 'one fifty-nine and fifty-nine seconds', Ellen correctly stated, 'the time is ... two o'clock.'[11]

Ellen's heightened auditory skills have given her abilities that could be interpreted as being 'extra-sensory'. Treffert reports that Ellen could tell if it was a different school bus coming to pick her up by the short horn beep that the driver used to announce its arrival. However, her parents told Treffert of occasions in which her abilities went far beyond acute auditory sensitivity. For example, she announced what her presents would be a week before Christmas Day: her parents assured Treffert that they had given her no clues about the gifts; and remember, Ellen was totally blind, so it was impossible for her to search around the house to discover hiding places. She also seemed to have an ability to know, in advance, who was going to telephone the house.[12]

As we have already discovered, these seemingly 'telepathic' abilities fascinated Bernard Rimland. According to his study of 5,400 autistic children cited earlier, he regularly witnessed what he believed were psychic abilities.[13] He suggested that whereas neurotypical people can choose to what degree they focus their attention, those with autism cannot:

> The autistic child and the savant do not have the option of deploying their attention to the narrow (physical) or broad (conceptual) ends of the spectrum, as the circumstances require. The adjusting knob on their tuning dial has come loose with the dial set at the narrow end of the range, so they are in effect locked into that attention mode.[14]

So exactly how rare is Savant syndrome? Surveys have shown that it has an incidence rate of 1:2,000 of the disabled population. This increases markedly in relation to individuals diagnosed with early infantile autism (EIA), where the incidence is as high 9.8 per cent. However, it must also be noted that for every 100,000 children, on average only seven will have EIA. It has been agreed by convention that there are two distinct types of savant: 'talented savants' and 'prodigious savants'. 'Talented savants' are those whose special skills and abilities are specialized and highly honed, making them conspicuous when viewed against the overall handicap. 'Prodigious savants' are individuals whose skills are so spectacular that they would be conspicuous even in a non-handicapped person. With regard to the latter, there have been around 100 reported cases in the last 100 years or so. As Treffert has suggested, prodigious savantism seems to manifest in children who are blind, particularly with regard to musical abilities.

Treffert is best known for his association with Salt Lake City resident Kim Peek, whose amazing savant abilities became the inspiration for the 1988 movie *Rain Man*. Peek was born in 1951 to a Mormon couple. At birth it was noted that his head was 30 per cent larger than normal, and subsequent tests showed that he had been born with no corpus callosum or anterior commissure. As we discovered earlier, the corpus callosum and the anterior commissure are two of the five 'commissures' that link the right and left hemispheres of the brain. Without these there is literally no communication between the brain's two sides. For communications related to conscious awareness the corpus callosum is by far the most important element. Kim's remaining three commissures, the posterior, hippocampal and habenular, will have contributed very little to any communication. In effect, he was two people located in one cranium. This led the specialists to believe that Kim would be mentally retarded. In many ways he was, in that he could not dress himself, cook, shave or brush his teeth without help. However, from a very early age he showed prodigious learning abilities aided by an uncanny memory for facts and figures. Treffert describes how from the age of 20 months he was able to memorize every book that was read to him after a single reading.

As he grew older he used telephone directories for exercises in mental arithmetic, adding each column of seven-digit numbers together in his head until he reached figures in the trillions. In his teens he had memorized the complete works of Shakespeare and every volume of the condensed *Reader's Digest* books.

However, until 1984, when he was 32, he had lived a very isolated life. This all changed when he accompanied his father Fran to the national conference of the Association of Retarded Citizens in Arlington, Texas. It was here that he was introduced to the screenwriter Barry Morrow. Morrow spent four hours chatting with Kim and during this time was astounded to discover that Kim knew every postcode, area code and road number in every state across America. Morrow went away and over the next two years wrote a film script loosely based upon Kim's uncanny abilities. He contacted the Peek family to say that a major studio had agreed to take the script and that a movie was planned. The film, *Rain Man*, was a huge success, and virtually overnight Kim became a celebrity.

Later it was discovered that Kim could read two pages of a book simultaneously – one with each eye, regardless of whether it was upside-down or sideways-on. His ability to retain 98 per cent of the information he absorbed led to his designation as a 'mega-savant'. In a 2005 article published in *Scientific American* Treffert and his associate Daniel D Christensen, the neurologist who scanned Peek's brain in 1988, describe how Kim read Tom Clancy's book *The Hunt for Red October* in one hour and 25 minutes and four months later, when asked, was able to recall the name of the Russian radio operator, refer to the page number on which he was mentioned and quote several passages verbatim.[15]

Sadly, Kim Peek died of a heart attack in December 2009, a month after his 58th birthday. He has left an amazing legacy, for he was responsible for giving the general public an insight into the world of savants.

We have already seen that individuals who show autistic behaviours have brains that work differently from the rest of us, and that this is probably to do with the way the cells of the brain communicate. A recent theory has suggested that this may relate to something that happens while the baby is still in the womb. At around the eighth month of gestation, something rather strange happens within the brain of the human embryo. Approximately 90 per cent of the neurons die in a process known as apoptosis. The reason for this is not fully understood.[16] However, it does have huge implications for children who are born prematurely. Any infant born at or before the end of the eighth month does not suffer this cell death and is born with 90 per cent more neurons than a child who goes to full term.

This revolutionary explanation of savant syndrome was first proposed by Norman Geschwind and Albert Galaburda in 1987.[17] As we have seen, Norman Geschwind, together with another associate, Stephen Waxman, argued that hyper-religiosity and hypergraphia were evident in certain individuals who experienced temporal lobe epilepsy (see p67).[18] In this work they also also suggest that the left hemisphere of the brain develops later than the right during embryo growth in the womb. This means that as gestation comes to its end, this hemisphere can be damaged. It is also known that the hormone testosterone, the chemical responsible for the development of the male reproductive tissues and therefore found in greater amounts in the male fetus, slows cortical growth and impairs neuronal architecture. Thus, in a male child the left hemisphere may be damaged before birth. The researchers suggest that this may explain why the incidence of autism is significantly higher in males than in females. Recent work, however, has brought this into question.

In the last chapter we discussed how individuals with Alzheimer's, in a process known as retrogenesis, seem to reverse back through childhood to effectively end their lives in an embryonic state, as if waiting for a rebirth. We have now seen evidence that autism, a neurological condition, mirrors many of the elements of Alzheimer's, with similar neurochemical causes and outcomes. For example, it seems that there is a five times greater chance of developing autism if a child is born prematurely than if he or she goes full term. This suggests that the avoidance of the cell die-off may facilitate autism and give access to the Huxleyan spectrum.

There is evidence that the brain functioning of premature individuals is different from that of full-termers. For example, back in 2006 University of California neurobiologists James McGaugh, Elizabeth Parker and Larry Cahill described a new neurological oddity which they termed 'hyperthymestic syndrome'. In effect, this is a super-memory for past-life experiences. To date, around 80 individuals from across the world have been found to have this syndrome. One of the most interesting is somebody identified only by the initials 'H K'. In June 2012 this blind 20-year-old could remember every day of his life from the age of about 11. Significantly, he was born very premature (27 weeks).[19] He clearly avoided the cell die-off. We have also discussed the case of Rebecca Sharrock who, unusually for a female, also remembers virtually her whole life in great detail.

Crucial to the ability of neurons to communicate with each other effectively is a process called myelination. Myelin is a fatty substance that acts as a sheath around nerve fibres and in doing so ensures the rapid transmission of electrical impulses along the axons. In effect, it works in a similar way to insulation around an electrical cable. At birth the human brain has no myelination: the process begins in infancy and continues into adulthood. Research has shown that the last part of the brain to develop myelination is the corpus callosum.[20] As a result, there is little or no communication in children between the dominant and non-dominant hemispheres.[21] Children are, in fact, split-brain patients. Further research has discovered that it is the right (non-dominant) hemisphere that is the major area of consciousness and cognitive processes in young children.[22]

This lack of myelination and the fact that children's consciousness seems to be processed in the child's non-dominant hemisphere suggests to me a possible explanation of why young children seem to be able to perceive elements of the Pleroma in a way that is denied neurotypical adults. Lack of myelination is also linked to two other areas of the Huxleyan spectrum: Alzheimer's and schizophrenia.

We know that Kim Peek's major neurological issue was the lack of a corpus callosum. This meant that he was also a 'split-brain' individual in exactly the same way that the patients evaluated by Roger Sperry and Michael Gazzaniga were in the late 1960s. Was this the cause of his savant skills?

You will recall that Temple Grandin, citing the experiences of Tito Rajarshi Mukhopadhyay and Carly Fleischmann, suggested that this 'two selves' model may be an explanation for autism. Using my Daemon-Eidolon dyad model, could it be that in some way Kim Peek was solely located in his non-dominant hemisphere and was therefore, in effect, in touch with his 'Daemonic consciousness'? If so, this would have given him limited but immediate access to the Pleroma and all the information encoded within it. Sadly, his initial brain damage severely limited how he was able to process the information and, in a similar way to other savants, simply regurgitated the information in a random and rather pointless way.

However, if a simple lack of inter-hemispheric communication creates Daemonic consciousness, why should it not be that all young children should show savant abilities?

We do know that young children certainly have access to certain elements of the Pleroma, a perceptual world denied to neurotypical adults. As we have already seen, many young children have 'quasi-corporal companions' (QCCs), as Michael J Hallowell terms them. Is such communication facilitated by the lack of inter-hemispheric communication that results in the child being located in the non-dominant hemisphere, and therefore able to perceive a much broader version of reality? An alternative argument is that the child permanently lives in a mental state similar to that evoked by Persinger's 'God Helmet' and/or Snyder's suppression of the left frontal temporal lobe (LATL) and that the 'sensed presence' is manifest as a QCC.

This again points to the operation of the 'intense world syndrome'. You will recall that there is strong evidence that autistic individuals perceive far more sensory inputs than neurotypicals. Could it be that they naturally tune in to the sensory domain facilitated by the 'God Helmet'? It seems that for autistics the sensory channels are not only wider, but also they overlap. It has been observed that autistic children will behave in a way considered inappropriate when dealing with loud noises or bright light. In reaction to a loud noise they will cover their eyes, whereas a bright light will make them cover their ears. It is as if all the channels are open and can pick up information using different receptors. This confusion of the senses is reported in a much higher frequency in autistics than in the general population.[23]

A modern-day individual whose autism has created for him a fascinating confusion of the senses is Londoner Daniel Tammet. Tammet experiences the world in a particular way, a way that is completely at odds with the everyday perceptions of neurotypicals. He experiences something known as synaesthesia.

For synaesthetics the external world presents itself to consciousness in a very different way from how it is perceived by neurotypicals. For example, Daniel was, according to his own sensory perceptions, born on a blue day: for him each day has a different colour. Wednesday for him is blue, as is the number 9 and the sound of loud voices arguing. All numbers evoke in Daniel's mind particular associations, moods and attitudes. Number 5 is loud, 11 is friendly. His favourite number is 4 because, like him, it is shy and quiet. Such interpretations apply to all numbers, not just single-digit ones.[24]

Interestingly enough, synaesthesia has also been reported in connection with migraine auras. Earlier we described the incident whereby one of Oliver Sacks's patients found himself in a timeless state experiencing a profound déjà vu sensation. As the hallucination came to an end, he described how 'The hum of the crickets was all around me, and when I closed my eyes this was immediately translated into a hum of colour, which seemed to be the exact visual translation of the sound I heard.'[25]

Synaesthesia suggests that the brain's Huxleyan reducing valve is being compromised in certain individuals, usually migraineurs, temporal lobe epileptics, schizophrenics and autistics. If this is so, then what these individuals perceive is a very different sensory world where sounds are blurred with colours and smells with tactile sensations. Although strange, these effects are nonetheless understandable with regard to how we believe the brain works. These perceptions are still 'sensory' rather than 'extrasensory'. However, there is growing evidence that extrasensory skills are also manifest in individuals on my Huxleyan spectrum. Recent research by American neuroscientist Diane Hennacy Powell is presenting powerful evidence that telepathy is also involved when the 'doors of perception' are opened.

## The Work of Diane Hennacy Powell

Diane Hennacy Powell trained as a neuroscientist at Johns Hopkins School of Medicine, Baltimore, Maryland, with a plan to become a neurosurgeon. However, it was at this time that psychiatry became her great interest, after she had read about autistic savants. She wanted to understand exactly how such amazing abilities can occur in individuals who are, in other ways, greatly challenged. Her brother, theoretical physicist Dr Ken Hennacy, an expert in artificial intelligence, shares her interests in savant skills; and in 2005 both of them gave a well-received presentation on calendar calculators at an international scientific conference in Copenhagen.

Her other great area of interest is telepathy. As a psychiatrist with a neurological science background, she is aware that mind-to-mind communication is simply impossible within our present understanding of science. However, she had heard of many anecdotal cases and was keen to test such skills under laboratory conditions. She considered that the best candidate would be somebody on the autistic spectrum, specifically an autistic savant. Her interest had been stimulated by the repeated comments by savants that the information just appears in their minds. There is no searching for the answer, no mathematical process, no prior calculations: the answers are spontaneous as if downloaded from somewhere outside of the individual. This process is particularly intriguing in mathematical savants who have had no previous training in mathematical processes.

In August 2013 Dr Hennacy Powell was contacted by Dr Darold Treffert, who informed her that he might have found the ideal candidate for her research. As we already know, Treffert is a world-recognized expert on savant syndrome, so it is no surprise that parents of children showing savant skills would contact him. Treffert had recently been approached by the parents of an 11-year-old autistic girl named Hayley. Hayley was, at that stage, effectively non-verbal but, unusually, could type fairly well. Her cognitive therapists had also discovered, through her use of a numeric keyboard, that Hayley had unusual mathematical skills, even though she had never been taught the relevant processes and procedures. However, they soon noticed something remarkable: Hayley's typed number would only be the correct answer to a mathematical question if the person working with her already knew the answer. It was observed that Hayley's answers switched from ordinary numbers to scientific or technical numbering systems such as binary notation when the display on the therapist's calculator was changed in the same way. The therapist asked Hayley how she did this and, in response, she typed: 'I see the numerators and denominators in your head.' She was then tested on her telepathic abilities. She was asked the name of her therapist's landlord and the name of a book the therapist was thinking about. On both occasions she typed the right answer. Another therapist, who was convinced that Hayley was reading her mind, half-jokingly asked Hayley to translate the words 'I love you' into German. Hayley had no knowledge of German, nor had she ever had any exposure to the language. Straight away she typed 'Ich liebe dich'.

Dr Hennacy Powell decided to test Hayley under controlled conditions and with new therapists. These sessions were videotaped. The team used a random number generator. In one 10-minute session she was asked to note down a series of 162 random numbers as seen by the therapist, but not by her. She made seven errors, correcting these straight away to give a 100 per cent success rate. There was a barrier between Hayley and the therapist, so no physical cues could have been picked up. There were also cameras in the laboratory recording the proceedings from five different angles.

The results of Hennacy Powell's work were presented to the San

Francisco Bay Area Parapsychological Association's annual meeting in August 2014. Her results were described as 'jaw-dropping'. She continues to work with Hayley in ever more controlled situations and the subject continues to show telepathic skills. However, as Hayley has now started to acquire verbal skills, Powell is concerned that her new-found means of communication may overshadow her need to use telepathy.

Diane Hennacy Powell informed me in early 2014 that she had discovered a handful of children who are all showing telepathic skills. Her plan is to continue testing them in an effort to understand exactly what is happening here. To facilitate this and take it forward she has set up what she calls the 'Telepathy Project'.[26]

We have now finished our review of the evidence for the Huxleyan spectrum. However, it is worth emphasizing that these glimpses through the doors of perception happen to real people, not statistical models. We can describe in detail the neurology and neurochemistry, but in the final analysis to appreciate what this really means requires us to perceive it through the eyes and ears of those who had glimpses of the Pleroma. Part Three of the book will look at the human aspects of this transformative experience.

PART THREE:

# GLIMPSES THROUGH THE DOORS

# CHAPTER NINE:

# The Entranced

## Who Are 'The Entranced'?

So far we have discussed the science and processes by which Aldous Huxley's doors of perception can be opened and the Pleroma can be glimpsed. We have also encountered a number of human beings who have seen through the veil of *maya*; and we have discussed what makes these individuals special. I would now like to turn our attention to a handful of individuals whom I call 'The Entranced'. By this I mean that they have 'entered' via 'trance-like' states the universe that can be found on the other side of Huxley's doors. These are famous artist Vincent van Gogh, Swedish playwright August Strindberg, temporal lobe epileptic Jayne Burton, Australian autistic author Donna Williams, American neurosurgeon Dr Eben Alexander and Alzheimer's patient Pat McCreath. This is a very small selection of the entranced from those I could have included. Unfortunately, space does not allow a more extensive, in-depth review of all the cases. However, I hope that these brief snapshots will give you some idea of just how powerful these experiences are.

## Vincent van Gogh

Towards the end of his life the great Dutch artist Vincent van Gogh (1853–1890) became more and more erratic in his behaviour. He attempted to murder his close friend Paul Gauguin and cut off part of his ear to give to a prostitute. Something was clearly disturbing his mind. He was plagued by hallucinations and terrifying nightmares. The tension can clearly be seen in his paintings of that period, specifically *The Starry Night*, painted in 1889. Other paintings from that period, including *Road with Cypress and Star* (1890) and *Wheat Field with Crows* (1890), also bear witness to his state of mind.

*The Starry Night*, completed between the 16 and 18 of June, has fascinated art lovers for over 100 years. There is something very strange about this picture. The stars are far too large, blazing like comets in the evening sky. The view has been identified as the one he would have seen from his east-facing second-story bedroom window. He was not allowed to paint in the bedroom, but he did make many ink and charcoal drawings which he would then take down to his ground-floor studio, where he would paint in oils. It is therefore reasonable to conclude that these images were drawn late at night as he looked out across the cornfields. It was at night that his nightmares and hallucinations were at their strongest. One can therefore reasonably surmise that this was a painting of how he saw the world during these states. However, recent astronomical observations have shown that this work may be able to tell us a great deal about one of the greatest mysteries of modern science: turbulence and chaotic flow.

On 8 February 2004 the Advanced Camera for Surveys on the Hubble Space Telescope took an image of an expanding halo of light around a distant star called V838 Monocerotis (V838 Mon). The research scientists were immediately reminded of the swirling stars in *The Starry Night*.

An article commenting on these similarities was posted on the web as part of a NASA press release.[1] This caught the attention of a Mexican physicist, José Luis Aragón, based at the National Autonomous University of Mexico in Querétaro. Aragón had long been interested in the challenges presented to science by the turbulent flow of gasses and fluids.

Aragón was intrigued to know if, in some as yet unknown way, the Dutch artist was perceiving a phenomenon that is invisible to most of us. Together with a group of associates, he embarked upon a series of experiments in which the theory of turbulence proposed by Soviet scientist Andrei Kolmogorov in the 1940s was applied to Van Gogh's paintings.

Kolmogorov had discovered a particular mathematical relationship between the fluctuations in a flow's speed and the rate at which it dissipates energy as friction. By applying his equations, Kolmogorov was able to calculate the differences in velocity between any two points in the fluid. In effect, big eddies transfer their energy to smaller eddies and in doing so repeat the patterns – hence the technical term, 'scaling law'.

Aragón and his associates took a series of high-resolution digital photographs of Van Gogh's paintings from the last year or so of his life, including *The Starry Night* and *Wheat Field with Crows*. They were then able to zoom in to view individual pixels and compare their brightness with others at a certain distance away. The researchers discovered that the repeating patterns Van Gogh was incorporating within his swirls mirrored the mathematical relationships described in Kolmogorov's equations. In effect, Van Gogh was painting turbulence.[2]

So how could a seemingly deranged and comparatively uneducated artist such as Van Gogh instinctively, and probably unconsciously, depict in his paintings a mathematical structure that has puzzled physicists for decades? In 2014 the conundrum was still taxing the best mathematical minds on the planet, as evidenced by the fact that the 2014 Abel Prize for Mathematics (often regarded as the Nobel Prize of maths) was awarded to

Russian mathematician Yakov Sinai for his work on turbulence and chaotic flow.

Vincent Willem van Gogh was born on 30 March 1853 in the manse of Groot-Zundert, a little village in northern Brabant, The Netherlands. His father was a pastor of the Dutch Reformed Church and his mother the daughter of a bookbinder. He had three sisters and two brothers. Art was in the family: three of his uncles on his father's side were art dealers and his younger brother, Theo, also followed this career path. Vincent's birth had been difficult. His mother had had an unusually long labour, and for a time he had been in the birth canal without oxygen. It is this lack of oxygen just prior to birth that may have caused Vincent's unusual perceptions.

From an early age Vincent was an intense, temperamental, isolated individual. Indeed, he showed all the signs of undiagnosed autism, possibly caused by his birth-induced hypoxia. As he was clearly 'high-functioning', this suggests Asperger's. He had to leave school at 15 owing to a family financial crisis, but thanks to his relationship with his uncles he was able to secure a post as a sales assistant at the Brussels branch of the famous French art dealership Goupil & Cie. In 1873 he was sent to London, and in 1876 to Paris. While in Paris, he became part of the Bohemian art scene in Montmartre. However, at this time it was not art itself that fired his enthusiasm but a fervour that channelled itself into religion. This compromised his work, and soon he found himself without a job. Vincent saw this as an opportunity to develop his religious vocation, but this too ended in disappointment. However, unemployment did allow him to concentrate on his other great enthusiasm, painting. In March 1886 he moved back to Paris. His paintings became brighter and charged with colour. He made friends with Émile Bernard, Henri Toulouse-Lautrec, Paul Signac, Georges Seurat and, most significantly, Paul Gauguin.

However, as usual with Vincent, his intensity alienated and eventually scared his new friends. He started to drink absinthe to excess and he became more and more aggressive. It was time for him to move on again. This time it was to the south of France. He visited Arles in late February 1888, and the light of Provence was to prove hugely beguiling. As winter turned to spring, Vincent decided that this was a place in which his art could really bear fruit. In September he moved into the 'Yellow House' and quickly invited Gauguin to join him. In a curious decision, bearing in mind Vincent's 'eccentricities' in Paris, Paul agreed, and moved in with Vincent in late October. By December both the weather and the atmosphere had become stormy. Vincent was back on a decline. Gauguin noted that his friend had a series of amnesiac sleepwalking episodes. These may have been caused by Vincent's excessive consumption of absinthe or else by a mental breakdown. Gauguin, fearing for his life, left Arles.

On 23 December Vincent cut off part of his ear, and the next day the police brought him to the hospital in the town. He was discharged on 7 January but by 9 January was suffering terrifying hallucinations. Such was the locals' fear of this individual that they wrote to the authorities requesting that 'this danger to the community' should be committed to their care. By the end of February the paperwork was in place and Vincent was re-admitted to the Arles Hospital. On 8 May 1889 he was admitted on a voluntarily basis to the Saint-Paul de Mausole Asylum in Saint-Rémy. Here he was allowed to paint, his style reflecting the inner turmoil and some new, intriguing changes in the way he applied the paint and depicted his chosen scenes. However, this new style may have been symptomatic of his deteriorating mental health. It is important to note that he was aware of his illness: he knew that his 'hallucinations' were related to a mental instability. However, one of the distinguishing characteristics of schizophrenic psychosis is that the subject believes the hallucinations to be true and acts accordingly. So if Vincent was suffering from a form of schizophrenia, it was of a particularly unusual variety. For example, in a letter to Theo he describes the behaviours of his fellow inmates in Arles

Hospital and compares them to his own:

> One of them here shouts and speaks all the time like me, for a
> fortnight, thinking he hears voices and speech in the echoes in
> the corridors, probably because his hearing nerve is diseased
> and oversensitive, and for me it's both vision and hearing.[3]

Rather than schizophrenia, this suggests to me that his life-long, possibly autism-related hyper-sensitivities were intensifying. It will be recalled that Henry and Kamila Markram have suggested that the core pathology of the autistic brain is the hyper-reactivity and hyper-plasticity of local neuronal circuits. This leads to hyper-perception, hyper-attention and hyper-memory: something they term the 'intense world syndrome'.[4] It is fair to say that at this stage in his life Vincent was becoming oversensitive to both visual and aural stimulations. His mind was opening up to a much broader visual canvas and his paintings were his attempt to depict, and possibly control, his perceptually overloaded world.

So how was it that he was acutely aware of his deteriorating condition? Some commentators have ignored or overlooked the autism links and suggested that Vincent was experiencing schizophrenia. Another suggestion has been made that it was not schizophrenia that was opening up his 'doors of perception' but temporal lobe epilepsy. Research has suggested that up to 90 per cent of temporal lobe epileptics present with symptoms that mimic schizophrenia, leading to frequent misdiagnosis.[5] As we have discovered, epilepsy can be caused by scarring on the brain. We know that Vincent's birth had been traumatic and that his brain had been, for a short time, starved of oxygen. This may have caused brain lesions. As autism, schizophrenia and temporal lobe epilepsy all feature on my Huxleyan spectrum, I feel that this comes down to a question of just how intense one believes Vincent's condition to have been. Epilepsy was in fact the diagnosis of Dr Felix Ray, the physician who had cared for Vincent during his December 1888 sojourn in Arles Hospital.

As we have seen, research has also shown that patients suffering from temporal lobe epileptiform illnesses have all the standard psychotic episodes evident in schizophrenia but, unlike schizophrenics, TLErs remain connected with reality and can function effectively within society.

It is known that schizophrenia normally stifles creativity and the sufferer cannot concentrate on any task. This was not the case with Vincent. After a week at Saint-Paul a room was made available for him to work on his paintings. The asylum was to subsequently provide him with the material for numerous works, including *Trees in Front of Asylum* and *Garden of Saint-Paul Hospital*. And in June 1889 he finished his famous *The Starry Night*.

This is not to say that this period was enjoyable for him. Although he had long periods of lucidity, his nightmares and hallucinations continued. In many ways it was this turmoil that drove him into an even greater creative frenzy. However, during one period of passivity in February 1890 he was allowed to leave.

So what evidence do we have that Van Gogh was actually a TLEr? An article by Shahram Khoshbin cited in the *Harvard Magazine* presents the evidence, concluding that Vincent may have been suffering from Waxman-Geschwind syndrome.

So were Van Gogh's doors of perception opened by his 'illness', whether we consider this to be epilepsy, migraine or autism?

Although at the time no brain-mapping technology was available, it is known that from their own knowledge and experience of the illness three of Van Gogh's physicians – Dr Rey, Dr Théophile Peyron and Dr Paul Gachet – diagnosed him as an epileptic. It is known that psycho-motor epilepsy seems to begin during the mid-30s, and we know that Vincent started showing signs of extreme personality changes in 1886, when he was 34.

One of the recognized factors is vivid and immediate recall of one's past. These are far more than memories: they are an actual *re-living* of a period in the past. As we have already discovered, experiments by Wilder Penfield showed that 'charged memories' can be evoked by the stimulation of the cortex, specifically the temporal lobes. However, I suggest that for those whose doors are beginning to open, past memories flood into the mind as part of present experiences: it is as if they are outside of time, viewing their lives from a location in the fifth dimension.

What can we make of the following comment by Van Gogh?: 'I saw again every room in the house in Zundert, every path, every plant in the garden, the views in the fields round about ... down to a magpie's nest in a tall acacia in the graveyard.'[6]

Individuals who experience TLE are known to sometimes show hyper-religiosity. Indeed, as we know, this is one of the symptoms of Waxman-Geschwind syndrome. Vincent had always had strong religious convictions. He had been a missionary in Belgium and his fervour was so intense that the Dutch Reformed Church, of which he was a member, decided that he was too extreme for them, and ceased using his services.

When he was living in Arles and as his 'illness' progressed, he became interested again in religion. We know that for a time he had lost his faith, but this returned with a vengeance now. After he left the hospital he wrote to Theo that his illness had taken on the character of religious exaltation, in which he experienced moments of enthusiasm, madness and prophesy.[7]

He also had physical symptoms that suggested epilepsy. For example, while painting a landscape in the fields near Saint-Paul de Mausole he described that he felt a pressure on his head which tightened like a metal band, and then he fell to the floor, his body went rigid and he blacked out. He was then carried back to Saint-Rémy and even after recovery he was in a state of agitated confusion for nearly three weeks. However, as we have already discussed in some detail, temporal lobe epilepsy aura states are very similar to another illness, migraine, and there is circumstantial evidence that this other element of my Huxleyan spectrum may have been another possible cause of Vincent's state of mind.

Vincent regularly reported that on occasion objects seemed to shrink in size as he looked at them.[8] As we have seen, this visual hallucination, known as 'Alice in Wonderland syndrome', is strongly related to migraine auras. He also described excessive sensitivity towards the visual world around him. However, we must be careful in this regard, since as we have already seen, such hypersensitivity is also a known feature of autism. I would like to suggest that the Markram's 'intense world syndrome' could readily be applied to migraineurs as well as autistics.

Of course, if the overall theme of this book is correct, then autism, migraine and temporal lobe epilepsy, all of which have been suggested as the causes of Vincent's erratic behaviour and wonderful artistic vision, are all related conditions and are simply points on the Huxleyan spectrum.

But there is another interesting factor in the mystery that was Vincent van Gogh. In a curious letter to his brother, Theo, written on New Year's Eve 1881, Vincent describes how he perceives colours:

> Some time ago you rightly said that every colourist has his own characteristic scale of colours. This is also the case with Black and White [sic], it is the same after all – one must be able to go from the highest light to the deepest shadow, and this with only a few simple ingredients. Some artists have a nervous hand at drawing, which gives their technique something of the sound peculiar to a violin, for instance, Lemud, Daumier, Lançon – others, for example, Gavarni and Bodmer, remind one more of piano playing. Do you feel this too? Millet is perhaps a stately organ.[9]

According to an article published in *Psychology Today* in August 2013, this suggests that Vincent was a synaesthetic, specifically experiencing a variation known as 'timbre synaesthesia'.[10] Interestingly, the article links this to Vincent's suspected Asperger's syndrome. According to synaesthetic artist Carol Steen, an artist's level of synaesthesia can be identified by the number of 'photisms' in their paintings. Photisms are shapes that artists see in response to inputs from those senses other than vision. Steen describes her discovery:

> One day, in the early 90s, I was searching deep in my painting and sculpture storage area for a painting to send to an art exhibition. Coincidentally, I had just read Richard Cytowic's wonderful book, *The Man Who Tasted Shapes*. In it I came across Mardi J Horowitz's illustration of Klüver's Form Constants (synesthetic photisms in response to peyote catalogued by Klüver). Something about the shapes in this illustration was familiar and as I was going through my works I came across a piece of sculpture I had made in 1980. I was really startled. It looked just like a Klüver Form Constant.[11]

It will be recalled from an earlier section of this book that the Klüver's Form Constants were categorized by German-American psychologist Heinrich Klüver in the mid 1920s. Klüver was later to work with American neurosurgeon Paul Bucy in isolating a behavioural disorder caused by the malfunction of the left and right medial temporal lobes. This was eventually named Klüver-Bucy syndrome in their honour. This syndrome, which has strong associations with Pick's Disease and Alzheimer's, is also regularly called 'temporal lobe syndrome'.

Steen noted a series of synaesthetic Klüver's Form Constants in Van Gogh's *Wheat Field with Crows* and – surprise, surprise! – *The Starry Night*. As we have seen, Klüver's Form Constants are now recognized as a central element of hallucinatory perceptions during altered states of consciousness and are directly associated with migraine, epilepsy, autism and hypoglycemia. Why the brain spontaneously, and for no apparent reason, reproduces such complex mathematical patterns is a huge mystery.

Paul Gauguin was also a friend of another intriguing individual who, like Van Gogh, is in my opinion a classic example of someone whose 'doors of perception' are well ajar. This is the great Swedish playwright August Strindberg.

## August Strindberg

Johan August Strindberg (1849–1912) was a hugely prolific playwright, novelist, painter and essayist. His work is known for its emotional intensity and its powerful subjectivity. Although Strindberg was never actually diagnosed with epilepsy or migraine, his life and works are littered with examples of an opening of the doors of perception.

An example of this is Strindberg's description of a 'cold wind' blowing over him just before a particularly bad period of delusions that took place when he was living in Paris. This suggests an 'aura' experience normally associated with temporal lobe epilepsy or migraine. Between 1894 and 1897 he experienced what he was later to term his 'inferno'. During this 33-month period he had no less than five 'episodes'. His experiences at this time have frequently led to a diagnosis of schizophrenia. In 1921 German psychiatrist Alfred Storch suggested this,[12] and two years later a similar diagnosis was made by fellow German psychiatrist Karl Jaspers.[13] However, there may be another cause, another common factor that Strindberg shared with Vincent van Gogh: a heavy consumption of absinthe.

Research by University of Maryland Medical School psychiatrist Russell R Monroe has shown that thujone, the toxic element in absinthe, produces bursts of electrical activity in the limbic system. Monroe argued that by this effect, absinthe reproduces neurological conditions similar to epilepsy.[14]

If this is the case, then Strindberg's 'doors of perception' may have been opened by absinthe-facilitated epilepsy. As we have already discovered, one of the syndromes associated with epilepsy is Waxman-Geschwind. This is hyper-religiosity. We have observed this in Van Gogh and there is strong evidence that Strindberg had similar predilections. In spring 1898 he received a letter from Axel Herrlin, a young academic. Herrlin had read Strindberg's autobiographical novel *Inferno* and in the letter he explained to the dramatist that he had had similar experiences and was keen to have an explanation. On 4 March Strindberg wrote back to Herrlin. In this revealing letter he asks some intriguing rhetorical questions and reveals something of his own state of mind at that time:

> Who stages these performances for us and with what purpose?
> Are they real? Is there a hell apart from this? Or is it to frighten
> children? My own crisis, which lasted nearly seven months, has
> given me no further certainty, except regarding certain points
> ...[15]

It is apparent from this that he is no nearer understanding the true nature of his glimpses of the world beyond the doors. However, what is perhaps significant with regard to our TLE/migraine interpretation is that he goes on to discuss religion and his fear lest he might

> ... be punished with religious fanaticism and led astray. But
> I'm not sure whether this is a trial which one must withstand
> or a calling which must be obeyed. My earlier fatalism has
> been translated into a belief in Providence, and I fully realize
> that standing alone I have nothing and can achieve nothing.[16]

It is evident that Strindberg showed strong religious convictions: it is just that he was never consistent in these beliefs. He professed, at different times in his life, to be Pietist, Protestant, Deist, Atheist, Occultist and Catholic.[17] This suggests a possible diagnosis of Waxman-Geschwind syndrome.

Later he addressed a letter to the Swedish poet Gustaf Fröding, another person who suffered from powerful hallucinations. In this he gives his own opinion of what hallucinations may be:

> Don't use the word hallucination (or even delirium) as though it stood for something unreal. Hallucinations and delirium possess a certain kind of reality – or they are phantasmagoria consciously designed by the Invisible One to frighten us.[18]

When he started writing, he discovered that there was a force within him that facilitated his creativity. In a letter written in June 1884 to his friend Karl Otto Bonnier he wrote: 'I sit and I write like a sleepwalker, and must not be awakened or it may stop in the middle.'[19]

He also showed many signs of clairvoyance. In 1893 a curious 'future memory' event was recounted by his wife, Frida. One day she went out for a walk. On her return Strindberg accused her of having met German dramatist Hermann Sudermann at four o'clock at the corner of Karlstrasse. It is clear from this exchange that Strindberg believed his young wife to be having an affair with the German. What was strange was that Strindberg said that he had 'seen' the meeting in his mind's eye and that Frida was wearing a different dress – a green one – from the one he saw her leave in earlier in the day. He further stated that this dress was the object of a conversation between his wife and Sudermann. According to Strindberg, Sudermann had commented that the dress reminded him of something. A week later, and by chance, Frida did meet with Sudermann in the location described. A conversation ensued, during which the German commented on Frida's green dress, adding that it reminded him of something.[20]

In 1903, while staying in Grisslehamm, Strindberg described another example of his precognitive abilities. He wrote in his diary: 'Today I shall get a telephone message that my daughter is ill.'[21] Later that day he did receive such a phone call. Of course, this may be a simple bending of the truth on his part. However, one has to take into account that Strindberg's diary was written simply for his own reading: he was not writing it for others, and so had no need to impress.

Between 1894 and 1897 Strindberg experienced what he was to term his 'Inferno crisis'. I am fascinated as to just how similar this is to Philip K Dick's experiences. Both writers came to identical conclusions about their respective 'theophanies', in that both believed in the profoundly Gnostic view that this universe is an illusion created by a mad demiurge. In 1897 Strindberg published his autobiographical novel *Inferno*. Like Philip K Dick's *VALIS*, this presents arguments that the Gnostic sages were correct: we are all trapped in an illusion created by an evil god. Strindberg's unnamed narrator makes the following comment:

> Earth, earth is hell – the dungeon appointed by a superior power, in which I cannot move a step without injuring the happiness of others, and in which others cannot remain happy without hurting me. Thus Swedenborg depicts hell, and perhaps without knowing it, earthly life, at the same time.[22]

In his preface to *A Dream Play* he describes the play's layout:

> Time and space do not exist; the imagination spins, weaving new patterns on a flimsy basis of reality: a mixture of memories, experiences, free associations, absurdities and improvisations. The characters split, double, multiply, evaporate, condense, dissolve and merge. But one consciousness rules them all: the

dreamer's; for him there are no secrets, no inconsistencies, no scruples and no laws.[23]

Here again we have the idea of a reality behind the everyday world of received perceptions. Strindberg believed that he was able to see beyond this illusion and perceive *true* reality.

There are other parallels between Strindberg and Philip K Dick. As well as the fact that both wrote fictionalized accounts of their experiences, they both kept secret journals describing in minute detail what they perceived and their attempts to understand what was taking place. Strindberg's journal has now become known as his *Occult Diary*, which he wrote over an 11-year period from 1897 to 1908. Philip K Dick spent a similar period of time writing his *Exegesis*. Both are powerful, if somewhat rambling, accounts of a mind experiencing a much more extensive universe than that presented by the everyday senses. As well as *Inferno*, Strindberg also fictionalized the contents of his *Occult Diary* in *Legends* (autobiographical sketches) and his *Road to Damascus* trilogy.

There is also evidence that, like Dick, Strindberg experienced migraine auras. For example, we know that he regularly described olfactory hallucinations such as the smelling of incense when none was present. Indeed, it seems that this smell was associated with altered states of consciousness. He wrote: 'This smell throws me into ecstasy and makes me happy as soon as I sense it, but happiness mixed with terror.'[24]

He also experienced auditory, specifically musical, hallucinations. While in Paris he kept hearing Schumann's melody *Aufschwung* playing over and over again. This was the favourite tune of his love rival, the Polish novelist Stanisław Przybyszewski. Now, it must be remembered that at this time recorded music was unknown, so such a phenomenon is unusual. As we have discovered, musicogenic epilepsy is a recognized variation on the epilepsy aura.

One of the standard 'hallucinations' described by migraineurs, TLErs and schizophrenics is the concept of the double, or doppelgänger. In *Inferno* Strindberg describes an entity he calls 'the other'. This being seemed very real and he wrote about it many times. For example:

> A stranger [...] was put into the room adjacent to my writing
> desk. This unknown man never uttered a word; he seemed to
> be occupied in writing something behind the wooden partition
> that separated us. All the same, it was odd that he should push
> back his chair every time I moved mine. He repeated my every
> movement [...] When I went to bed the man in the next room
> next to my desk went to bed as well.[25]

Strindberg describes how this went on for three days, a mirror image of his own movements sounding through the partition back at him. Strindberg's encounters with the 'sensed presence', as Persinger calls it, are a regular theme in *Inferno*. Indeed, here the playwright virtually uses the same term:

> Enter your room at night-time and you will find that someone
> has got there before you. You will not see him but you will sense
> his presence.[26]

Strindberg describes many of the elements of the Huxleyan spectrum that I have presented in this book. For example, we have discussed how humming noises in the head are related to out-of-body experiences and the near-death experience. These auditory hallucinations seem to involve tuning in to a background noise that can only be heard as the doors of perception slowly open. They are also strongly related to the various 'aura' states of TLE and migraine. Is this what Strindberg is trying to describe here?:

175

Have you had in your ears the humming that resembles the noise of a water mill? Have you noticed, in the stillness of the night, or even in broad daylight, how memories of your past life stir and are resurrected, one by one or two by two? All the mistakes you have made, all your crimes, all your follies [...] You re-live the life you have lived, from your birth to the very day that is ... Do you recognize the truth of all this?[27]

Note that from the humming he swiftly moves on to associate this liminal state with a description strongly reminiscent of the 'panoramic life review' associated with the classic near-death experience? Strindberg calls these experiences the 'Mills of God'. It is also reasonable to conclude from sections of his *Occult Diary* that he regularly experienced sleep paralysis and REM intrusion. He describes how, late at night, he was 'visited' by his estranged wife Harriet Bosse and how she forced him down on the bed to have sexual relations with him. This is the classic 'succubus' scenario that has been described for centuries, an illusion now associated with sleep paralysis. For Strindberg this is another manifestation of 'the other'.

At the height of his fame he turned to full-blown esotericism. Under the influence of the writings of Swedish mystic Emanuel Swedenborg, he became consumed with what Swedenborg termed the 'science of correspondences'. In general terms this was the idea that everything had significance and even the most trivial event contained a message – again a classic example of Waxman-Geschwind syndrome.

In his later years Strindberg was able to look back on these experiences rather dispassionately in his *Inferno*. The jury is out as to what caused Strindberg's strange worldview. It may simply have been an excess of absinthe, or it may have been undiagnosed temporal lobe epilepsy. But one thing is for sure: whatever the cause, clearly he had glimpsed things beyond the doors of perception.

The suggestion given thus far is that a position on the Huxleyan spectrum brings about extreme creativity. However, this is not always the case. A very normal individual can also experience something extraordinary as part of their daily life. I would now like to move our enquiry to lesser-known but nevertheless important Huxleyans such as my friend Jayne Burton.

## Jayne Burton

After my first book was published, I was approached by quite a few TLE experiencers who were intrigued by my 'angle' on the condition. One of these, fellow Merseysider Jayne Burton, became a good friend, and we occasionally met up to have a chat and a catch-up. As I have already mentioned, Jayne is the only person I know who has experienced something known as the 'WADA test'. This is where the dominant hemisphere is effectively 'switched off' and the non-dominant hemisphere allowed a fleeting period of control.

Jayne and I had agreed to meet at a bookstore in a retail park in Speke on the outskirts of Liverpool. This bookstore had a café located on a mezzanine floor, and from this elevated location the whole shop could be viewed, together with the only entrance. Jane and I had settled down to have a coffee. She explained to me that she had just left her son in the city centre, about six miles away, and that she would be going into the city later to meet up with him again. Jayne experienced occasional TLE 'absences' but at that stage I had never witnessed one. I was therefore surprised when she literally stopped in mid-conversation and stared at me. She had become immobile. She was quite silent and then suddenly she spoke: 'What is he doing here?' she exclaimed with surprise. I realized that this was not Jayne but her unconscious speaking, while she was in her 'absence' state. She then blinked quickly and came to. I was about to tell her what she had said when she looked over the balcony towards the entrance to the shop and said, 'What is he doing here?' I was totally stunned to see her son walk in through the entrance and make his way up to see us. Jayne looked at me and reiterated her surprise at his unexpected arrival. For me this was irrefutable evidence of a precognition while in an altered state of consciousness. Jayne had absolutely no recollection of what she had said during her absence, but it seemed to me that part of her was perceiving the contents of her immediate future.

Is such an ability of any use? By the time the subject realizes that something has been foreseen, it is taking place. However, it can be argued that such a short-term foreknowledge of events can carry a huge evolutionary advantage. Knowing that danger awaits in a second or two may allow avoiding action to be taken – for example, if a dangerous animal is about to attack or a rock is about to hit you on the head. Is this why temporal lobe epileptics have survived to carry through their genetic blueprint to the next generation? Clearly, regular and potentially debilitating seizures cannot in any way contribute to genetic survival. In most cases they will leave the subject vulnerable to attack, particularly if the 'absence' is followed by a tonic-clonic seizure. But for some reason the genes that carry epilepsy have survived.

There is strong empirical evidence that this ability to monitor the immediate future is a skill that we all have: it is just that for neurotypicals the skill remains totally unconscious. In 1997 a series of experiments was carried out by Dean Radin and Dick Bierman. They used something called the 'galvanic skin response'. The body's sweat glands are directly controlled by the sympathetic nervous system. This means that any form of arousal, be it fear, anger or stress, will bring about changes on the surface of the skin, specifically in the skin's electrical resistance. In order to measure these tiny changes, each of the volunteers had a sensor placed on their left index and middle fingers. This, in turn, sent signals to a device that could measure these changes. It is important to note that the sympathetic nervous system goes about its business with no self-aware consciousness.

Such responses have the same source as the blink and yawn mechanisms.[28] To clarify the automatic nature of this process, Radin and Bierman were careful to call what they were searching for 'presentiment' or 'pre-feeling'.

The subjects were placed in front of a computer monitor. When they were ready they were able to start the test by pressing a button. After a delay of 7.5 seconds, a randomly selected picture was displayed on the screen for a specific exposure period. The pictures had been carefully selected to bring about a sense of relaxation or to elicit a strong emotional response. Relaxing pictures of fruit, household objects or beautiful landscapes were interspersed with images of horror – car crashes, murder victims or animals about to attack. The skin conductance was measured before, during and after each image was shown at a rate of five samples per second.

The results showed that most subjects could unconsciously anticipate the contents of the next picture before it was shown on the screen. If the anticipated picture was threatening or disturbing, the galvanic skin response reflected arousal. However, if the picture was relaxing, no response was recorded. For the researchers this was strong evidence that something within us can monitor our immediate future. With most of us, this aptitude is entirely unconscious; but for some temporal lobe epileptics this subliminal awareness leaches into the self-aware brain.

This may explain how Jayne could subliminally perceive the contents of her own immediate futures. This suggests that time itself is, for certain individuals, more flexible in the length of the perceptual 'moment'. However, there is a little-known psychological state in which subjective time can also speed up. This is known as the 'Zeitraffer-Elebnis phenomenon'.

In German a Zeitraffer is an apparatus that accelerates the apparent motion of a film. This is used in a similar way to time-lapse photography. However, it seems that for some people this apparatus is not needed. Under certain, little-understood neurological conditions, the world is suddenly perceived to be speeded up. One particularly fascinating case is cited by Ferdinand Binkofski of the Department of Neurology, Heinrich Heine University, Dusseldörf, and Richard A Block of the Department of Psychology, Montana State University.[29]

Block and Binkofski report that a right-handed, 66-year-old retired clerk with no history of neurological disease was driving his car along a German road. The man (known as 'B W') was horrified to discover that suddenly external objects starting rushing towards him at great speed. As he described it, it was as if somebody had pressed a fast-forward button. He also found that his car was also running fantastically fast. He could not control it, as his reaction time remained 'normal'. He found himself driving through a set of red traffic lights because he simply could not stop. But he managed to slam his brakes on and come to a halt. He watched in horror as the world around him still ran around him in super-speed.

This experience continued for him, and two days later, in a state of great stress, B W was admitted to the Heinrich Heine Neurological Hospital. He described what was happening as an 'accelerated motion of events, like a time-lapse film'. He complained that he could no longer tolerate watching TV because the progression of events was too quick for him to follow. He also described how life itself had begun to pass too quickly for him.

On his admission to hospital, a CT scan was done, showing that he had a lesion on his dorsolateral pre-frontal cortex. He was then given a series of tests. He showed no problem with time orientation: it was just that for him it was going faster. However, when asked to decide how long a 60-second period was for him, some strange things were discovered. B W was told to say when he wished to start, then remain silent until he felt that a minute had gone by. He was then to say 'Stop'. They repeated this test many times and B W's subjective average 'minute' turned out to be 286 seconds.

It was subsequently discovered that B W had a glioblastoma tumour centred in the 'Brodmann area' in the pre-frontal cortex of his left hemisphere. Sadly, he died soon afterwards without ever regaining normal time perception. Now what is interesting about this paper is that the two scientists suggest some intriguing possible explanations, including the idea that we all have an internal 'pacemaker' that controls how we subjectively perceive time duration. However, they finish by writing: 'It is unclear how best to explain the phenomenon.' In a personal communication Dr Block has informed me that to his knowledge there has been no other case of this sort ever recorded.

Such temporal anomalies are regularly reported to me by other individuals who experience temporal lobe epilepsy. If this sensation were purely an element of TLE, we could at least isolate it to neurological and neurochemical activity in the temporal lobes. However, there is powerful evidence that precognition is also a central experience of another element of the Huxleyan spectrum, namely autism.

## Donna Williams

In 1992 a book came from literally 'nowhere' to become the number one bestseller in the USA, Japan and Norway, spending 15 weeks in the *New York Times* bestseller list. Written by a young Australian woman named Donna Williams, it had the curious title, *Nobody Nowhere*.[30] In this book, an autobiography, Williams describes growing up in Australian suburbia, a place of almost stifling ordinariness. But Donna was far from ordinary. She had curiously vivid dreams. One occurred the night after her 21st birthday:

> In the dream I had been sharing a house with this man but was now sharing a house with a woman who, curiously, I had recognized as an acquaintance I had met through my friend Stella when I was 14 [...] I dreamed that it was again my birthday. The three of us stood around the dining room table draped in an antique lace tablecloth. We had raised our glasses (the crystal

glasses I had later been given by a friend) ...[31]

Two years later she was celebrating her 23rd birthday with three friends when she found herself literally re-living her dream, in perfect and precise detail. She was, as she had been in the original dream, standing with the people she had dreamed of, holding the very crystal glasses she had been given two years before:

> The glasses were raised in a toast. 'Happy Birthday!' came the announcement as the entire scene began to run in slow motion. Awake, yet in a dream state, Donna stood, frozen. My mouth hung open in shock ...[32]

Like others we have encountered in this book, Donna Williams was, and still is, able to peep through the doors of perception. Her faculty was something virtually unknown at the time – unknown, that is, outside specialist circles. Williams's book gave voice to millions of people across the world who were experiencing the strange, the anomalous and the downright weird every waking moment of their lives.

The book opens with Donna Williams recalling her first ever dream. This involved her moving through a whiteout with bright spots of fluffy colour passing through her. This must have been before she was three years old. What she then noticed was that the air was, as she terms it, 'full of spots'. She describes how, in her visual field, people got in the way of the spots, effectively obscuring them. As we have seen earlier, this suggests two sorts of 'hallucination', one creating the spots and another obscuring parts of consensual reality – in effect a hallucination of omission.

Donna describes how she enjoyed giving herself what she calls the 'wizzies': that is, she would spin around with her arms outstretched. She also began to encounter the 'wisps'. These she describes as tiny creatures that hung in the air directly above her and looked like wisps of hair. These creatures were almost transparent, but if she 'looked through them, they were very much there'.[33] These sound to me like 'floaters' – small flecks of a protein called collagen that can accumulate on the vitreous humour at the back of the eye, and are sometimes 'seen' as thread-like strands floating across the visual field. I assume that everybody sees these: they are not in any way unusual. However, the 'spots' that she perceived surrounding her bed are. She called these images 'stars'. These totally enveloped her bed. She explains that later she was told that she was seeing 'air particles'. I am intrigued by exactly what was meant by this. She has been informed that these were evidence of her visual hypersensitivity. They became so numerous that the rest of the world 'faded away'.[34] Again, this is of importance. If she was actually seeing 'air particles' in three-dimensional space, how did they make the world 'fade away'? This suggests that these particles obscured the other objects in consensual space. Air is transparent, which is why we can see the world. This suggests that they were hallucinations. If this is the case, we again have a powerful example of a negative hallucination that takes out elements of the visual field as well as adding to it.

'Willy' was the name she gave to a pair of piercing green eyes that could only be seen in the darkness. Young Donna regularly encountered this being, and over time she 'became' Willy: soon this was the personality that she presented to the world. Later she meets a girl called Carol. Again she internalizes the personality of this associate, and 'Carol' becomes a third focus of consciousness within Donna's rapidly compartmentalizing mind. Carol's personality is the total opposite of Willy's. She acts normally when interacting with others. Such was Carol's power that by the time 'they' were five years old, this surrogate self had taken over. It took many years for the original personality to take control back.

As I have already suggested, infants and young children regularly report having imaginary friends. This suggests to me that the doors of perception are naturally slightly ajar for younger children. These glimpses of the world beyond seem to be specifically facilitated during the liminal sleep states known as hypnagogia and hypnopompia, which some children experience profoundly. Of course, the label 'autistic' is somewhat arbitrary for the under-sixes: the condition could just as easily be diagnosed as childhood-onset schizophrenia. The 'Willie' Donna first encounters seems very similar to my concept of the 'Daemon'. Willy is male, which is in keeping with the general observation that for most people the Daemon is of the opposite sex.

Donna Williams's books *Nobody Nowhere* and *Somebody Somewhere* are, in my opinion, the most powerful descriptions of the inner world of autistics ever written. However, I am also of the opinion that Donna's 'world' is crafted by something far more powerful than autism. As we have seen, she is precognitive and has super-senses – witness her ability to actually see the flashing of a fluorescent light, something that neurotypicals are totally unaware of. But it seems that Donna has other perceptions that suggest temporal lobe epilepsy. For example, in *Somebody Somewhere* she gives a harrowing description of a state of mind she calls the 'Big Black Nothingness'. When reading the following account, bear in mind the descriptions of pre-seizure aura states given to us by TLErs:

> A feeling kept washing over me. It began with the feeling one gets from eating lemons. It was like a tingle that ran up my neck and then spread out to every thread and fibre of my body like the emergence of cracks in an earthquake. I knew this monster. It was the Big Black Nothingness and it felt like death coming to get me.[35]

She first experienced this sensation at four years of age. It then became a regular part of her life, sometimes occurring up to three or four times a day. As she grew older, these episodes decreased, but even in her mid-20s they visited her three or four times a year. It was after her first book deal that the 'monster' returned on a more regular basis. Again, consider this description:

> My body trembled like a building in an earthquake, my teeth hit together with the sound of a fast typist attacking the keys of a typewriter. Every muscle tensed as though it would squeeze the life out of me and relax just long enough to be hit and hit and hit again by 'tidal waves'.[36]

But there are also elements of classic migraine here. We know that Donna has a great dislike of bright lights and loud noises. By her own admission this is hypersensitivity. The actual brightness of the light and the noise levels are not that high, it is just that her sensitivities are higher. This seems to be a permanent issue for Donna and her fellow autistics. As we have discovered, this is now known as the 'intense world syndrome'. However, migraineurs also suffer the same discomforts when in a migraine state. It is just that for migraineurs this is an occasional sensation rather than a continual one.

When she was young, it seems that Donna experienced perceptions that can be interpreted as either out-of-body experiences (OBEs) or a form of remote viewing. These took place in a semi-dream state reminiscent of hypnagogia. Here she describes what happened:

> At school strange things were happening. I would have daydreams in which I was watching children I knew. I would see them doing the most trivial things: peeling potatoes over the sink, getting themselves a peanut butter sandwich before

going to bed. Such daydreams were like films in which I'd
see a sequence of everyday events that didn't relate in any
way to myself. I began to test the truth of these daydreams,
approaching the friends I'd seen in them and asking them to
give a step-by-step detailed picture of what they were doing at
the time I had the daydream. Amazingly, to the finest detail,
I would find I had been right. This was nothing I controlled, it
simply came into my head, but it frightened me.[37]

In her own work, Temple Grandin mentions that some autistics have visual
perceptions so acute that they can see the flicker of fluorescent tubes.
Donna has this ability. She describes being disturbed at a college lecture:

I had been tortured by sharp white fluorescent light, which
made reflections bounce off everything. It made the room
race busily in a constant state of change. Light and shadow
dancing on people's faces as they spoke turned the scene into
an animated cartoon.[38]

Her eyesight does seem exceptionally acute. She is fascinated by 'charged
energy particles that fill the air and that most people tune out as irrelevant
background information or do not have sensitive enough vision to see'.[39]
These again seem to be related to a migraine state rather than autism.
Of course, if autism, migraine and temporal lobe epilepsy are all related
experiences, then it is not at all surprising that there may be perceptual
overlaps. But Donna is convinced that these 'stars and spots' are things
out there in consensual reality: it is just that neurotypicals are not sensitive
to them. I am intrigued as to what she means by this. Clearly she believes
these 'spots' to be a natural phenomenon. Could she be referring to
those objects that are popularly known as 'orbs'? These do show up on

photographs. Does she actually mean dust motes? She cannot really mean 'charged energy particles', because nobody can see these, however sensitive they are. I am of the opinion that what she is intimating here is that the brains of neurotypicals cut out these floating objects, whereas her autistic brain, facilitated by its 'intense world syndrome', sees everything.

I have repeatedly suggested that precognition is a central element of the Huxleyan spectrum. It therefore comes as no surprise that Donna Williams has regularly experienced powerful and convincing incidents in which her unconscious foresaw an aspect of her future. We have already looked at her birthday party precognition. She describes another in her second book, *Somebody Somewhere: Breaking Free from the World of Autism*. She describes how she was visiting New York as part of a publicity tour and had been asked to bring with her copies of some of her paintings. She was staying in a huge hotel overlooking Central Park. On arrival she was allocated a room on the 15th floor, one that would give her a wonderful view across the park. As she entered the room she could see through the windows the vivid colours made apparent by the setting sun. This is how she described what happened next:

> I had brought my paintings with me. Among them was a copy of the painting I had given my solicitor. It was a day scene with a hazy blue and purple sky, with lights of the buildings playing in the reflection of the water stretching out before them. I raced to the window with my picture. My heart was thumping. Fifteen stories up, I found I had painted the scene outside my window, building for building, steeple for steeple, in the same order, complete with the cranes now towering over them in the process of construction work. There was one thing wrong. I had painted the picture four months before coming to New York, and had never been there before.[40]

Later she was given information that proved just how powerful this 'precognition' was. There was one element of Donna's painting that did not match the scene. She had painted a small surface of water that was not in the view from the window. This is how she describes what happened next:

> 'There is no water down there, though, in Central Park,' I said. 'There is in my picture.' My agent pointed out that, out of sight, there was a vast reservoir, just beyond the trees that met the road in front of the buildings. The light reflected in just the way I had painted.[41]

What can we make of this? Donna had not known about the reservoir until she was told about it at that moment. This suggests a precognition involving a future scene incorporating information received after the scene was first observed. So how can this be explained? This is nothing to do with being able to sense by mysterious skills the environment as it is now. This is sensing a *future* image in the past. This is pure precognition. Not only that but the premonition is *proved* – by a painting.

Donna Williams is now a very successful writer and has contributed hugely to the public's understanding of autism. She travels the world lecturing. Her work is of crucial importance. It is only through personal experience of the Pleroma that individuals can really appreciate just how powerful these altered states can be. Donna Williams has lived all her life with the Pleroma as an ever-present reality.

Autism is recognized as an 'illness' that is being diagnosed in ever-increasing numbers. This suggests that it is more than a neurological anomaly, and more something that is ingrained within most of us to a greater or lesser extent. It is usually associated with the early period of life rather than the later. However, I believe that an association can be made between autism and that other great mystery of our times: the huge increase in numbers of people suffering from Alzheimer's disease.

## Pat McCreath

In 2015 a fascinating book was published in the UK, entitled *The Gift of Alzheimer's* and written by Scottish holistic therapist Maggie La Tourelle. This was the first book to discuss the regularly observed, but little commented upon, cases of Alzheimer's that suggest that in this state individuals begin to perceive a universe denied to us neurotypicals. As we have already discovered, Alzheimer's seems to open up the 'doors of perception' through visual hallucinations and heightened senses. However, in her book Maggie La Tourelle describes how she witnessed, in her mother, a series of ever-developing cognitions that defy explanation and suggest that Alzheimer's is far more than a simple degenerative disease, and more a 'preparation' for moving on from this perceptual plane to another.

In 2000 her mother, Pat, was diagnosed with Alzheimer's disease. In February 2002 things became so bad that Pat was sent to a local care home to give Maggie a period of respite. Sadly, she never returned to live with her husband, instead becoming a permanent resident in the home. Soon Pat entered what is technically known as stage 6 (late-stage) Alzheimer's. This is the stage when people have given up struggling: they have no choice but to surrender to their condition. It was at this time that Maggie decided that she would keep notes of her conversations with her mother. What initially became simply a note-taking exercise became something far more, as Pat slipped deeper and deeper into her Alzheimer's and, in doing so, another part of her seemed to 'wake up' and become hypersensitive to the messages the universe was giving her. It was then that Pat made an incredible statement about her condition. She explained to her daughter: 'It's difficult being ... working between two worlds.'[42]

I have met Maggie and discussed with her in great detail the significance of her records, and I am totally convinced that her work will,

189

in years to come, be considered a lens through which we can see exactly what is taking place as the microtubules are shattered and communication with the Pleroma becomes more direct and less processed by the dominant hemisphere of the brain.

I now offer a small selection from the discussions Maggie had with Pat, together with my own interpretation using the Huxleyan model as my guide. Pat described how she was in the process of being taught things in preparation for her full transition into the Pleroma. She spoke of how 'we are learning we're immortal'. My question here is, who is doing the 'teaching'? It seems, too, that Pat was not alone in the process. Of course, what she may mean here in her use of the word 'we' is humankind in general: the idea that life itself is a preparation to be 'immortal'.[43]

Pat regularly refers to the way in which her brain was being re-programmed. She states that 'they' have 'taken things out'[44] of her mind, and that 'they are very skilful'.[45] Later she describes how she has had 'three or four operations'.[46] This reminds me of the regularly reported incidents in DMT 'dreams' whereby subjects describe how they find themselves in operating theatres having organs surgically removed or implanted. This theme parallels the UFO-abduction scenario where 'aliens' operate on the helpless abductees who are in a state of paralysis. As we have already suggested, endogenous DMT may be the facilitator of such perceptions.

Pat mentions the 'inspectors'. They usually announce when they are coming. She seems to be in a timeless zone when interfacing with them. On one occasion she comments on how her deceased sister Kathleen is 'very polite to them'.[47] But rather than being friendly bystanders, they may alternatively suggest that she can perceive the life force of individuals who have already moved over into the Pleroma. These 'inspectors' also ask her questions, which she finds straightforward and easy to answer. Later Pat makes a comment that astounded me when I read it, something that Maggie herself did not pick up on: it seems that the 'inspectors' had been very *effective*. Pat was keen to impart her new knowledge of the brain to her daughter: 'Do you want to continue asking me questions?,' she asked, 'about how the four parts of my brain are connected?'[48]

Each hemisphere of the brain consists of an occipital, temporal, parietal and frontal lobe. Four parts, each of which interfaces with the others in various ways. When I met Maggie in London to talk about her book, I discussed with her just how strange this was. Maggie assured me that as far as she was concerned, her mother had never shown any interest in the structure of the brain. So how did she know that it is commonly recognized that the brain has four lobes?

As she approached the 'crossover', Pat made a very curious reference to 'programming' – it is unclear if what she meant by 'programme' is a TV broadcast or a computer program.

If my model is correct, individuals suffering from Alzheimer's will, in similar ways to TLErs, autistics, migraineurs and schizophrenics, manifest what are generally known as 'psychic' abilities. These may involve telepathy, precognitions or general extrasensory perception (ESP). It is therefore not surprising that Maggie cites many examples of her mother proving beyond all reasonable doubt that she was accessing information from areas outside of her five senses. Pat calls this information field 'television'. She informed her daughter that she had got her brain 'organized': 'I think of something, anything,' she said, 'and take it from there. Television.'[49] In an uncanny echo of my own mother's behaviour as her Alzheimer's progressed, Maggie notes that Pat had started a new tic of rubbing her nose and her brow with her index finger.[50]

In a fascinating development Pat then started to show seemingly precognitive abilities. The first example was fairly mundane. Pat seemed to be aware that Maggie was having problems with her teeth, which was quite true but had not been discussed previously.[51] Later Pat shows that she is, in some subliminal way, aware of what is taking place in Maggie's life. She advises her daughter that she should 'take it easy moving house. You need to take it easy, Margaret.'[52] This could be an example of 'remote viewing' but for me the explanation is more likely to be telepathy.

As we have discovered, there is mounting evidence that children with autism have telepathic abilities. The work of Dr Diane Hennacy Powell has virtually proven this. There are also known links between autism and Alzheimer's – for example, the brains of people with Alzheimer's have been shown to have much higher levels of aluminium,[53] as have the brains of young people with autism.[54] There is a similar link with regard to mercury and lead.

The most astounding case of telepathy was recorded by Maggie on Sunday 21 May 2006. In a general conversation, and in relation to nothing that had been said before, Pat suddenly said, 'My Mini'. Maggie was stunned by this. This is how she describes the background:

> In London the previous day a friend asked where I was going, so I zoomed in on an aerial photo of my parents' house on my computer to show him. There, to my surprise, sitting in the driveway was Mum's old Mini. Her car had been sold years ago when she was no longer fit to drive so the photo was clearly out of date.[55]

I discussed this with Maggie in the summer of 2015 and she confirmed to me that she had used Google Earth to check out the house on the Internet. Here we have evidence of something very strange. The Google Earth image was clearly years out of date and this was what caught Maggie's attention. Here we have powerful evidence that Pat's telepathic skills were becoming very powerful. It has been suggested with regard to autistic children who are 'locked in' – that is, who have no ways of communicating with the outside world – that they develop new skills to accommodate this. I suggest that exactly the same compensatory effects are developed by individuals at the other end of the age spectrum who have similar restrictions.

In late August 2006 Maggie's father had a fall at home. It became clear that he could no longer live independently, and Maggie began a series of meetings to discuss moving him into a care home. On 25 October Maggie travelled from her home in London to have another meeting about her father's future. She called in to see her mother. The first thing her mother said to her after the general 'How are you?' question and response was: 'I want to be at all the meetings.'

In his book *The Man Who Mistook His Wife for a Hat* Oliver Sacks describes how a young Indian woman called Bhagawhandi was dying of a malignant brain tumour. As her illness progressed, she spent much of her time in a semi-dream state facilitated by the sad fact that the tumour was growing into her temporal lobes. Initially, she had suffered a series of tonic-clonic seizures, but as the tumour worked its way into her temporal lobes, the seizures ceased and she moved into a semi-permanent 'dreamy state' as described by epilepsy pioneer John Hughlings Jackson in connection with temporal lobe epilepsy and its associate altered state, déjà vu. It was confirmed by EEG scans that these dreamy states were, indeed, temporal lobe seizures. But her 'dreams' in this state, manifesting as profound hypnagogic or hypnopompic sequences, involved her going back to her childhood in India. She was re-living long-lost incidents of that time. Sacks was fascinated by this time-reversal.[56]

It seems that something similar was happening to Pat. At various times during their meetings Pat had mentioned that she was re-living her past and remembering long-forgotten incidents. But one particularly intriguing conversation suggested that these were far more than simple reveries. On 14 November 2006 Maggie noted that her mother was looking 'particularly radiant'. When her daughter commented on this, she replied that she felt like she was 'seventeen, ten years older'.[57] A few weeks later Pat announced that she had 'entered the first stage'.[58]

Such insights seem to be perceived from a timeless location, a looking in from outside. Pat felt dislocated within time. On one occasion she said to Maggie: 'I feel I have no past, present or future.'[59]

I found this very familiar. In 2012 my own mother was sliding into the final stages of Alzheimer's. She was still able to chat with me on the phone and seemed to recognize me when I visited her. However, I felt that she was not really sure who I was and had no idea where she was, how old she was or, indeed, who she was. Then one evening I received a phone call from the home, asking me if I would speak with my mother. I could hear her in the background and the voice was my mother's, but not the 89-year-old Alzheimer's patient's. This was somebody far younger, and far more engaged with life. The nurse handed the phone over to my mother. What happened next was simply astounding – and witnessed by my wife (she was in the room with me listening in) and the staff of the Wirral nursing home. My mother said, 'Tony, I really need your help.' She then explained how she had been sitting watching TV with my father and seemed to have nodded off to sleep. The next minute she woke up and she was 'in this place', as she termed it. She believed that she had been imprisoned by the staff and they were holding her against her will. She then said, 'Wait until your father hears about this.' My father died in 1988 and this was 2012. I tried to explain this. Her response stunned me. She said, 'Your father is not dead, a few minutes ago I was watching television with him at home'. She then went quiet for a second or two and said: 'You are not my son, you sound too old. My son is 20 years old and away at university.' She then accused me of being an imposter in collusion with her captors, and slammed the phone down. I phoned back immediately and was told that they needed to give her a sedative to calm her down. This they did. When I phoned next day she was back in her Alzheimer's twilight state.

I was absolutely convinced that I was speaking to my 50-year-old mother, not to an 89-year-old. It was exactly her way of speaking when she was younger – the phrasing, the tonality. It was as if I had telephoned the past. I am sure that the events had happened in exactly the way my mother described them. When she dropped off to sleep, it was a cozy evening at home in 1974. She then finds herself in a nightmare in which she has been transported to her future, held prisoner by persons unknown and trapped in the body of a frail, elderly woman. I would like to believe that when she woke up from her 'future slip' she would return to a world where my long-dead father was sitting next to her and Morecambe and Wise were on the TV.

It has long been reported that in the final stages of Alzheimer's the patient, for a few moments, becomes totally lucid: the fully aware personality seems to surface for a short time before they slide into unconsciousness. This is known as 'terminal lucidity'. Virginia-based psychiatrist Bruce Greyson has researched this subject over many years and has drawn some interesting conclusions.

In a paper published in 2011, Greyson describes how he and his associates, Michael Nahm, Emily Williams Kelly and Erlendur Haraldsson, had identified no fewer than 83 cases of terminal lucidity, and of these a fair number involved Alzheimer's patients. They cite one case of a woman who had suffered from the disease for 15 years and for the last few years of her life she was totally unresponsive. However, a few minutes before she died she started a completely normal conversation with her daughter. Not surprisingly, this left the daughter totally confused. Another case, cited from the files of Erlendur Haraldsson, featured an 81-year-old Icelandic woman who had been unresponsive and recognized none of her family. A month before she died, she suddenly sat up in bed, looked directly at her son, Lydur, and said, 'My Lydur. I am going to recite a verse to you.' She then recited with very clear and precise Icelandic enunciation a five-line poem ... whereupon she lay back on her pillow and become totally unresponsive again until her death. Her son remembered the words and discovered that it was the first stanza of a psalm by an Icelandic poet.[60]

It is known that at the terminal stages of Alzheimer's the cortex of the brain is almost totally destroyed. There should be no conscious awareness, let alone ability to hold a rational conversation or to recall a poem and repeat it with total accuracy. What has been observed in these cases is medically impossible. And yet it happens.

Greyson has associated terminal lucidity with another phenomenon known as 'Peak in Darien' experiences, whereby the terminal lucidity actually involves a broadening of perceptions to such an extent that a glimpse of the Pleroma is gained.[61] This term was first used by Frances Power Cobbe in 1882 as the title of a book of essays. She was making a reference to a sonnet by John Keats, 'On First Looking into Chapman's Homer,' in which he describes how the Spanish conquistadors, led by Cortéz, looked out from a peak in Darien (now Panama) to see an unknown ocean, the Pacific. Cobbe presented anecdotal evidence suggesting that at the point of death we all find ourselves looking from this world at the vistas of another.[62]

Greyson reports many cases of individuals, like Pat, who are in a state of advanced Alzheimer's and yet recover lucidity days or hours before they die.

Pat McCreath seemed to have experienced such perceptions. She regularly mentioned to Maggie that she had been speaking to Fiona and that she 'was fine' – Fiona was her second daughter who had tragically died a few years earlier. She also commented that her father was in the room with them and that her deceased brother had asked her to 'visit him'.

This phenomenon of seeing dead relatives is surprisingly common. I did a general search of Alzheimer's websites and web-based support groups and I found scores of examples. For example, here are two quotes that I found particularly intriguing. The first concerns an elderly Alzheimer's sufferer who started hearing music late at night:

Then she started reporting seeing her sister (who passed two years ago) walking in the house late at night. Next, she heard people working on the house during the day – no one was working on the house. More recently, she has made supper for my father (who passed 12 years ago) and made lunch for people she thought were working on the house.[63]

This seems to contain elements of both Peak in Darien experiences and CBS.

The second quote, taken from an article on Alzheimer's disease published on the Planet Waves website is even stranger:

My father had emphysema and dementia (at least according to the doctors). He was born in South Dakota, USA. He died four years ago on May 18th. One evening he was sitting on his couch reading, and glanced down his hallway. He saw his grandmother in the hallway, she turned, smiled and waved at him and continued on. He used to wake up in the morning thinking our dog (from childhood days, gone over 30 years) was lying beside him, asleep. And he would wake up petting the dog. And then he said he woke up in the middle of the night, and my mother was sleeping beside him. He asked her if it was time for him to leave with her, and she told him – not yet, but she would be with him until the end. For the last month of his life, he said he woke up in the morning with mom at his side, and believed she had snuck out to make him his favorite breakfast. And the last day of his life he said mom had run out to get things ready, but he would like us to chat with his old army buddies while she was gone.[64]

This is a case of not so much encounters with dead people, more of time slips in which the past seems to overlap into the present – in a similar way to that perceived by my mother. If she really was experiencing sitting watching television with my father, then his appearance would in no way be ghostly to her: it was just a matter-of-fact evening interrupted for a short time by a disturbing dream. However, for the elderly American gentleman things were far more complex. He recognizes that he is seeing dead people. But even stranger is the fact that his deceased wife responds precisely to the question he addresses to her. This is the behaviour of a seemingly sentient and independent entity, rather than simply a hallucination. The incident with the dog is also intriguing. as this suggests a tactile sensation as well as a visual one.

In many ways the experiences of Pat McCreath seem to me to be an extended near-death experience that took place over a period of years rather than a few seconds. During this time, Pat slowly had her consciousness transferred from one level of perception to another. However, it is of great importance to note that subjective time within an NDE is totally different from time as perceived by a witness to that NDE. In a classic NDE, the subject can experience many perceptions over an extended period of personal time that will be only a few seconds for the witness. Could it be that within an Alzheimer's state, time shrinks so that a period of months or even years can be perceived as a few hours or even minutes from the viewpoint of the Alzheimer's patient? Clearly what relates Alzheimer's and the NDE is that they are both part of the dying process, and must be related in some way or other. For Pat and her daughter Maggie La Tourelle, accessing the Pleroma was an unexpected but gradual feature of the Alzheimer's. For others, the Pleroma comes crashing in unannounced, and when it does a lifetime's prejudice about the paranormal simply falls apart. This is exactly what happened to Eben Alexander one fall morning in 2008.

## Dr Eben Alexander

On that fateful morning Alexander, a neurosurgeon at the Lynchburg General Hospital in Virginia, awoke with an extremely intense headache. He was rushed to hospital in a state known as 'status epilepticus': in effect, he was going from one epileptic seizure to another. This seizure state was brought about by a bacterial meningitis infection. This had seeped through his cerebral spinal fluid into his brain, attacking his neocortex, hippocampus and other parts of the limbic system. Within a few hours his cerebral cortex was totally shut down and he fell into a deep coma. He was in this state for six days. His neurological examinations revealed deeply pathological cortical reflexes, and scans revealed cortical disruption throughout his neocortex. Much to the surprise of the physicians caring for him, on the seventh day he came out of the coma state. What was even more surprising was that he had experienced something extraordinary while in his deep coma state – a state in which no such experience was possible. His cortex was not just malfunctioning: effectively it had been switched off. On his initial awakening, his brain function was devastated – he had no memories of the life of Eben Alexander before coma; even his language had been deleted. He did not even recognize beloved family members at the bedside – at least, not at first. Words came back to him over hours, personal memories over weeks, and all his knowledge from decades working as a neurosurgeon returned completely over a few months. His rich and ultra-real memories from deep within coma, which completely violated all neuroscientific principles about the relationship of the neocortex to consciousness, became an increasingly haunting mystery that demanded better explanation. Over a period of months it became clear that his near-death experience was far more than a simple hallucination.

Alexander claimed that after he had lost consciousness within this world, he found himself in another. He was aware that he was submerged in a kind of transparent mud with tree roots all around him. He was surrounded by a deep rhythmic pounding. This description is uncannily similar to those described by DMT experiencers. American writer Terence McKenna, considered one of the foremost experts in the DMT experience, describes here what is perceived when the 'traveller' arrives in the DMT universe:

> First of all (and why, I don't know) you have the impression that you are underground – far underground – you can't say why, but there's just this feeling of immense weight above you but you're in a large space, a vaulted dome. People even call it 'The DMT dome'. I [have had] people say to me, 'Have you been under the dome?' and I knew exactly what they meant.[65]

Alexander pulls himself out of the underground state to see a series of grotesque faces appear and screech at him. This is very reminiscent of hypnagogic or hypnopompic imagery experienced during states of REM intrusion. He then sees a white-gold rotating light accompanied by a complex melody. Music is also often reported as part of a TLE 'aura' state. The rotating light is reminiscent of the DMT perception commonly known as the 'Chrysanthemum'. This is what Terence McKenna believed was happening at this stage:

> [The 'Chrysanthemum'] represents some kind of disequilibrium state that has its roots in the synapses. What's happening as you're watching this Chrysanthemum is that millions and then hundreds of millions of DMT molecules are rushing into these serotonin bond sites in the synaptic cleft and disrupting the serotonin and switching the electron spin resonance signature of these neural junctions in this 'other' direction ...[66]

Two other intrepid 'psychonauts'(the semi-serious term explorers within the DMT universe call themselves), known by the pseudonyms 'Gracie' and 'Zarkov', describe the 'Chrysanthemum' as follows:

> At the end of the 'flash' of the visions you will have an after-vision of circular interlocking patterns in exquisite colors. It has been described as looking at a vaulted ceiling or dome. If you did not 'break through' to the levels described above, this 'chrysanthemum' pattern, as we call it, is all you will see. It is worth the trip, too.[67]

It is also significant that some of Rick Strassman's subjects spoke of a 'spinning golden disc'. Gracie and Zarkov also described the strange, powerful alien music that accompanies the journey. Of course, this is the same location as Myron Dyal's 'High Place', the difference being that Myron's form of transport is temporal lobe epilepsy whereas Eben Alexander's is a near-death experience; while Terence McKenna and Gracie and Zarkov use the DMT superhighway. Different journeys to the same place.

Alexander then finds himself high in the air over a beautiful landscape. As he looks down, he realizes that he is not alone. He is accompanied by a guiding spirit of some description. This is how he describes this strange companion:

> She was young, and I remember what she looked like in complete detail. She had high cheekbones and deep-blue eyes. Golden brown tresses framed her lovely face. When first I saw her, we were riding along together on an intricately patterned surface, which after a moment I recognized as the wing of a butterfly. In fact, millions of butterflies were all around us – vast fluttering waves of them, dipping down into the woods and

coming back up around us again. It was a river of life and color, moving through the air.[68]

The 'intricately patterned surface' that he describes as a butterfly's wing is very similar to the vivid colours and swirling geometric patterns described by individuals who have taken DMT. Here is a typical description from an anthology of 'true life' psychedelic adventures: 'A kaleidoscopic array of shifting patterns scrolled across the sphere. Luminous blue balls circulated around it on a kind of track.'[69]

This flying on the wings of a butterfly has an uncanny similarity to Myron Dyal's finding himself flying through a cloudscape on the black wings of a gigantic crow. Dyal and Alexander are obviously describing a similar experience. Alexander points out that the degree of destruction of his neocortex, which made it unlikely that his ultra-real conscious awareness was produced by his physical brain, also suggests that DMT (which acts mainly through receptors in the neocortex) did not play a role in his extraordinary experience deep in coma. It is possible that some of Alexander's NDE may have taken place when he was in a state of status epilepticus, whereby a person goes from one epileptic seizure to another. In other words, both Dyal and Alexander might have been experiencing seizures when they had their visions.

We have already shown how these patterns recur in all altered states of consciousness, whether natural (during migraine and TLE aura states, synaesthesia, NDEs, hypnagogia and hypnopompia, and so on) or chemically induced (DMT/ayahuasca journeys, light stimulation responses, sensory deprivation). These Klüver's Form Constants are a consistent link. Moreover, these patterns seem to reproduce the complex mathematical structures of fractal geometry found in the famed Mandelbrot set.

In DMT journeys, specifically ones involving ayahuasca, the 'spirit guide' is a central character. This entity is also regularly reported in the NDE literature, where it is known as the 'being of light'. It manifests in a way that will put the dying person at ease. It may therefore be a dead relative, a religious figure or a cultural icon. It may come as a surprise to discover that Elvis Presley is now regularly encountered by old rock and rollers. And in reports of children's NDEs the 'being of light' may be a very much alive school friend, a school teacher or even a popular cartoon character. In the case of Eben Alexander, it was a young woman with 'high cheekbones and deep-blue eyes'. Four months after his coma, he received a photograph of a birth sister he had never known (Alexander had been adopted and spent most of his life not knowing his birth family). To his shock, she looked just like his beautiful companion on the butterfly wing! At no time does the 'entity' claim to be his sister, however, and this, to me, is significant. In other NDE reports Christians describe how they met 'Jesus', but again the entity never announces that this is who they are. I would suggest they take such forms because this is how they wish to come across: as something to reassure the dying person and put them at ease.

In my book *Is There Life After Death?: The Extraordinary Science of What Happens When We Die* I present evidence that the 'being of light' is, in fact, the 'Higher Self', the being I call the Daemon. With regard to Eben Alexander, I humbly suggest that his 'sister' had the same provenance as Myron Dyal's 'Charon'. They are both Daemons using the best avenue they know for communication – the opening of the doors of perception facilitated by the 'altered states' known as the near-death experience and temporal lobe epilepsy.

Alexander is convinced that his experience taught him that separation is an illusion, that everything is a single unity, and that this unity is God. This is exactly the message that psychonauts bring back from their DMT and ayahuasca journeys. Dr Martin W Ball, an Oregon-based anthropologist, has written a book about his experience with 5-MeO-DMT, which he calls *The Entheological Paradigm*. By this title he means that, as Bill Hicks stated so eloquently in his famous monologue, 'we are all one entity experiencing itself subjectively'.

So what was really happening to Eben Alexander and all the other thousands, if not millions, of people who have reported uncannily similar experiences over the centuries. What *is* the near-death experience?

## The NDE and Neurochemistry

Earlier in this book (p28) we discussed the work of University of Wisconsin-Madison pharmacologist Arnold Ruoho. In 2009 Ruoho and his team discovered that the powerful hallucinogen dimethyltryptamine (DMT) activates one of the brain's many receptor sites, the sigma (σ) receptor. After their discovery in 1976, it was quickly found that sigma receptors are located across the body and particularly in the brain. Their role was initially something of a mystery. Tests showed that they 'bind' (are stimulated by) the hallucinogen opium and its derivatives such as morphine.[70] There are now two known sigma receptors, sigma-1 and sigma-2 . As we already know from our earlier discussions, all receptor sites will have a corresponding neurotransmitter. To date no internally generated (endogenous) neurotransmitter has been discovered for either of the sigma sites. However, this has not stopped neurochemists suggesting a name for this substance. The initial name was the wonderful 'angeldustin' but sadly this has been replaced with a more prosaic, but probably more accurate, term, 'endopsychosin'.[71]

In 1990 London-based psychiatrist Karl Jansen suggested a revolutionary new model to explain the near-death experience.[72] He had noted that the recreational drug ketamine is reported to reproduce all the elements described in a near-death experience. For example, in 1991 a research paper on psychedelic drugs reported that ketamine brings about the sensation of being disembodied and visiting other worlds. It also has a powerful dissociative effect whereby the subject loses all sense of personal identity. These sensations are so powerful that most subjects genuinely believe that they have left their body.[73]

Ketamine, once in the brain, attaches itself to a glutamate receptor called the 'N-methyl-D-aspartate' or NMDA receptor for short. It is reasonable to imagine these receptors to be a like tiny harbour with several docks. What ketamine does is, in effect, blockade the harbour, thereby stopping any glutamate from getting through to its receptors. As we have already discovered with regard to cortical spreading depression (CSD), generally glutamate is not harmful, but when present in excess it causes massive neuronal die-off due to excitotoxicity.

The circumstances that lead to this glutamate flood are times of extreme threat or crisis, as in a life-threatening situation. However, it is counterproductive to have a potentially damaging flood of chemicals in the brain, particularly if the life-threatening situation proves to be a false alarm.

Evidence has shown that ketamine prevents neurotoxic damage by blockading the NMDA receptor and thus preventing glutamate from transferring from cell to cell. However, as a psychedelic drug it also causes psychological effects similar to those of a typical NDE. Jansen believes that during a real near-death event the glutamate flood is prevented by the internal generation of a substance that protects the NMDA receptors by binding to one of the 'docks' in the NMDA 'harbour'. This 'dock' is called the phencyclidine (PCP) receptor. This substance must, by its very nature, have a very similar effect to that of ketamine on the psychological state of the individual concerned. This endogenous (internally created) drug is the trigger for natural near-death experiences.

In 1984 endogenous substances were found in the brain that bind to the PCP receptor, and one of these was a peptide called 'alpha-endopsychosin'.[74] Peptides are a peculiar group of neurotransmitters discovered in the 1970s. Initially they were found only in the intestine, and it caused great surprise when they were also discovered in the brain. What was even more curious was that small amounts of one type (TRH) can induce euphoric states, and this type been used as an anti-depressant. Another (beta-endorphin) causes muscular rigidity and immobility (catatonia), whilst the wonderfully named 'luteinizing-hormone-releasing-hormone' (LHRH) is reputed to stimulate the libido. Alpha-endopsychosin is a member of an ever-growing group of internally generated drugs that are called endogenous morphines (shortened to 'endorphins'). These are the body's own opiates, and as well as controlling pain they can also bring about euphoria and hallucinations. Until the discovery of alpha-endopsychosin it was believed that in some way endorphins were responsible for the hallucinatory and euphoric effects reported during NDEs.[75][76] But there was a problem with this endorphin hypothesis: endorphins are simply not powerful enough to bring about the massive perceptual changes reported. As it has now been discovered that endopsychosins have exactly the same effect as ketamine in stopping the glutamate flood, it is reasonable to conclude that the conditions that trigger an NDE may also trigger an endopsychosin flood to protect cells. As such the NDE is, in reality, a side-effect caused by a purely physical reaction.

This information allows us to finally make a neurochemical link between migraine, TLE, schizophrenia and NDEs. There is a fair degree of evidence that the similarities between the major factors of my Huxleyan spectrum are brought about in some way by glutamate.[77][78] However, this is an indirect facilitation, because the actual key to the doors of perception may be alpha-endopsychosin working in association with glutamate. This idea is supported by the growing evidence that alpha-endopsychosin is the neurotransmitter that binds with the sigma-1 receptor.[79]

In 2009 Dominique Fontanilla at the University of Wisconsin-Madison published a paper in *Science* suggesting that the mysterious endopsychosin is none other than dimethyltryptamine (DMT), the substance we discussed earlier with regard to the creation of the 'sensed presence' and profound aural hallucinations.

Fontanilla and her associates experimented on a strain of mutant mice that do not have sigma-1 receptors. When the team injected DMT into *non-mutant* mice, it caused increased motor activity or 'hypermobility'; whereas with mutant mice, without sigma-1 receptors, no hypermobility occurred.[80] They also found that DMT binded so strongly to sigma-1 receptor sites that it simply could not be displaced.

In 2014 yet more evidence was discovered that DMT and its close cousin 5-MeO-DMT works directly with the sigma-1 receptor sites of human immune cells.[81]

So the evidence suggests that one of the mystical endopsychosins is DMT, probably the most powerful hallucinogen known to humankind. We are now starting to pull together some of the threads that we have collected on our journey. But first we need to understand more about this intriguing chemical compound.

## Rick Strassman and the 'Spirit Molecule'

Inspired by this intriguing discovery by the University of Wisconsin-Madison team with regard to DMT and the sigma-1 receptors, Rick Strassman began a research programme with two associates, Dr Steven Barker of the Analytical Systems Laboratory at Louisiana State University and Dr Jimo Borjigin of the University of Michigan. Strassman was keen to discover if his long-held suspicion that the pineal gland synthesized internally-generated DMT was correct (see p28). As we already know, Strassman and his team were successful, and in December 2013 they published their findings in an article that appeared in the academic journal *Biomedical Chromatography*.[82]

But if DMT is created by the brain, what is its purpose?

Research has suggested that the same areas of the brain are activated when a person sees an object in the phenomenal world and when they experience a similar object within the mind's eye in the inner world created by a DMT-based hallucinogenic brew called ayahuasca. A research team based in Brazil and lead by Dr Dráulio de Araújo of the Brain Institute at the Federal University of Rio Grande do Norte were keen to discover just how 'real' the vivid images facilitated by ayahuasca actually were. Using functional magnetic resonance imaging (fMRI), they discovered that during an ayahuasca experience exactly the same parts of the brain were activated as when a person is actually looking at the objects. This was not the case when they were asked to visualize the objects when not under the influence of the drug.[83] As the team stated in the abstract of the paper describing the results:

> Our results indicate that ayahuasca seeings stem from the activation of an extensive network generally involved with vision, memory and intention. Ayahuasca lends a status of reality to inner experience.

These results suggest that hallucinations, specifically those created artificially by hallucinogens such as DMT and ayahuasca and those experienced naturally by individuals on my Huxleyan spectrum, are as neurologically 'real' as any percepts of the Pleroma. As we have discovered, this is exactly the position taken by McCreery and Green with regard to their 'metachoric model'.

The mystery here is that these substances exist in the external world and seem to have been designed to override the reducing valve and allow access to the Pleroma. What is even stranger is that the human brain seems to have evolved in such a way as to allow itself to be manipulated like this. The brain creates a number of substances that act as internal facilitators apparently ready to open the Huxleyan doors of perception.

This suggests one thing only: that these perceptions have evolved in some way and are central to the human condition. They seem to have developed hand in hand with the evolution of self-conscious awareness and are part of the ongoing development of life within the universe. The doors of perception are real and the place beyond, which I call the Pleroma, is probably just another staging post along a route that leads to who knows where.

I would now like to move onto the final section of our journey, where I will attempt to pull together my personal interpretation of what is taking place and of how it works. Of course, this is all pure speculation on my part. But it makes sense to me: let's see if it makes sense to you.

# What Is on the Other Side?

## Accessing the Pleroma

Central to this book is the idea that the brain acts as a receiver and that consciousness is located somewhere else. In this respect the brain is analogous to a radio in that it processes and 'embodies' information from elsewhere. No one would think of taking the back off a radio to meet the musicians whose work they have just been listening to!

However, this mistake is made consistently when reviewing brain processes. The assumption is that the person who is speaking to you is located within the brain. However, on taking the brain apart the actual location of the person cannot be found, nor can her memories, hopes, fears or even any kind of facsimile of her personality.

Most scientists accept that every discharge from the synapse of a neuron is an individual event. But what makes up you with regard to your hopes, your dreams, your memories, your experience of a beautiful sunset, a subtle red, a richly flavoured chocolate, a sharp pain, a moving passage of Mozart, a puzzling dream, the all-encompassing love you have for your children and/or partner, and the very source of your referential self-consciousness ... all this is created by trillions of these individual events. How can a collection of individual electrical discharges create any of these sensations? How can these firings of electromagnetic energy (facilitated by neurochemicals called neurotransmitters), each one of which seemingly has no life, let alone awareness, create the perceived sensations that are presented, fully formed, to consciousness; and how can that self-consciousness spontaneously 'appear'. Indeed, at what point does 'consciousness' appear? How many cell firings are needed to bring it about? Ten billion? A hundred billion? Is there a 'tipping point' whereby the firing of one more neuron brings up 'consciousness' from somewhere? Where was consciousness before that 'tipping point' and is there a point where consciousness disappears into non-consciousness when the increasing complexity of synaptic firing goes into reverse?

Can a single cell be said to be conscious in any way? Possibly not. However, there are many single-celled organisms that seem to function extremely effectively within their particular environment. They can swim and find food and seem to show a very rudimentary ability to learn things from the environment. From this comes the million-dollar question: how can something with one cell learn anything? Indeed, if a single cell shows motivational behaviours, then could it be that that sentience can be individual or collective? Does this suggest that neurons are individual 'receivers' of information and each receiver contributes to a web of information that in turn creates consciousness? Is this analogous to individual cells of another variety: the ones that collectively make up a solar panel? Each solar panel is made up of thousands of individual solar cells. The source of the energy is not the cells themselves but the sun, 93 million miles (150 million km) away. I suggest that an analogous process is taking place in the brain. Each neuron is picking up 'energy' from within itself.

This 'energy' is actually information (or, as David Bohm termed it, 'in-formation') and is drawn up, to use Bohm's term, from the zero-point field (Ervin László's 'Akashic Field'). I believe that the process is akin to that suggested by Stuart Hameroff and Roger Penrose in their ORCH-OR model. As we discovered earlier (p18), within each neuron are billions of structures called microtubules. The internal walls of each microtubule are known to give off pulses of single-photon light. These are fired inwards and towards each other inside the cylindrical, hollow microtubule. These photons (collectively manifest as electromagnetic waves) 'interfere' with each other and in doing so create interference patterns. As many of you will know, holograms are created by interference patterns of coherent light. Now we know that holograms are odd, in that each part of a holographic image contains the whole image. David Bohm, in his book *Wholeness and the Implicate Order*, suggested that in this respect the universe itself may be holographic in nature. Coincidently, at the same time, psychologist Karl Pribram was suggesting that memory location in the brain worked on holographic (distributed) principles.

If the above model has any validity, it would explain how a brain can 'create' sentience and consciousness. It is in fact not creating it, but is uploading it from a digital in-formation field, a field that fills everything and is, in effect, everything. Matter is created from in-formation. This means that it is matter that is the brain-generated hallucination. But, more importantly, the physical processes within the brain (the neurochemicals, the neurons themselves and all the other physical processes) are themselves created from digital information. This is the famous 'it from bit' concept we owe to quantum physicist John Archibald Wheeler. The phrase came from a paper that Wheeler wrote in 1989, wherein he stated:

> I suggest that we may never understand this strange thing, the
> quantum, until we understand how information may underlie

reality. Information may not just be what we 'learn' about the world. It may be what 'makes' the world. An example of the idea of *it from bit*: when a photon is absorbed, and thereby 'measured' – until its absorption, it had no true reality – an unsplittable bit of information is added to what we know about the world, 'and', at the same time, that bit of information determines the structure of one small part of the world. It 'creates' the reality of the time and place of that photon's interaction.[1]

Of course materialist-reductionists will argue that it is self-evident that the brain processes information and that all we are is the 'epiphenomenon' of all the neurological interactions, the neurochemical exchanges and the electrical energy surging around our brains. They will argue that, working together, individual components can create something that is not evident in their individual parts. For example, the atoms of individual elements can come together and create something very different from their individuated reality. Oxygen and hydrogen come together to create water, which is very different from either of its 'parent' elements. The coming together of the atoms in certain configurations creates additional functionalities. However, water is not a brain, although interestingly enough the human brain is made up of around 78 per cent water, the remainder consisting of 10 per cent lipids, 8 per cent proteins, 1 per cent carbohydrates, 2 per cent soluble organic substances and 1 per cent inorganic salts.[2]

In recent years it has been discovered that the brain shows incredible abilities to repair itself after damage. In a continuous process known as neuronal plasticity, it can re-organize its internal structures to compensate for damage in one area by recreating the lost functionality in another.[3]

All this suggests that the brain has access to information fields that are not part of the structure evident from the present scientific model. Indeed, there is evidence that the brain uses quantum-field information in its processes of rejuvenation.

We know from research that the hippocampus is the place in the brain where memories are processed and recalled. This was powerfully proven by the famous case of 'H M', a young man whose hippocampi were removed in an attempt to cure him of his seizures. In that regard the operation was totally successful. However, there was an unfortunate side-effect. After the operation H M was unable to lay down any new memories. He existed in the 'now', believing that he was still 25 years old and consulting a surgeon about a possible operation to cure his epilepsy. He had no new memories after 1953. This famous case proved the role the hippocampus has in the initial processing of memories.

However, though the hippocampus may be able to reconstitute memories, it is not where memories are physically located. In an intriguing paper published in the late 1950s, James McConnell of the University of Michigan did a series of experiments with planeria worms. McConnell's team taught a group of worms to react to light in a non-instinctive way. They were then killed, chopped up and fed to a new group of planeria. McConnell claimed that the new worms acquired the same non-instinctive behaviours. This caused a sensation and created something known as the 'molecular theory' of memory.

Three years later a group of Californian researchers had similar results with rats. This suggested that memories could be transferred, via molecules, from one animal to another.

In 1972 a paper by George Ungar of Baylor University, Waco, Texas, was published in *Nature*. In this peer-reviewed article Ungar described how his research team had trained rats to fear the dark. The rats were then killed and their brain cells transferred to the brains of a new set of rats who had the natural affinity to darkness found in other rodents. Subsequent tests showed that fear of darkness had been transferred to the new group.

The implications of Ungar and McConnell's discoveries caused a great deal of consternation in conservative scientific circles. In an attempt to discredit them, it was argued that if memories were carried in molecules, then on the basis of the known informational storage capacity of computers, a lifetime of memories would need 220 pounds of molecules to be encoded. However, from our present knowledge of holographic storage methods, and the potential of the microtubule model, we know that a much smaller amount of storage material would be needed. Indeed, if memory is stored non-locally in a variation on our modern 'cloud' storage, the whole objection disappears and we are back looking at the raw evidence supplied by McConnell and Ungar. Of course, the major objection regarding storage capacity could be explained away if the encoding mechanism was not weighty molecules but digital information encoded within microtubules.

Much to the consternation of those wedded to the 'brain-entrapped mind' model, the plucky little planeria raised their heads (or lack of them) above the parapet again recently. In July 2013 a paper by biologists Tal Shomrat and Michael Levin of Tufts University (Medford, Massachusetts) appeared in the *Journal of Experimental Biology*. Shomrat and Levin were aware of the original McConnell paper and were keen to revisit his findings using new protocols. Unlike McConnell, the Tufts researchers did not need to kill and feed the planeria to other planeria: they simply cut their heads off. This may sound rather drastic but planeria have an amazing ability to regrow a replacement head or tail if it is lost in an accident. Indeed, the head will grow a new body and the tail likewise. In 2011 it was discovered that a whole worm can be cloned from one single cell.[4]

Of probably less interest to most people is that planerians do not like light. If light is shone on them, they will try to find shade. This is because they associate light with being visible to predators. Apparently they are also very partial to liver. The researchers placed a piece of liver on a plate located underneath a bright source of light. The worms were then placed next to the plate. They initially moved away from the light, but over a period of time the more adventurous learned that underneath the light was food and that there was no danger there. The worms that showed the most effective learning were subsequently beheaded and the researchers waited for two weeks for new heads to grow. The newly headed worms 'remembered' the location of the liver and showed no fear of bright light.[5] In an interview with *National Geographic* magazine Levin was asked how a worm can remember things after losing its head and brain. His response was very interesting: 'We have no idea. What we do know is that memory can be stored outside the brain – presumably in other body cells – so that [memories] can get imprinted onto the new brain as it regenerates.'[6]

This suggests that despite the negative reactions at the time, McConnell was quite right in his conclusions. Of course, such findings beg huge questions of the present materialist-reductionist paradigm. If the 'mind' of a lowly worm can be totally destroyed only to reappear again in a seemingly identical form in another brain, what does this suggest with regard to the human brain? After all, we are simply a more evolved version of the humble planeria. If we consider that the destruction of the brain equals death, and this is the criterion applied by modern medicine, then what we have here is clear evidence of life after death and the potential demise of the 'brain-entrapped mind' model.

The question here is whether the brain is actually needed for consciousness to exist within consensual reality. I would argue that just as a receiver is needed in order to convert radio waves into sound and vision, as facilitated by a TV set (the analogy can be adapted by those who prefer to talk about laptops, tablets or smartphones), so it is with the brain. All that happened with the planeria was that they grew new 'receivers' in the same way that a new radio can be quickly tuned to pick up your favourite stations. So the real question here is, what is actually doing the signal modulation in the brain? Some have suggested that it may be the most curious organ in the brain, something we have touched on many times: the pineal gland.

WHAT IS ON THE OTHER SIDE?

## Beach Barrett and 'Metatonin'

For centuries the role of the pineal gland has been the subject of intense speculation. The philosopher René Descartes suggested, in all seriousness, that this tiny organ located at almost the direct centre of the brain was the seat of the soul. Others, including many mystical schools and even some religions, have believed that the pineal gland is the 'third eye' and that by developing it adepts could use it to 'see' the real universe, the hidden world denied to us by our everyday senses.

In 1958 Aaron Lerner discovered a new hormone which he called 'melatonin'. This was of great interest because a few years earlier, two researchers at the Harvard Medical School, Mark Altschule and Julian Kitay, had published a landmark monograph which suggested that the pineal gland had a direct effect on the sexual maturation of mammals. They extracted the pineal glands from young rats and found that in these particular individuals sexual maturation came earlier. In 1960 a Dr Virgina Fiske of Wellesley College made the related discovery that if rats were exposed to continual light, their pineal gland decreased in weight. This stimulated researcher Richard J Wurtman to try and discover what the substance responsible for this inhibition was. This led him to a collaboration with Dr Julius Axelrod, and together they discovered that the substance responsible for these mysterious effects was none other than Lerner's melatonin.

The link between hallucinations and Alzheimer's disease has long been known. Until recently the source of the effect has been located within the visual cortex of the brain. In July 2014 two groups of researchers, one Australian and one American, announced at the Alzheimer's Association International Conference (AAIC) that a huge breakthrough had been made in this respect. Both their research results had shown that these odd visual images may originate within the eye itself, not the brain. Of course, this is not that surprising. The retina is recognized as being a developmental outgrowth of the brain and may therefore be vulnerable to the same inflammatory injury that causes neurodegenerative disease.

The Australian team, from the Commonwealth Scientific and Industrial Research Organization (CSIRO), reported that that all 40 subjects who had tested positive to high levels of plaque within the brain had also tested positive for ß-amyloid (Aß) within the retina.[7] This protein has been associated with cell death in individuals experiencing schizophrenia. Later in the conference the American team, led by Paul D Hartnung of Cognoptix Inc., reported results identical to those of their Australian associates.

You will recall that earlier in our discussions I suggested a link between Alzheimer's disease and Charles Bonnet syndrome (CBS). The 2014 papers present us with direct experimental proof that Alzheimer's involves retina-generated hallucinations. But there is more. It has been discovered that the retina has another role: the indirect generation of melatonin. The retina is responsible for signalling to the pineal gland that external light levels are dropping. This in turn stimulates the pineal to excrete sufficient amounts of melatonin to bring about drowsiness and sleep. So any damage to the efficacy of the retina will, it is reasonable to conclude, bring about disruption of melatonin production. And this seems to be the case. It is known that the creation of melatonin decreases with age[8] and some researchers have linked this directly to the development of Alzheimer's.[9] Others have suggested that it is Alzheimer's that brings about this decrease in the creation of melatonin. I would like to suggest that the observed link between Alzheimer's and decrease of melatonin production is related to the disruption of retinal-pineal communications brought about by the proliferation of ß-amyloid within the retina. This would, in turn, explain a known Alzheimer's-associated behaviour popularly known as 'sundowning', whereby patients with advanced cases of the disease develop extremely agitated behaviours during the evening hours.

What is potentially significant here is that we now seem to have a direct link between the effective functioning of the pineal gland and the development of Alzheimer's. It has been discovered that melatonin and other structurally related indolic compounds, such as indole-3-propionic acid, are very effective in preventing the deposition of ß-amyloid (Aß) plaques. In effect the decrease of melatonin production facilitates the development of the disease.

Other papers have shown that Alzheimer's is also linked to the calcification of the pineal gland.[10] So it seems that Alzheimer's seems to damage the pineal gland's abilities to keep the communication channels open. However, long-term administration of externally generated melatonin seems to act as a therapeutic agent in the relief of some Alzheimer's symptoms.

Here we have direct links between Alzheimer's, the pineal gland and the production of melatonin. Related to this is the work of American researcher Beach Barrett. In a fascinating paper Barrett suggests that the pineal gland secretes both melatonin and a related substance that he terms 'metatonin'.[11] In effect, metatonin is his term for endogenously generated DMT. This works with the melatonin to bring about a liminal state of consciousness whereby alternative realities can be perceived. Of course, modern neurology has an alternative explanation. The technical term for this is 'REM intrusion', which proposes that the subject is actually in a dream state which superimposes itself upon the waking mind. We have already encountered this surprisingly common state under the label of sleep paralysis (see p22).

Of further significance, Barrett also suggests that metatonin is found in high concentrations in the blood of embryos and children up to the age of three, adding that the concentration increases again at the point of death and in doing so brings about the near-death experience.

As we have already seen, during early childhood many youngsters report powerful hallucinations (p137). Many of these involve encounters with 'imaginary friends', including entities similar to those reported by adults during DMT 'trips', alien abductions and near-death experiences. I would like to suggest that Barrett's 'hypothetical' metatonin may be responsible for the facilitation of similar experiences in adulthood. I would further argue that Alzheimer's-induced metatonin release in old age creates the 'hallucinations' associated with CBS.

In fact, however, Barrett's metatonin is far from hypothetical. You will recall that in 2009 Dominique Fontanilla at the University of Wisconsin-Madison published a paper in *Science* stating that the mysterious neurotransmitter that binds with the sigma-1 receptors in the brain, endopsychosin, is actually endogenous dimethyltryptamine.[12] This was followed up with a paper published in 2014 showing that DMT and its close cousin 5-MeO-DMT work directly with the sigma-1 receptor sites of human immune cells.[13] The final proof, if final proof were needed, came when Steven Barker and Jimo Borjigin reported the discovery of DMT in the brains of live rats.[14] Barrett's 'metatonin' actually exists.

So have we, at long last, discovered a crucial piece of evidence that all perceptions are, in a real sense, hallucinations? In which case, what is the actual source of these hallucinations? Could it be that everything we perceive is a form of brain-facilitated simulation?

## Epilogue: Playing the Game

So far I have proposed that there is one single universe. This is the totality of all that is and it is created out of information. Information is non-physical, in the same way that the digital information that creates the illusion of a three-dimensional space in a computer graphic is non-physical. What processes the image is a conscious observer who through various sensory organs creates a representation of the information. The great physicist David Bohm used the term in-formation to describe information that is processed in this way.

Imagine that you are playing a computer game in which you take the role of the central character – in computer terminology this in-game character is known as an 'avatar'. Such games are designed as a totally immersive experience. To create this, the 'game player' is given a sense of embodiment within the avatar: he or she sees on screen a three-dimensional environment rendered as if it were being viewed through the eyes of the avatar. Stereo sounds from the computer speakers create a three-dimensional sound-field identical to how sounds are processed in the non-game world. Some modern games involve tactile body suits in which the game player's movements are reproduced on screen as movements by the avatar. These movements can be seen on screen as the game player looks down at their avatar body. Tactile feedback software is also incorporated into the suit, together with ambient temperature responses and possibly even pain and pleasure simulations.

Incorporated into these suits is a headset with a pair of wide-angle goggles with a screen in each goggle. The images projected on these two screens are designed to create a three-dimensional reproduction of the game environment and a perfect facsimile of the visual field as seen in normal life. A pair of headphones reproduces a similar three-dimensional sound-field.

To make the game even more real, let us say you agree to take a short-acting amnesiac drug. This temporarily wipes clean all your memories. So when the game begins, you have no memories of who you are or, indeed, of the existence of an environment outside of the game. You are, in effect, born into the game; and for you, the game is all that there is. All your sensory feedbacks confirm that this is the case.

Now imagine a game that is designed to be a whole lifetime. Using exactly the same protocols as above, you are dropped into the game as a newly born avatar. The digital body that you find yourself in is a helpless infant. You have no memories of who you are and therefore no prior

221

knowledge of anything. As your in-game visual systems get used to the new environment, so you begin to orientate yourself in this new world. Like any new-born, it will take time for you to control your body and to make sense of what you are seeing, hearing and feeling. Now remember you are no longer you, you are that baby, and future in-game experiences will develop and nurture you into a personality totally different from your 'real world' personality.

A few years ago a computer 'life simulation' called *Second Life* became hugely popular. This was a three-dimensional world that could be explored within game play. What made this interesting was that each game player shared the virtual environment with others who had created their own avatars. In effect, this meant that all entities with whom you engaged within the game were real people who could be located anywhere on Earth. Each onscreen avatar had its own out-of-game motivations sourced from the mind of the game player, and each game player interfaced with the *Second Life* environment from an avatar-embodied viewpoint.

To make my 'life game' even more powerful, imagine that my hypothetical designers have placed another active agent into the amnesiac drug. This is a time dilator. In effect, this expands the subjective in-game time so that a few hours in the external world becomes 70 or 80 years within the game. This is not such a weird idea. Time dilation effects are regularly reported by individuals who take DMT, ayahuasca and many other psychedelics. Indeed, many of us experience time dilation effects every night when we dream.

So here we have a scenario where a full life of 70 years can be experienced in a few hours. Now here is my twist. Imagine that the avatar that you are born into is you at the moment of your birth. Imagine that the environment in which the game is experienced is a re-creation of your actual real-life environment. You are born to the same parents in the same town in the day you were actually born. So now you are a version of yourself existing in a virtual-reality re-creation of your life. How would you ever know that this was a simulation? In which case could your *actual* life be a simulation?

This is not as crazy as it seems. In 2003 Oxford University philosopher Nick Bostrom had an article published in *Philosophical Quarterly*. In it he suggested that it was almost certain that we are all living in computer-generated simulations of our lives. In simple terms, his argument goes as follows. We know from the famous 'Moore's law' that computer processing power is doubling every two or three years. There is no reason to believe that this will not continue for some time to come, the only restrictions being how small we can make printed circuit boards. A new area of research called 'quantum computing' suggests that processing power may be almost limitless for future generations. So what will our descendants do with this processing power? Bostrom suggests that it is inevitable that they will create what he calls 'ancestor simulations'.

Bostrom argues that a single, planet-sized computer could, using less than a millionth of its capacity, 'simulate the entire mental history of humankind'. By 'mental history' he means all the memories, hopes, dreams and anticipations of every single human being that has ever lived. He further suggests that when uploaded into an in-simulation 'avatar' (a digital facsimile of an individual existing within the simulation), this personality data would create self-awareness in that entity. In effect, the avatar will become sentient, aware of itself within the simulated environment. However, as the avatar is unware that it exists within a simulation, it will believe that all that exists is the sensory information it receives from the program. Also, because it has no other knowledge base, it will have no option other than to believe that it is the person whose original perceptions and experiences populate its mind.[15]

There is a raging argument in both philosophy and computing as to whether it would ever be possible to simulate self-referential consciousness within a computer program. This, of course, goes back to the David Chalmers debate discussed earlier (p17). But let us assume that Chalmers' 'hard problem' (that is, that modern science has absolutely no idea how the inanimate matter that makes up the brain can spontaneously 'create' self-referential consciousness) can be overcome. This would mean that future scientists could use this knowledge to create self-awareness within the 'avatars' populating their ancestor-simulation. I am sensitive to the difficulties of grasping the enormity of what Bostrom and his supporters are suggesting. Space does not allow me to expound more on this intriguing idea. I therefore advise that any interested readers should invest some time reading Bostrom's original paper and the various on-line websites discussing this hypothesis.

Physicist Tom Campbell has carried this argument forward to suggest that everything around us is made up of digital information, and in his *Big Toe Trilogy* he presents an all-encompassing theory that explains in great detail the workings of the simulation and effectively deals with every objection to the simulation argument.

Recently, some startling discoveries have been made with regard to the fine-structuring of the observed universe. These findings are the first to show that the perceptual cosmos may, indeed, be created out of digital information, and that it is, in effect, a huge hologram. The work is being done by a team of Fermilab scientists, in Batavia, Illinois, near Chicago, led by cosmologist Craig Hogan.

In physics there is something known as 'entropy'. In effect, any system moves from a state of order to a state of disorder in a gradual but inexorable process. This only ever goes in one direction. It has never been observed that something in a state of disorder gradually changes to order. For example, an egg in its initial state is in a state of total order: its shell is intact and the yoke and white are perfectly separated. If that egg is dropped onto the floor, it smashes. The shell is shattered and the yoke and white

its gravitational field – not even light. Let me explain this. Gravity is caused by the mass of an object. The more massive the object, the greater the gravitational force it contains. You and I are held on the surface of the Earth because the Earth is much more massive than we are. However, at certain speeds – known as 'escape velocities' – an object can escape the gravitational force of a much more massive object. To overcome Earth's gravitational force an object needs to travel away from the surface at a speed of 25,020 miles per hour (40,270 km/h). As the moon is much less massive (and is, in fact, captured by the Earth's gravitational field, which is why it is in orbit around us) the required escape velocity there is only 5,324 miles per hour. However, black holes are so massive that the escape velocity is greater than the speed of light. This is why it is a black hole: it gives off no electromagnetic energy (light) and therefore is totally black. However, as nothing can travel faster than the speed of light, nothing can escape a black hole once it has been sucked in. But this is where things get weird. According to modern science, when anything is sucked into a black hole, it is totally destroyed: it ceases to be. However, this violates the law of the conservation of energy. The universe is an enclosed system and yet, in certain 'areas' within that system, energy and its accompanying information are totally destroyed – not converted into anything else.

Theoretical physicist Juan Martín Maldacena has suggested a solution. This works in a similar way to holograms. Indeed, the process may be directly linked to holographic principles and may therefore be yet more evidence that what we believe to be a three-dimensional, physical universe is, in fact, created out of non-physical digital information. If we look at a holographic image we see a three-dimensional object located in the space in front of us. But this is simply a trick of the light. What is actually there is a two-dimensional image projected into three-dimensional space. Maldacena argues that the answer to the mystery of how energy is lost from an enclosed system is that our three-dimensional universe is actually a huge two-dimensional hologram. This universal 'image' is created by this no-longer-lost energy spilling back out from the 'surfaces' of trillions upon trillions of tiny black holes that pepper the inner surface of the ever-expanding universe. I am aware that this is a very difficult concept to grasp. For those readers interested in the details, I suggest that they check out an article written by Jacob D Bekenstein in the August 2003 edition of *Scientific American*. A link to a full pdf of the article can be found in the endnotes.[16]

In a later article published in July 2014, astrophysicist Craig Hogan hypothesized that our macroscopic world is like a 'four-dimensional video display'. He argued that if we stare deeply enough into the structure of matter we will discover the bitmap of our holographic universe, in the same way that if you look closely enough at a computer screen you will eventually spot the individual pixels.[17] In 2013 the German GEO600 gravity wave-detector found the 'pixilation' that Hogan had suggested would exist if the universe was a hologram.

In other words, there is strong reason to believe that this universe and everything in it is a super-hologram created out of digital information. If this is so, then Bostrom may be right: we may be all existing in a computer game of our own lives created by our descendants.

This has huge implications with regard to the life-as-a-computer-simulation model with which I started this chapter. If our descendants can program one life for each of us, why would they not program in all possible lives as well? One of the leading theories of modern quantum physics is the 'many worlds' or 'many minds' hypothesis. This suggests that in order to explain certain observed quantum effects, the only solution would be that the outcome of each and every quantum effect brings about an alternative universe. First suggested by American physicist Hugh Everett III in 1957, this has become the accepted theory by an ever-growing number of quantum physicists. This would explain, for example, why this particular universe has been seemingly hard-wired for the evolution of humanity

227

since the first nanoseconds of the Big Bang. This is extremely fortuitous if this is the only universe there has ever been; but following the many worlds model, we can see it as a totally logical outcome. Humanity, according to this view, has evolved in the one universe that contained all the elements needed for its evolution; it has not evolved in the trillions of others that were not right.

Interestingly, the 'many worlds interpretation' (MWI) is being accepted by more and more scientists as the best explanation we have for the way in which the observed universe presents itself. Bostrom's ancestor-simulation similarly suggests that all possible outcomes of all decisions also exist in potentiality.

In 2006 Stephen Hawking, with his CERN-based associate Thomas Hertog, proposed a new variation on the Everett hypothesis that presents an even closer match to the ancestor simulation model. It is known as the 'top-down interpretation' (TDI). In simple terms, Hawking and Hertog argue that the universe did not have one single unique beginning but a countless number of them, each one following its own unique path. We exist in the universe that was fine-tuned for our own evolution. Over billions of years each quantum event brings about a change in the evolution of our particular universe and the alternate paths remain in potentiality with regard to our own point of observation.[18]

So if Everett's MWI and Hawking and Hertog's TDI are accepted as powerful explanatory models of how the universe actually works, then Bostrom's ancestor-simulation hypothesis fits in very well within this overall structure. Just as MWI and TDI propose that the outcomes of all actions are contained as potentialities within the developing universe, Bostrom's model locates all the potentialities as digital information encoded within a huge quantum computer. If we accept this as a possibility, then within Bostrom's ancestor simulation can be found the data for each and every possible life a sentient ancestor-avatar can experience.

The ancient Greeks believed that when a person passed away and they had been taken to the land of the dead, they were presented with a choice. They were offered a drink from one of two chalices. One chalice contained water from the 'Spring of Memory' and the other held water from the 'River of Forgetting', the tributary of the Styx known as the Lethe. If the person chose to drink from the 'Spring of Memory', they walked along a path leading off to the right, to heaven. If they chose the waters of the Lethe, they took the left path and were reborn with all their past-life memories wiped clean.

The Gnostic *Book of the Saviour* says the same thing. It explains that the righteous person will be born into his next life without forgetting the wisdom he has learned in his last life. He will not be given the 'draughts of oblivion' before his next birth: rather, he will receive a 'cup of intuition and wisdom' which will cause the soul to 'seek after the Mysteries of Light, until it hath found them'.[19] Many esoteric texts throughout the centuries have proposed that enlightenment involves the realization that we are living in a simulated universe, unaware of the fact that all we perceive is *maya*, an illusion. When we 'wake' from this we experience 'anamnesis', a loss of forgetting. Of course, most modern people will recognize the connection with taking either the blue pill or the red pill in the hugely popular *Matrix* movies.

In my computer game analogy, this is exactly what I suggest. The game player takes an amnesiac and for the duration of the game forgets that they may have played the game before – possibly many, many times.

So how does this all relate to my Huxleyan spectrum? Well, as you recall, I have consistently maintained that conscious awareness has not one but two locations. I call these Eidolonic and Daemonic consciousness. In my model described above, the amnesiac in-game avatar is Eidolonic consciousness. It has no idea that it is experiencing its whole life in a simulation. It is embedded within *maya*, or, if you prefer, the Matrix. It can play the game many, many times, and at the start of each game it has its memory banks swept clean and a new life is started. A game can only come to an end with the in-game death of the avatar. This is exactly what happens in modern first-person role-playing computer games: the avatar is killed and the game player restarts the game, either at the point just before the sudden death or right back at the start of the game.

In this way, multiple in-game lives can be experienced, each one feeling totally unique as far as Eidolonic consciousness is concerned. As long as the 'waters of the Lethe' keep Eidolonic consciousness in a state of amnesia, there is no awareness of the true nature of reality, the place I have called the Pleroma.

In effect, the Pleroma is the location of the *Nebuchadnezzar* ship in the *Matrix* movies (where, not with any originality, it is termed the Real World). It is the place outside of the program, the reality that is seen when Blake's 'doors of perception' are cleansed.

The word 'Pleroma' is taken from the Gnostics, a group of very early Christians who explained the existence of evil in the world by arguing that this world is an illusion created by a false god known as the Demiurge. The realm of the true God, outside of the illusion, is known as the Pleroma. The word is from the ancient Greek *pleroma*, 'that which fills'. It is the totality of everything that is, including the illusory universes of the Demiurge.

In my model the Pleroma is simply the place outside of the Eidolonic program. It is the location of the game player who, you will recall from the start of this discussion, is the person actually doing the perceiving – from an exterior viewpoint. The game player is embodied within the game as Daemonic consciousness. Imagine playing a normal first-person role-playing game (RPG). As the game player you are always aware of who you are and you remember all the previous iterations of the game that you may have played. You plan the onscreen movements of your avatar based upon this knowledge. You know where to avoid the monsters and you remember the oncoming dangers before they are actually rendered on screen. In effect you are, with regard to the game, a precognitive.

I would argue that this is what may actually be happening. We are all Eidolons trapped within a *Matrix*-like program of our lives. Our Eidolonic consciousness suffers from amnesia with regard to any knowledge of previous games and of the Pleroma in general. However, we all have an element of the Pleroma within us: this is the Daemon which, through its state of anamnesis, can remember all the events that took place in previous lives (previous runs through the game).

And this is where the Huxleyan spectrum comes in. In this book I have given scores of examples of how certain individuals can break out of the program and, for a few seconds or longer, can glimpse a universe outside of the controls of Eidolonic consciousness. They can throw off William Blake's 'mind-forged manacles' and see through the bars of Philip K Dick's 'Black Iron Prison': they are like the prisoner in Plato's Myth of the Cave who breaks free and realizes that everything he had, until that moment, thought to be real was just shadows on a wall.

Unfortunately, the rest of us are firmly trapped within the manacles and cannot move sufficiently to see through the prison bars. We firmly believe that what our senses tell us is real actually is real – and that is all there is. In Plato's myth the escaped prisoner returns to his fellow inmates and tells them that by turning around he has seen the true nature of the universe. They simply do not believe him. They wish to be left alone to enjoy their illusions. To use another *Matrix* trope, they prefer to remain under the control of the blue pill. Meanwhile, the escaped prisoner, feeling the effects of the red pill, becomes more and more frustrated. In the end he is simply labelled as insane. In our modern world we would simply announce that he is hallucinating, and that the world he sees is just a creation of his addled mind.

I have discussed the many different ways that the Pleroma can be perceived by migraineurs, temporal lobe epileptics, schizophrenics, Alzheimer's patients, autistics and people who have near-death experiences, out-of-body experiences and many other 'altered states'. I also have given examples of how certain neurological states can open up everyday Eidolonic consciousness to Daemonic consciousness. The individuals who experience this can tune in to the information sources usually available only to the Daemon. In doing so, these Eidolons sense the presence of their silent partner.

Remember that the Daemon has lived its life many times – that is, it has 'played the game' many times. Therefore it has access to information from the previous games. To an Eidolon trapped in the linear nature of the game, such information will be interpreted as precognitive. It will seem to the Eidolon that they are glimpsing the future. In fact, they are remembering the past. Sometimes they will have sudden recognition of the circumstances in which they find themselves. Some will sense that they know what is about to happen next. This is interpreted as a déjà vu or deja vécu sensation. All that is happening is that they are receiving a vague lifting of amnesia and an accessing of Daemonic consciousness.

The farther along the spectrum one goes, the greater the access to the Daemonic. You will recall the Japanese TLErs who believed that they had already lived this life many times. The simple truth is that they had. The sad thing is nobody believed them. But why would they? All we have here is another example of Plato's escaped prisoner.

It is our changing from one game to another that is particularly fascinating, and this is why I placed the chapters on autism and Alzheimer's back-to-back at the end of the book. This is because this is literally what they do: they are the same 'illness' working in different temporal directions. Alzheimer's happens at the end of a long, probably successful game – by which I mean that to survive to a great age suggests that other potential death situations have been avoided; while autism is the start of a new game.

The above model also explains near-death experiences. It accommodates the panoramic life review, the sensation of time slowing down, the encountering of one's own Daemon. In fact, all the phenomena discussed in this book, with one exception, take their place within a comprehensible worldview. The one situation that does not is the encounters with seemingly sentient entities, human or otherwise, that those on the Huxleyan spectrum regularly experience. These inhabitants of Magonia are a mystery to me. They suggest that within the Pleroma there are places inhabited by all kinds of wonderful and possibly even dangerous creatures. Usually the barriers of Eidolonic consciousness protect the Eidolon from such encounters. However, when the doors of perception are opened, all kinds of entities can come through into this world.

I am intrigued by the consistency in the reports of aliens and other beings during DMT trips, CBS encounters and TLE auras and also in the fairy folk and cuddly creatures that fill childhood with such wonders. The location of Jacques Vallée's Magonia and the motivations of its inhabitants are a great enigma to me, which I hope will become the subject of another book.

Thus far, I have discussed in passing what I think may be the neurochemical and neurophysiological facilitators of the Pleroma. I have argued that Daemonic consciousness resides in the non-dominant hemisphere and its Eidolonic counterpart in the dominant hemisphere. There is strong evidence in support of this case, and I still believe that this is the best model available. However, I am also of the opinion that there is another bicamerality of consciousness, which may mirror or even override the hemispheres model. It is to this I now turn our attention.

## The Glutamate Connection

We have already discussed the role of glutamate with regard to the near-death experience (NDE) and its involvement in migraine-related cortical spreading depression (CSD) and epilepsy. Glutamate, probably the most fascinating of all neurotransmitters, is the one I suspect may be the major facilitator of my Huxleyan spectrum.

Technically speaking, glutamate is the monoamide of glutamic acid. It is the only amino acid that can readily cross the barrier between blood and brain. With glutamic acid, it is thought to account for about 80 per cent of the amino nitrogen of brain tissue. The majority of large neurons in the cerebral cortex use glutamate as their neurotransmitter. Glutamate is the key chemical messenger in the temporal and frontal lobes, and is central to the function of the hippocampus. It plays a vital role in the cognitive processes involving the cerebral cortex, including thinking, memory formation of memories and recall, and is vital in perception.

Glutamate was discovered together with the other three amino acids (aspartate, GABA and glycine). These four organic compounds were found in high concentrations in all cells and organs, and it was clear that they were involved in a great many metabolic highways. As glutamate participates in virtually all mammalian brain functions, it has also been speculatively identified as the major nutrient within the 'primordial soup' in which life on Earth presumably originated. Glutamate is essentially the same substance that adds flavour to food, particularly in oriental cooking. As well as being a neurotransmitter, it is also a precursor for the inhibitory neurotransmitter gamma-aminobutyric acid (GABA). It has a number other roles as well, so it is impossible to tell exactly what role it is fulfilling when discovered in a synapse.

Glutamate may also have a major role in another element of the Huxleyan spectrum, schizophrenia. It has been discovered that a major site of changes in the schizophrenic brain is the dosolateral prefrontal cortex (DLPC). The DLPC consists of mostly pyramid cells, and these cells use glutamate as their neurotransmitter. This suspected linkage between glutamate and schizophrenia has been further reinforced by the way in which a drug popularly known as 'angel dust' (phencyclidine) can induce schizophrenia-like psychosis in otherwise normal people. It does this by acting upon glutamate receptors, and in doing so creates a feeling of euphoria, combined with hallucinations and paranoia. It has also been proposed that in some way glutamate and dopamine work together to bring about schizophrenia-like symptoms and, in doing so, open the doors of perception. This would certainly explain why phencyclidine is so effective in generating schizophrenic-like behaviours.[20]

A curious feature of glutamate is that it interacts with glial cells, or glia: little-understood brain cells that outnumber neurons by a ratio of at least 10 to one. There are around 100 billion neurons in the human brain and therefore a trillion glial cells. This accounts for approximately 90 per cent of the brain (this is where the much-discussed idea that we only use 10 per cent of our brains came from). Unlike neurons, glia lack axons and dendrites, and they do not directly participate in synaptic signalling: they were considered to be simply the glue that held the brain together. In fact, the word 'glia' is from the German for 'glue'. In effect, they were considered to be simply the insulators for the much more important neurons. At least seven types of glial cell have been observed: Schwann cells, Müller cells, ependymal cells, oligodendrocytes, tanycytes, microglial cells and astrocytes. Of these, astrocytes are the most numerous and have been observed only in the brain and spinal cord. Many of them are star-like in appearance: hence the 'astro' part of the name.

In 1963 Stephen Kuffler and David Potter at Harvard Medical School decided to test out the idea that glial cells were neuronal insulators. They took some astrocytes from the brain of a leech and added potassium. They discovered that the cells responded to the potassium in a similar way to neurons in that they exhibited an electrical potential.[21] These results surprised many neurologists, and research began into the role of these hitherto neglected elements of the brain. It was discovered that the further you go up the evolutionary ladder, the number and size of the astrocytes increases within the cortex. Humans have the most astrocytes and the largest of any animal. This suggested that in some way astrocytes are involved in increased intelligence and the development of self-aware consciousness. It therefore came as no real surprise that, in 1989, a team of researchers at Yale School of Medicine discovered that astrocytes can communicate with each other and are capable of sending information to neurons.[22] This is a finding of great importance. It suggests that glial cells have their own, exclusive communication system across the brain, and this web of cells contains at least 10 times as many cells as the neurological network. Some have termed this the 'other brain' network. Glial cells do not have synapses but they have structures called 'gap junctions'. These work electrically rather than chemically, in that they release calcium ions. This is a far more effective method of cell communication than the neuron-to-neuron synaptic process. Astrocytes join together and in this way create a 'intercellular calcium wave'[23] (ICW) of information that spreads out from the source in all directions. This form of communication may solve one of the big mysteries of neuroscience, the so-called 'binding problem'. We touched upon the question earlier: how does everything seem to come together in the brain to create the illusion of simultaneity when information is being received from many sources and at different speeds. We perceive sensory information as all happening 'now', and with the personal sense of being a focal point, a unity. Could it be the astrocytes that create this sense of unity? Well, this certainly seems to be the opinion of Brazilian biologists Alfredo Pereira Jr and Fábio Augusto Furlan. They describe the 'astroglial' network as a 'master hub' that integrates conscious states by bringing together processing from various parts of the brain.[24]

It is significant that the neurotransmitter responsible for this release of calcium ions is glutamate. It was also discovered that astrocytes control blood flow within the brain, sending it to regions involved in brain activity.

For 'brain activity' read thought and conscious awareness.

In his book *The Root of Thought*,[25] neuroscientist Andrew Koob argued that glial cells and calcium waves are directly responsible for thought. Koob is fascinated by the generation of imagery in dreams and during periods of sensory deprivation. In an interview published in *Scientific American* in October 2009 he made this astounding claim:

> Without input from our senses through neurons, how is it that we have such vivid thoughts? How is it that when we are deep in thought we seemingly shut off everything in the environment around us? In this theory, neurons are tied to our muscular action and external senses. We know astrocytes monitor neurons for this information. Similarly, they can induce neurons to fire. Therefore, astrocytes modulate neuron behavior. This could mean that calcium waves in astrocytes are our thinking mind. Neuronal activity without astrocyte processing is a simple reflex; anything more complicated might require astrocyte processing. The fact that humans have the most abundant and largest astrocytes of any animal and we are capable of creativity and imagination also lends credence to this speculation.[26]

I would like to add to this speculation that when we discuss imagery created during periods of sensory deprivation or dream sequences, what we are actually describing are hallucinations. From this it can be proposed that hallucinations of all kinds, all of which fall within Koob's description of mental activity 'without input from our senses', are facilitated by ion exchanges between astrocytes stimulated by glutamate. This, in turn, suggests that glutamate may be the neurochemical facilitator of consciousness, the processor that assists the glial cells in downloading consciousness from the Pleroma.

What strikes me as potentially significant here is glutamate's double effect. It is responsible for both the cortical spreading depression (CSD) that moves across the neuronal networks and the ICW that fulfils a similar function in the communications within the astroglial network. Could it be that these are two separate areas of consciousness existing in parallel within the human brain? If this is correct, then the consciousness created by the astroglial network has at least 10 times the processing power of the neuronal network. Could the former be the source of Daemonic consciousness and the latter be responsible for Eidolonic consciousness? And could it be the accidental accessing of the information-processing capacity of the astroglial network by Eidolonic consciousness that brings about fleeting glimpses of the Pleroma?

I would like to suggest that the astroglial network is the neurological equivalent of dark matter/dark energy and junk DNA – the three mysterious substances that have prompted a huge degree of speculation in recent years.

Dark matter has been proposed to explain a huge anomaly in how the universe functions. Ever since the concept of the Big Bang has been used to explain the expansion of the universe, it has been assumed that the rate of expansion is slowing down. As with all explosions, the farther away in time from the source explosion ejected material is, the slower its movement away from that source. However, in 1998 the Hubble Space Telescope, on observing very distant supernovae, discovered that many billions of years ago the universe was expanding more slowly than it is today. This discovery was totally unexpected. The only explanation could be that roughly 68 per cent of the universe is made up of a totally unknown form of energy. Because it seems to be totally undetectable by our present measuring devices, it is known as 'dark' energy. A further 27 per cent is made up of a form of matter that is similarly undetectable. Not surprisingly, this is known as 'dark' matter. In effect, this means that everything we can observe using our senses and our best detection machines makes up around 5 per cent of what there really is. One candidate for dark energy is something I have already discussed: zero-point field.

DNA (deoxyribonucleic acid) is a molecule that carries all the genetic instructions to create a living organism. It stores biological information in a series of codes. However, there is one fact about DNA that tends not to be generally known, and that is that only 2 per cent of DNA actually carries code. The other 98 per cent of it is technically known as 'non-coding' DNA. Modern scientists have no idea what role this non-coding DNA fulfils. Its seeming uselessness is reflected in the fact that it is known as 'junk' DNA.

For centuries the defenders of materialist-reductionism have used the 'law of parsimony' as defined by William of Occam's much-quoted statement, 'Entities must not be multiplied beyond necessity.' In simple terms this advises that among any competing hypotheses, the one with the fewest assumptions is the most reliably accurate. This has been long argued to be a reflection of the workings of nature. As Galileo famously wrote: 'Nature does not multiply things unnecessarily; she makes use of the easiest and simplest means for producing her effects; she does nothing in vain.'[27] The idea was supported a few years later by Isaac Newton, who stated in his *Principia Mathematica* (1687) that 'Nature is pleased with simplicity, and effects not the pomp of superfluous causes.'

So the question must be asked, why does a seemingly parsimonious nature create such huge amounts of unnecessary and seemingly useless DNA? To have only 2 per cent of anything being of any use is, in my opinion, the total opposite of parsimony. The same logic can be applied to dark energy and dark matter. If our universe has any deep significance, why is it that everything we can observe and perceive is less than 5 per cent of what really exists. Is that 95 per cent similarly superfluous? In which case, why has nature created it?

The mystery of the astroglial network in the brain is similar in character. Why would evolution bother with such a huge number of useless cells within a brain that clearly needs more space within the cranium. Why evolve sulci and gyri, the furrows and ridges found on the surface of the cerebral cortex, when additional space could have been made millions of years ago by simply not having a seemingly useless astroglial network?

Materialist-reductionism has been a wonderful tool that has helped humankind mould its environment and create the wonders of modern technology. Newtonian science and its powerful child, quantum mechanics, have created a model of understanding that can effectively explain most of what is taking place in the consensual reality accessible to our collective senses. We now have telescopes that can extend our perceptions to the edge of the universe and microscopes that can show us individual atoms. We are within a few percentage points of understanding everything regarding the workings of our consensual reality. However, here lies the problem. Our consensual reality seems to be but a tiny part of a much greater universe, of whose workings we have no real understanding. Dark matter, dark energy in cosmology; junk DNA in biology and the medical sciences; and the astroglial network in neurology and consciousness ... these things have given us fleeting glimpses of the Pleroma. Now is the time to open the doors of perception and glimpse the true universe.

In my last book for Watkins, *The Infinite Mindfield*, I referred to a story told by Israeli psychologist Benny Shanon regarding the location of the last great mystery. Please forgive me for repeating it here, but for me it sounds a note as true for this book as it was for that one.

On one of his many trips to Latin America, Shanon met up with an indigenous ice cream salesman deep in the Amazonian jungle. This most unlikely of sources shared with Shanon a popular myth known to his people. He explained:

God wanted to hide his secrets in a secure place. 'Would I put them on the moon?' He reflected. 'But then, one day, human beings could get there, and it could be that those who would arrive there would not be worthy of the secret knowledge. Or perhaps I should hide them in the depths of the ocean?' God entertained this as another possibility. But again, for the same reasons, he dismissed it. Then the solution occurred to Him: 'I shall put my secrets in the inner sanctum of man's own mind. Then only those who really deserve it will be able to get to it.'[28]

In my humble opinion the next great scientific frontier will not be outer space, but inner space. We will break out of the confines of our present consensual reality and in doing so will begin the first few tentative steps in creating a new science to explain the wonders of the Pleroma. But to do that we have to first open the doors of perception a little more.

# Reference Notes

**Introduction** (pp2–9)

1 Osmond, H, and Smythies, J, 'Schizophrenia: A New Approach', *The Journal of Mental Science*, Apr 1952, xcvii

2 Huxley, A, 'A Treatise on Drugs', *Chicago Herald and Examiner*, 10 Oct 1931

3 Letter to A Huxley from Humphry Osmond, quoted in *Moksha: Writings on Psychedelics and the Visionary Experience (1931–1963)*, ed. Michael Horowitz and Cynthia Palmer, Stonehill Publishing, New York, p31

4 Huxley, A, letter to Humphry Osmond, 10 Apr 1953, quoted in *Moksha: Writings on Psychedelics and the Visionary Experience (1931–1963)*, ed. Michael Horowitz and Cynthia Palmer, Stonehill Publishing, New York, p29

5 Huxley, A, letter to Harold Raymond, 21 Jun 1953, quoted in *Moksha: Writings on Psychedelics and the Visionary Experience (1931–1963)*, ed. Michael Horowitz and Cynthia Palmer, Stonehill Publishing, New York, p42

6 Huxley, A, *The Doors of Perception*, Chatto & Windus, London, 1954; Random House, 2010, p8

7 Published in 'Neural correlates of the psychedelic state as determined by fMRI studies with psilocybin', *Proceedings of the National Academy of Sciences*, 7 Feb 2012, pp2138–43

**PART ONE: THE KEY**
**Chapter One: Hallucinations** (pp12–32)

1 Hameroff, S R, and Penrose, R, *Orchestrated Reduction of Quantum Coherence in Brain Micro-tubules: A Model for Consciousness*, MIT Press, Cambridge, MA, 1996

2 Emerson, D J, Weiser, B P, Psonis, J *et al*, 'Direct Modulation of Microtubule Stability Contributes to Anthracene General Anesthesia', *Journal of the American Chemical Society*, Apr 10 2013, 135(14): pp5389–98

3 Roland, P E, and Gulyas, B, 'Visual imagery and visual representation', *Trends in Neuroscience*, 17(7), pp281–6, 1994

4 Kosslyn, S M, and Ochsner, K N, 'In search of occipital activation during visual mental imagery, *Trends in Neuroscience*, 17(7), pp290–91, 1994

5 Gregory, Richard L (ed.), *The Oxford Companion to The Mind*, Oxford University Press, Oxford (UK), 1998, p299

6 Ramachandran, V S, and Blakeslee, S, *Phantoms in the Brain: Human Nature and the Architecture of the Mind*, Fourth Estate, London, 1998, p107

7 Green, C, and McCreery, C, *Apparitions*, Hamish Hamilton, London, 1975

8 McCreery, C, *Perception and Hallucination: The Case for Continuity*, Oxford Forum, Oxford (UK), 2006, p9

9 Bostrom, N, 'Are You Living in a Computer Simulation?', *Philosophical Quarterly*, 2003, vol53, no.211, pp243–55

10 Russell, B, *Human Knowledge: Its Scope and Limits*, 1st edn, Routledge, London,

2009, p186

11 Carhart-Harris, R L, Erritzoe, D, Williams, T *et al.*, 'Neural correlates of the psychedelic state as determined by fMRI studies with psilocybin', *Proceedings of the National Academy of Sciences*, 2012, 109, pp2138–43

12 Monroe, R R, and Heath, R G, 'Effects of lysergic acid and various derivatives on depth and cortical electrograms,' *Journal of Neuropsychiatry*, 1961, 3, pp75–82

13 Schwarz, B E, Sem-Jacobsen, C W and Peterson, M C, 'Effects of mescaline, LSD-25, and adrenochrome on depth electrograms in man', *AMA Archives of Neurology and Psychiatry*, 1956, 75(6), pp579–87

14 Carhart-Harris, R L, Nutt, D, 'Was it vision or a waking dream?', *Consciousness Research*, 2-14, 5, 255

15 Megavand, P, Groppe, D M, Goldfinger, M S *et al.*, 'Seeing Scenes: Topographic visual hallucinations evoked by direct electrical stimulation of the parahippocampal place area', *Journal of Neuroscience*, Apr 2014, 34(16), pp5399–405

16 Ruoho, A E *et al.*, 'The Hallucinogen N,N-Dimethyltryptamine (DMT) Is an Endogenous Sigma-1 Receptor Regulator', *Science*, 13 Feb 2009, 323(5916), pp934-7

17 Cozzi, Nicholas V, *et al.*, 'Indolethylamine N-methyltransferase expression in primate nervous tissue', *Society for Neuroscience* abstract, 2011, 37, 840.19

18 http://www.cottonwoodresearch.org/dmt-pineal-2013/

19 Barker, S A, Borjigin, J, Lomnicka, I and Strassman, R, 'LC/MS/MS Analysis of the endogenous dimethyltryptamine hallucinogens, their precursors, and major metabolites in rat pineal gland microdialysate', *Biomedical Chromatography*, 2013, 27(12), pp1690-700.

20 Peake, A, The *Daemon: A Guide to Your Extraordinary Secret Self*, Arcturus, London, 2008, pp277–8

## Chapter Two: Accidental Tourists (pp34–44)

1 Persinger, M A, 'Religious and mystical experiences as artifacts of temporal lobe function: a general hypothesis', *Perceptual and Motor Skills*, 1983, 57, pp1255–62

2 Horowitz, M J, and Adams, J E, 'Hallucinations on Brain Stimulation: Evidence for Revision of the Penfield Hypothesis', in *Origin and Mechanisms of Hallucinations*, ed. W. Keup, Plenum Press, New York, 1970, pp13–22

3 Gloor, P, 'Temporal Lobe Epilepsy: Its Possible Contribution to the Understanding of the Significance of the Amygdala and of Its Interaction with Neocortical-Temporal Mechanisms', in *The Neurobiology of the Amygdala*, ed. B E Eleftheriou, Plenum Press, New York, 1972, pp423–57

4 Persinger, M A, 'Vectorial cerebral hemisphericity as differential sources for the sensed presence, mystical experiences and religious conversions', *Perceptual and Motor Skills*, 1993, 76 (3 Pt 1), pp915–30

5 Persinger, M A, and Healey, F, 'Experimental Facilitation of the Sensed Presence', *Journal of Nervous and Mental Diseases*, 2002, pp533–41

6   http://www.innerworlds.50megs.com/God_Helmet/god_helmet.htm

7   Strassman, R, *DMT: The Spirit Molecule*, Inner Traditions, Rochester (Vermont), 2001, p224

8   Gysin, Brion, diary entry, 21 Dec 1958, quoted in Brion Gysin and Terry Wilson, *Here To Go: Planet R101*, RE/Search Publications, San Francisco, 1982

9   Walter W G, *The Living Brain*, W W Norton & Co., New York, 1963; Penguin, Harmondsworth, 1968

10  Gysin, Brion, interviewed by Jon Savage, from Vale, V, and Juno, Andrea (eds), *William S. Burroughs, Brion Gysin, Throbbing Gristle: Search #4/5 San Francisco 1982*

11  Sacks, O, *Migraine*, University of California Press, Berkeley, CA, 1970; Picador, London, 1993, p28

12  http://www.migraine-aura.org

## PART TWO: AT THE DOORWAY
### Chapter Three: Migraine (pp48–60)

1   Moskowitz, M A, Henrikson, BM, Markowiz, S, Saito, K, 'Intra- and extracraniovascular nociceptive mechanisms and the pathogenesis of head pain', in Olesen, J, and Edvinsson, L (eds), *Basic Mechanisms of Headache*, Elsevier, Amsterdam, 1988, pp429–37

2   Leão, A A P, 'Spreading depression of activity in the cerebral cortex', *Journal of Neurophysiology*, 1944, 7, pp359–90

3   Olney, J W, et al., 'Excito-toxic mechanisms of epileptic brain damage', *Advances in Neurology*, 1986, 44, pp857–7

4   Mody, I, and Heinemann, U, 'NMDA receptors of dentate gyrus granule cells participate in synaptic transmission following kindling', *Nature*, 1987, 326, pp701–3

5   Anttila, V, Stefansson, H, Kallela, M, Todt, U, Terwindt, G M, *et al.*, 'Towards an understanding of genetic predisposition to migraine', *Nature Genetics*, 2010, 42, pp869–73

6   Lippman, C W, 'Certain hallucinations peculiar to migraine', *Journal of Nervous and Mental Disease*, 1952, 116, pp346–51

7   Lippman, C W, 'Certain hallucinations peculiar to migraine', *Journal of Nervous and Mental Disease*, 1952, 116, p348

8   Lippman, C W, 'Reoccurring dreams in migraine: an aid to diagnosis', *Journal of Nervous and Mental Disease*, 1954, 120, pp273–6

9   Lippman, C W, 'Hallucinations in Migraine', *American Journal of Psychiatry*, 107(11), p856

10  Ibid.

11  Ibid.

12  Podoll, K, Topper, R, Robinson, D, and Sass, H, 'Recurrent dreams as migraine aura symptoms', *Fortschritte der Neurolologie-Psychiatrie*, 2000, 68(4), pp145–9

13  Irwin, H J, 'Out-of-the-body experiences and dream lucidity: empirical

perspectives', in J Gackenbach and S LaBerge (ed.), *Conscious Mind, Sleeping Brain: Perspectives on Lucid Dreaming*, Plenum Press, New York, 1988, p367

14  Jackson, J H, 'Hospital for the epileptic and paralyzed: case illustrating the relation between certain types of migraine and epilepsy', 1985, *Lancet*, 2, pp244–5

15  Pace, B Pm, 'JAMA 100 years ago: migraine and epilepsy', *Journal of the American Medical Association*, 1998, 279, 1126

16  Andermann, F, 'Clinical features of migraine-epilepsy syndrome', in Andermann, F, and Lugaresi, E (eds), *Migraine and Epilepsy*, Butterworth, Oxford (UK), 1987, pp3–30

17  Ibid., p30

18  Andermann, F, 'Migraine-epilepsy relationships', *Epilepsy Research*, 1987, 1(4), pp213–26

19  Marks, D A, and Ehrenberg, B L, 'Migraine-related seizures in adults with epilepsy, with EEG correlation', *Neurology*, 1993, 3, 43(12), pp2476–83

20  Ottman, R, and Lipton, R B, 'Comorbidity of migraine and epilepsy', *Neurology*, Nov 1994, 44 (11), pp2105–10

21  Velioglu, S K, Boz, C, Ozmenoglu, M, 'The impact of migraine on epilepsy: a prospective prognosis study', *Cephalalgia*, 2005, 25(7), pp528–35

22  Ludvigsson, P, Hesdorffer, D, Olafsson, E, Kjartansson, O, and Hauser, W A, 'Migraine with aura is a risk factor for unprovoked seizures in children', *Annals of Neurology*, 2006, 59, pp210–3

23  http://cep.sagepub.com/content/33/9/629.full.pdf+html

24  Ito, M, Adachi, N, Nakamura, F, *et al.*, 'Characteristics of postictal headache in patients with partial epilepsy', *Cephalalgia*, 2004, 24(1), pp23–8

25  Gaustaut, H, 'A new type of epilepsy: benign partial epilepsy of childhood with occipital spike-waves', *Clinical Electroencphalography*, Jan 1982, pp13–22.

26  Barre, M, Hamelin, S, Minotti, L, Kahane, P, and Vercuil, L, 'Epileptic seizures and migraine visual aura: revisiting migralepsy', *Revue Neurologique*, Paris, Mar 2007, 164(3), pp246–52

27  Wei, Y, Ullah, G, and Schiff, S J, 'Unification of Neuronal Spikes, Seizures, and Spreading Depression', *Journal of Neuroscience*, 2014, 34(35): 11733 DOI: 10.1523/JNEUROSCI.0516-14.2014

## Chapter Four: Temporal Lobe Epilepsy (pp62–85)

1  Evans, M, *A Ray of Darkness*, John Calder, London, 1978

2  Ibid., p154

3  Ibid.

4  Evans, M, *Turf or Stone*, Parthian Books, Swansea, 2011, p38

5  Ibid., p124

6  Evans, M, *A Ray of Darkness*, John Calder, London, 1978, p40

7  Ibid., p178

8  Armstrong, K, *The Spiral Staircase*, 2004; Harper Perennial paperback, 2005, p74

9  Ibid., p75

10 Ibid., p205

11 https://www.youtube.com/watch?v=vs0hfhSje9M

12 Ide, M, Mizukami, K, Suzuki, T, and Shiraishi, H, 'A case of temporal lobe epilepsy with improvement of clinical symptoms and single photon emission computed tomography findings after treatment with clonazepam', *Psychiatry and Clinical Neurosciences*, Oct 2000, 54(5), pp595–7

13 Funkhouser, A T, 'The "dream" theory of déjà vu', *Parapsychological Journal of South Africa*, 1983, 4, pp107–23

14 Brown, A S, 'A review of the déjà vu experience', *Psychological Bulletin*, 2003, 129, pp394–413

15 Pick, A, 'On reduplicative paramnesia', *Brain*, 1903, 26, pp242–67

16 Murai, T, and Fukao, K, 'Paramnesic Multiplication of Autobiographical Memory as a Manifestation of Interictal Psychosis', *Psychopathology*, 2003, pp49–51

17 Pethö, B, 'Chronophrenia: a new syndrome in functional psychosis', *Psychopathology*, 1985, 18, pp174–80

18 Ibid., p177

19 Ibid.

20 Ibid., p178

21 Hallowell, M J, *Invizikids: The Curious Enigma of 'Imaginary' Childhood Friends*, Heart of Albion Press, Marlborough, Wiltshire, 2007

22 Dyal, M, *The Boy Nobody Wanted* (unpublished), p27

23 Ibid., p23

24 Ibid., p85

25 Ibid., p110

26 Eliade, Mircea, Shamanism: *Archaic Techniques of Ecstasy*, 1951; Penguin Arkana, London, 1989, p24

27 Ibid., p34

28 Dyal, M, *The Boy Nobody Wanted* (unpublished), p117

29 Mellors, J D, Toone, B K, and Lishman, W A, 'A neuropsychological comparison of schizophrenia and schizophrenia-like psychosis of epilepsy', *Psychological Medicine*, 2000, 30(2), p325

30 Kraepelin, E, *Psychiatrie*, 8th edn, vol.2, Barth, Leipzig, 1910

31 Kraepelin, E, *Dementia Praecox and Paraphrenia*, E & S Livingstone, Edinburgh, 1919, p274

32 Gibbs, F A, and Gibbs, E L, *Atlas of Electroencephalography*, Addison-Wesley, Cambridge, MA, 1952, pp167–9

33 Hill, D, 'EEG in episodic psychotic and psychopathic behaviour: a classification of data', *Electroencephalography and Clinical Neurophysiology*, 1952, vol4, issue 4, pp419–42

34 Slater, E, Beard, A W, and Glithero, E, 'The schizophrenia-like psychosis of epilepsy', *The British Journal of Psychiatry*, 1963, 109, pp95–150

## Chapter Five: Schizophrenia (pp86–96)

1   McGrath, M E, *Schizophrenia Bulletin*, 1984, edn 10, pp 638–40.
2   Gottesman, I I, *Schizophrenia Genesis*, W H Freeman & Co., New York, 1991, p43
3   Ibid.
4   McDonald, N, 'Living With Schizophrenia' in *Consciousness, Brain, States of Awareness and Mysticism*, ed. Goleman, Daniel, and Davidson, R J, Harper Row, New York, 1979
5   Ferguson, M, *The Brain Revolution*, Taplinger Pub. Co., New York, 1973, p226
6   McCreery, C, *Dreams and Psychosis*, Oxford Forum, Oxford (UK), 2008
7   Robbins, P R, *The Psychology of Dreams*, McFarland and Co., Jefferson, NC, 1988
8   Oswald, I, 'Experimental studies of rhythm, anxiety and cerebral vigilance', *Journal of Mental Science*, 1959, 105, p269
9   Stevens, J M, and Darbyshire, A J, 'Shifts along the alert-repose continuum during remission of catatonic "stupor" with amobarbitol", *Psychosomatic Medicine*, 1958, 20, 99–107
10  Douaud, G, Groves, A R, Tamnes, C K, Westlye, L T, Duff, E P *et al.*, 'A brain network links developing, ageing and vulnerability to disease', *Proceedings of the National Academy of Sciences (PNAS)*, Dec 2014, vol.111, no. 49, pp17648–53

## Chapter Six: Alzheimer's Disease (pp98–118)

1   Bickerstaff, E R, 'Basilar artery migraine'
2   http://www.northerneye.co.uk/more-info/lost-in-lilliput
3   Sacks, O, *Hallucinations*, Picador, London, 2012, p6
4   Ibid.
5   Ibid., note 10
6   Ibid., note 12
7   Ibid., p20
8   Ibid., p27
9   Bensimon, G, and Chermat, R, 'Microtubule disruption and cognitive defects: effect of colchicine on learning behavior in rats', *Pharmacology Biochemistry and Behavior*, 1991, 38, pp141–5
10  James, F F, and Dennis, W L, 'Long-term memory: disruption by inhibitors of protein synthesis and cytoplasmic flow, *Pharmacology Biochemistry and Behavior*, 1981, 15, pp289–96
11  Gentleman, S M, *et al.*, 'Quantitative differences in the deposition of beta A4 protein in the sulci and gyri of frontal and temporal isocortex in Alzheimer's disease', *Neuroscience Letters*, 1992, 136(1), pp27–30
12  Chance, S A, Tzotaoli, P M, Vitelli, A, Esiri, M M, Crow, T J, 'The cytoarchitecture of sulcal folding in Herschl's sulcus and the temporal cortex in the normal brain and schizophrenia: lamina thickness and cell density,' *Neurscience Letters*, 2004, 367(3), pp384–8
13  O'Connor, A R, Moulin, C J A, and Cohen, G, *Memory and Consciousness*, https://research-repository.standrews.ac.uk/bitstream/10023/1646/1/O_Connor_et_al_Memory_and_Consciousness_Chapter.pdf
14  Moulin, C J A, Conway, M A, Thompson, R G, James, N, and Jones, R W,

'Disordered memory awareness: recollective confabulation in two cases of persistent déjà vécu', *Neuropsychologia*, 2005, 43(9), pp1362–78

15  Reisberg, B, 'Alzheimer's disease: stages of cognitive decline', *American Journal of Nursing*, 1984, 84, p225

16  Douaud, G, Groves, A R, Tamnes, C K, Westlye, L T, Duff, E P, *et al.*, 'A brain network links developing, ageing and vulnerability to disease', *Proceedings of the National Academy of Sciences (PNAS)*, 2014, vol.111, no.49, pp17648–53

## Chapter Seven: Autism (pp120–139)

1  Kanner, L, and Eisenberg, L, 'Early infantile autism 1943–1955, *American Journal of Orthopsychiatry*, 1956, 26, pp55–65

2  Asperger, H, trans. and anno. Frith, U, 'Autistic psychopathy in childhood' (1944) in Frith, U, *Autism and Asperger Syndrome*, Cambridge University Press, Cambridge (UK), 1991, pp37–92

3  Kanner, L, 'Autistic Disturbances of Affective Contact', *Nervous Child*, 1943, 2, pp175–219

4  Asperger, H, 'Die "Autistischen Psychopathen" im Kindesalter', *Archiv für Psychiatrie und Nervenkrankheiten*, 1944, vol.117, issue 1, pp76–136

5  Grandin, T, *The Way I See It: A Personal Look at Autism and Asperger's*, Future Horizons, Arlington, TX, 2008

6  Bergman, P, and Escalona, S K, 'Unusual sensitivities in very young children', Psychoanalytical Study of the Child, 1949, 3/4, pp333–52

7  Creak, M, 'Schizophrenia syndrome in childhood: progress report of a working party', *Cerebral Palsy Bulletin*, 1961, 3, pp501–504

8  Wing, L, 'The handicaps of autistic children', *Communications*,  June 1972, pp6-8

9  Delcato, C, The Ultimate Stranger: *The Autistic Child*, Academic Therapy Publications, Noveto, CA, 1974

10  Casanova, M F, Buxhoeveden, D P, Switala, A E, and Roy, E, 'Minicolumnar pathology in autism', *Neurology*, 2002, 58, pp428–32

11  Casanova, M F, *Brains of autistic individuals*, International AWARE On-line Conference Papers, 2006

12  Courchesne, E, 'Abnormal early brain development in autism', *Molecular Psychiatry*, 2002, 7, suppl.2, S21–3

13  Courchesne, E, 'Brain development in autism: early overgrowth followed by premature arrest of growth', *Mental Retardation and Developmental Disabilities Research Reviews*, 2004, 10, pp106–11

14  Casanova, M F, 'White matter volume increase and minicolumns in autism,' *Annals of Neurology* 2004, 56, 3, p453

15  Bogdashina, O, *Sensory Perceptual Issues in Autism and Asperger's Syndrome: Different Sensory Experiences, Different Perceptual Worlds*, Jessica Kingsley, London, 2003

16  Williams, D, *Autism: An Inside-Out Approach: An Innovative Look at the Mechanics of 'Autism' and its Developmental Cousins*, Jessica Kingsley, London,1996

17 Williams, D, *Autism and Sensing: The Unlost Instinct*, Jessica Kingsley, London, 1998

18 Ouspensky, P D, *Tertum Organum*, Alfred Knopf, New York, 1981, p258

19 Moorjani, Anita, *Dying To Be Me*, Hay House, London and New York, 2012, p63

20 Walker, N, and Chantelle, J (eds), *You Don't Have Words to Describe What I Experience*, 1994, www.autism

21 Williams, D, *Like Colour to the Blind: Soul Searching and Soul Finding*, Jessica Kingsley London, 1999

22 Stillman, W, *The Autism Prophecies*, New Page Books, NJ, 2010, p141

23 Rawn-Joseph, R E, Gallagher, W H, and Kahn, J, 'Two Brains: One Child: Interhemispheric Information Transfer Deficits and Confabulation in Children Aged 4,7 and 10', *Cortex*, 1984, 20, pp317–31

24 Baron-Cohen, Simon, *Autism and Asperger Syndrome*, Oxford University Press, Oxford (UK), 2008, p2

25 Ibid.

26 'Perception and the Senses', *In Our Time*, 28 Apr 2005, BBC Radio 4

27 Grandin, T, *The Autistic Brain: Exploring the Strength of a Different Kind of Mind*, Rider Books, London, 2014, p70

28 Ibid., p72

29 Ibid., p27

30 Peake, A, *The Daemon: A Guide to Your Extraordinary Secret Self*, Arcturus, London, 2008

31 Grandin, T, *The Autistic Brain: Exploring the Strength of a Different Kind of Mind*, Rider Books, London, 2014, pp78–9

32 Ibid., p79

33 Fleischmann, A, and Fleischmann, C, *Carly's Voice: Breaking through Autism*, Touchstone, New York, 2012

34 Sperry, R, 'Mental Phenomena as Causal Determinants in Brain Function', in Globus, G, *Consciousness and the Brain*, Plenum Press, New York, 1976

35 http://www.mentalhealthamerica.net/conditions/psychosis-schizophrenia

36 http://www.mayoclinic.org/diseases-conditions/childhood-schizophrenia

37 Rapoport, J L, *Childhood Onset of 'Adult' Pathology: Clinical and Research Advances*, American Psychiatric Press, Washington, DC, 2000

38 http://www.schizophrenia.com/family/childszsym.htm

39 'Practice parameters for the assessment and treatment of children, adolescents and adults with autism and other pervasive developmental disorders', *Journal of the American Academy of Child and Adolescent Psychiatry*, 1999, 38(12), 32S–54S

40 Hallowell, M J, 'Jok Zottle and the Invizikids', *Fortean Times*, 2009, T250, p30

41 Hallowell, M J, *Invizikids: The Curious Enigma of 'Imaginary' Childhood Friends*, Heart of Albion Press, Marlborough, Wiltshire, 2007

42 http://www.scientificamerican.com/article/is-there-really-an-autism-epidemic/

43 http://www.cdc.gov/ncbddd/autism/addm.html

## Chapter Eight: Savant Syndrome (pp140–156)

1 Hoffman, E J, 'The idiot savant: a case report and review of explanations', *Mental Retardation*, 1971, 9, pp17–21

2 Rubin, E J, and Monaghan, S, 'Calendar calculation in a multiple-handicapped blind person', *American Journal of Mental Deficiency*, 1965, 70, pp478–85

3 Rimland, B, 'Savant capabilities of autistic children and their cognitive implications', in Serban, G (ed.), *Cognitive Defects in the Development of Mental Illness*, Brunner/Mazel, New York, 1978

4 Treffert, D, *Extraordinary People*, Black Swan, London, 1990, p97

5 Ibid.

6 Snyder, A W, Mulcahy, E, Taylor, J L, Mitchell, D J, Sachdev, P, and Gandevia, S C, 'Savant-like skills exposed in normal people by suppressing the left fronto-temporal lobe', *Journal of Integrative Neuroscience*, Dec 2003, 2(2), pp149–58

7 Treffert, D, *Extraordinary People*, Black Swan, London, 1990

8 Penfield, W, *Mystery of Mind: A Critical Study of Consciousness and the Human Brain*, Princeton University Press, Princeton, NJ, 1975

9 Kanner, L, 'Early Infantile Autism', *Journal of Paediatrics*, 1944, 25, pp200–17

10 Cain, A C, 'Special isolated abilities in severely psychotic young children', *Psychiatry*, 1970, 33, pp137–49

11 Treffert, D, *Extraordinary People*, Black Swan, London, 1990, p98

12 Ibid., p97

13 Rimland, B, 'Savant capabilities of autistic children and their cognitive implications', in Serban, G (ed.), *Cognitive Defects in the Development of Mental Illness*, Brunner/Mazel, New York, 1978

14 Ibid.

15 Treffert, D A, and Christensen, D D, 'Inside the Mind of a Savant', *Scientific American*, Dec 2005, 293, pp108–13

16 Hamburger, V, and Oppenheim, R W, 'Naturally occurring neuronal death in vertebrates', *Neuroscience Commentaries*, 1982, 1 pp39–55

17 Geschwind, N, and Galaburda, A M, *Cerebral Lateralization: Biological Mechanisms, Associations and Pathology*. MIT Press, Cambridge, MA, 1987

18 Waxman, S G , and Geschwind, N, 'Hyperreligiosity in temporal lobe epilepsy: redefining the relationship', *Journal of Nervous Mental Disease*, 1975, 175, pp181–4

19 Ally B, Hussey, E, and Donahue, M, 'A case of hyperthymesia: rethinking the role of the amygdala in autobiographical memory', *Neurocase*, 2012, 19, pp1–16

20 Yakovlev, P I, and Lecours, A R, 'The myelenetic cycles of regional maturation of the brain' in Minkowski, A (ed.), *Regional development of the brain in early life*, Blackwell Scientific, Oxford (UK), 1967), pp3–70

21 Johnstone, J, Galin, D, and Herron, J, 'Choice of handedness measures in studies of hemispheric specialization', *International Journal of Neuroscience*, 1979, 9, pp71–80

22 Rawn-Joseph, R E, Gallagher, W H, and Kahn, J, 'Two Brains: One Child:

Interhemispheric Information Transfer Deficits and Confabulation in Children Aged 4,7 and 10', *Cortex*, 1984, 20, pp317-31

23 Cytowic, R E, 'Synaesthesia: phenomenology and neuropsychology – a review of current knowledge' in *Synaesthesia: Classic and Contemporary Readings*, ed. Baron-Cohen, S, and Harrison, J E, Blackwell, Oxford (UK), 1997, pp17-39

24 Tammet, Daniel, *Born on a Blue Day* (unpublished), p2

25 Sacks, O, *Migraine*, University of California Press, 1970; Picador, London, 1993, p86

26 Details of D Hennacy Powell's 'Telepathy Project' can be found at http://dianehennacypowell.com/consciousness/telepathy-project/

## PART THREE: GLIMPSES THROUGH THE DOORS
### Chapter Nine: The Entranced (pp160-209)

1 http://hubblesite.org/newscenter/archive/releases/2004/10/]/

2 Aragón, J L, Naumis, G G, Bai, M, Torres, M, and Maini, P K, 'Turbulent luminance in impassioned van Gogh paintings', *Journal of Mathematical Imaging and Vision*, 2008, 30, pp275-83

3 http://vangoghletters.org/vg/quickguide.html

4 Markram, H, Rinaldi, T and Markram, K, 'The Intense World Syndrome: An Alternate Hypothesis for Autism', *Frontiers in Neuroscience*, Nov 2007, 1(1), pp77-96

5 Gastaut, H, 'La Maladie de Vincent van Gogh Envisagée a la Lumière des Conceptions Nouvelles sur L'epilepsie Psychomotrice', *Annales Médico-Psychologiques: Revue Psychiatrique: bulletin officiel de la Société Médico-Psychologique*, 1956, pp114-236

6 Van Gogh, V, letter to Théo Van Gogh, 23 Jan 1889

7 Van Gogh, V, letter to Théo Van Gogh, 3 Feb 1889

8 LaPlante, E, *Seized: Temporal Lobe Epilepsy as a Medical, Historical, and Artistic Phenomenon*, 1993; iUniverse, 2000, p6

9 Van Gogh, V, letter to Théo Van Gogh, 31 Dec 1882

10 Quiñones, R D, *Vincent Van Gogh Was Likely a Synesthete*, Sensorium (*Psychology Today*), 26 Aug 2013

11 Ibid.

12 Storch, A, *August Strindberg im Lichte seiner Selbstbiographie*, J F Bergmann-Verlag, 1921

13 Anderson, E W, 'Strindberg's Illness', Psychological Medicine, 1971, 1(2), pp104-17.

14 Monroe, R R, *Creative Brainstorms: The Relationship between Madness and Genius*, Ardent Media, London, 1992, p110

15 Strindberg, A, *Strindberg Plays: 3 'To Damascus' (Introduction)*, Bloomsbury Methuen, 2014, p185

16 Ibid.

17 Heller, Otto, *Prophets of Dissent*, Alfred A Knopf, New York, 1918, pp71-105

18 Strindberg, A, Strindberg Plays: 3 '*To Damascus' (Introduction)*, Bloomsbury

Methuen, 2014, p186

19  Meyer, M, Strindberg: *A Biography*, Secker & Warburg, London, 1985, p128

20  Strindberg, F, *Marriage with a Genius*, Jonathan Cape, London), 1937, pp236–7

21  Engström, A, *August Strindberg og jag*, Albert Bonnier, Stockholm, 1923, p11

22  Strindberg, A, *Inferno*, William Rider & Son, London, 1912, p120

23  Strindberg, A, *Dream Play: Introduction*, 1901

24  Meyer, Michael, *Strindberg: A Biography*, Secker & Warburg, London, 1985, p438

25  Strindberg, A, *Inferno*, William Rider & Son London, 1912, pp172–3

26  Ibid., p263

27  Ibid., p264

28  Radin, DI, 'Unconscious Perception of Future Emotions: An Experiment in Presentiment', *Journal of Scientific Exploration*, 1997, 11(2), pp163–80

29  Binkofski, F, and Block, R A, 'Accelerated Time Experience after Left Frontal Cortex Lesion', *Neurocase*, 1992, vol.2, pp485–93

30  Williams, D, *Nobody Nowhere*, Doubleday, New York, 1992

31  Williams, D, *Nobody Nowhere: The Remarkable Autobiography of an Autistic Girl* (revised edn), Jessica Kingsley, London, pp120–21

32  Ibid., p132

33  Ibid., p16

34  Ibid., p17

35  Williams, D, *Somebody Somewhere*, Doubleday, New York, 1994, p99

36  Ibid., p101

37  Quoted in Stillman, D, *Autism and the God Connection*, Sourcebooks, Naperville, Illinois, p76

38  Ibid., p74

39  Stillman, W, *Autism and the God Connection: Redefining the Autistic Experience through Extraordinary Accounts of Spiritual Giftedness*, Sourcebooks, 2006

40  Williams, D, *Somebody Somewhere*, Doubleday, New York, 1994, p180

41  Ibid., p181

42  La Tourelle, M, *The Gift of Alzheimer's*, Watkins, London, 2015, p38

43  Ibid., p47

44  Ibid., p40

45  Ibid.

46  Ibid., p50

47  Ibid.

48  Ibid., p71

49  Ibid., p50

50  Ibid., p102

51  Ibid., p75

52  Ibid., p174

53  Rusina, R, *et al.*, Neurotoxicity Research, Nov 2011, 20(4), pp329–33

54  Blaurock-Busch, E, *et al.*, *Maedica*, Bucharest, Jan 2012, 7(1), pp38–48

55  La Tourelle, M, *The Gift of Alzheimer's*, Watkins, London, 2015, p180

56  Sacks, O, *The Man Who Mistook His Wife for a Hat*, Picador, London, 1985, p147

57  Ibid., p148

58  La Tourelle, M, *The Gift of Alzheimer's*, Watkins, London, 2015, p194

59  Ibid.

60  Ibid., p59

61  Nahm, M, *et al.*, 'Terminal lucidity: a review and a case collection', *Archives of Gerontology and Geriatrics*, 2011, doi:10.1016/j.archger.2011.06.031

62  Greyson, B, 'Seeing Dead People Not Known to Have Died: "Peak in Darien" Experiences', *Anthropology and Humanism*, 2010, vol.35, issue 2, pp160–61

63  Cobbe, F P, 'The Peak in Darien: The Riddle of Death', *New Quarterly Magazine*, July 1877, 8, pp283–93

64  http://mikegamble.websitetoolbox.com/post?id=93255&trail=15

65  '"Greenbriar" Living on the Threshold: Alzheimer's and the Elderly', www.planetwavesweekly.com/parallel/articles/alzheimer.html

66  http://deoxy.org/timemind.htm

67  Ibid.

68  http://deoxy.org/h_vnotes.htm

69  http://www.newsweek.com/proof-heaven-doctors-experience-afterlife-65327

70  Hayes, C (ed.), *Tripping: An Anthology of True-life Psychedelic Adventures*, Arkana, London, 1999

71  Mach, R H, Smith, C R, and Childers, S, R, 'Ibogaine possesses a selective affinity for sigma 2 receptors,' *Life Sciences*, 1995, 57(4), pp57–62

72  DiMaggio, DA, Contreras, PC, *et al.*, 'Biological and Chemical Characterization of the Endopsychosins: Distinct Ligands for PCP and Sigma Sites. Sigma and Phencyclidine-Like Compounds as Molecular Probes in Biology', in Domino, E F, and Kamenka, J-M (eds), *Sigma and Phencylidine-like Compounds as Molecular Probes in Biology*, NPP Books, Ann Arbor, MI, 1988, pp157–71

73  Jansen, K L R, 'Neuroscience and the near-death experience: roles for the NMDA-PCP receptor, the sigma receptor and endopsychosins', *Medical Hypotheses*, 1990, 31, pp25–9

74  Grinspoon, L, and Bakalar, S, *Psychedelic Drugs Reconsidered*, Basic Books, New York, 1981

75  Quirion, R, *et al.*, 'Evidence for an endogenous peptide ligand for the phencyclidine receptor', *Peptides*, 1984, 5, pp967–77

76  Carr, D B, 'Endorphins at the approach of death', *Lancet*, 1981, 1, p390

77  Carr, D B, 'On the evolving neurobiology of the near death experience', *Journal of Near Death Studies*, 1989, 7, pp251–4

78  Persinger, M, and Makarec, K, 'Temporal lobe epileptic signs and correlative behaviours displayed by normal populations', *Journal of General Psychology*, 1987, 114, pp179–95

79  Saavedra-Aguilar, J, and Gomez-Jeria, J, 'A neurobiological model of near-death experiences', *Journal of Near-Death Studies*, 1989, 7, pp205–22

80  DiMaggio, D A, Contreras, P C, *et al.*, *Biological and Chemical Characterization of the Endopsychosins: Distinct Ligands for PCP and Sigma Sites. Sigma and*

*Phencyclidine-Like Compounds as Molecular Probes in Biology*, NPP Books, Ann Arbor, MI, 1988

81  Fontanilla, D, Johannessen, M, Hajiipour, A R, Cozzi, N V, Jackson, M B, and Ruoho, A E, 'The Hallucinogen N,N-Dimethyltryptamine (DMT) Is an Endogenous Sigma-1 Receptor Regulator', *Science*, 2009, vol.323, no.5916, pp934–7

82  Szabo A, Kovacs, A, Frecska, E, Rajnavolgyi, E, 'Psychedelic N,N-Dimethyltryptamine and 5-Methoxy-N,N-Dimethyltryptamine Modulate Innate and Adaptive Inflammatory Responses through the Sigma-1 Receptor of Human Monocyte-Derived Dendritic Cells', *PLoS (Public Library of Science) ONE*, Aug 2014, 9(8), e106533

83  Barker, S A, Borjigin, J, Lomnicka, I, and Strassman, R, 'LC/MS/MS analysis of the endogenous dimethyltryptamine hallucinogens, their precursors, and major metabolites in rat pineal gland microdialysate', *Biomedical Chromatography*, 2013, 27(12), pp1690–700

84  Araújo, D B, Ribeiro, S, Cecchi, G A *et al.*, 'Seeing with the eyes shut: neural basis of enhanced imagery following ayahuasca ingestion, *Human Brain Mapping*, 16 Sep 2011, Wiley-Liss, DOI: 10.1002/hbm.21381

## Conclusion: What Is on the Other Side? (pp210–241)

1  Wheeler, J A, and Ford, K, Geons, *Black Holes, and Quantum Foam*, W W Norton & Co., 1998

2  McIlwain, H, and Bachelard, H S, *Biochemistry and the Central Nervous System*, Churchill Livingstone, London, 1985

3  Wojtowicz, J M, 'Adult neurogenesis. From circuits to models', *Behavioural Brain Research*, 14 Feb 2012, 227(2), pp490–6

4  Wagner, D E, Wang, I E, and Raddien, P W, 'Clonogenic Neoblasts Are Pluripotent Adult Stem Cells That Underlie Planarian Regeneration', *Science*, 2011, vol.332, no.6031, pp811–16

5  Shomrat, T, and Levin, M, 'An automated training paradigm reveals long-term memory in planarians and its persistence through head regeneration', *Journal of Experimental Biology*, 2013, 216, pp3799–810

6  http://voices.nationalgeographic.com/2013/07/16/decapitated-worms-regrow-heads-keep-old-memories/

7  Frost, S, Kanagasingam, Y, Macauley, L, *et al.*, 'Retinal amyloid fluorescence imaging predicts cerebral amyloid burden and Alzheimer's disease', *Alzheimer's & Dementia*, 2014, vol.10, issue 4, pp234–5

8  Pandi-Perumal, S R, Zisapel, N, Srinivasan, V, Cardinali, D P, 'Melatonin and sleep in aging population', *Experimental Gerontology*, Dec 2005, 40(12), pp911–25

9  Srinivasan, V, Pandi-Perumal, SR, Cardinali, DP, Poeggeler, B, and Hardeland, R, 'Melatonin in Alzheimer's disease and other neurodegenerative disorders', *Behavioural and Brain Functions*, May 2006, 4, pp2–15

10  Mahlberg, R, Walther, S, Kalus, P, Bohner, G, Haedel, S, Reischies, FM, Kühl, KP, Hellweg, R, and Kunz, D, 'Pineal calcification in Alzheimer's disease: an *in*

*vivo* study using computed tomography', *Neurobiology of Aging*, Feb 2008, 29(2), pp203–9

11  http://metatoninresearch.org/

12  Fontanilla, D, Johannessen, M, Hajiipour, A R, Cozzi, N V, Jackson, M B, and Ruoho, A E, 'The Hallucinogen N,N-Dimethyltryptamine (DMT) Is an Endogenous Sigma-1 Receptor Regulator', *Science*, 2009, vol.323, no.5916, pp934–7

13  Szabo, A, Kovacs, A, Frecska, E, and Rajnavolgyi, E, 'Psychedelic N,N-Dimethyltryptamine and 5-Methoxy-N,N-Dimethyltryptamine Modulate Innate and Adaptive Inflammatory Responses through the Sigma-1 Receptor of Human Monocyte-Derived Dendritic Cells', PLoS *(Public Library of Science)* ONE, Aug 2104, 9(8), e106533

14  Barker, S A, Borjigin, J, Lomnicka, I and Strassman, R,'LC/MS/MS analysis of the endogenous dimethyltryptamine hallucinogens, their precursors, and major metabolites in rat pineal gland microdialysate', *Biomedical Chromatography*, 2013, 27(12), pp1690–700

15  http://www.simulation-argument.com/simulation.html

16  http://www.phys.huji.ac.il/~bekenste/Holographic_Univ.pdf

17  Hogan, Craig, 'Now Broadcasting in Planck Definition', *2014, arXiv:1307.2283 [quant-ph] FERMILAB-PUB-13-685-A*

18  Hawking, S W, and Hertog, Thomas, 'Populating the landscape: A top-down approach', *Physical Review*, 23 Jun 2006, D73, 123527 (http://journals.aps.org/prd/abstract/10.1103/PhysRevD.73.123527)

19  Mead, G R S, *Fragments of a Faith Forgotten*, 1900; 2nd edn, Theosophical Publishing Society, London and Benares, 1906, p475

20  http://www.biomed.ee.ethz.ch/research/tnu/teaching/schizophrenia/iglesiasdagt

21  Kuffler, S W, and Potter, D D, 'Glia in the leech central nervous system: Physiological properties and neuron-glia relationship', *Journal of Neurophysiology*, 1964, vol.27, no.2, pp290–320

22  Cornell-Bell, A H, Finkbeiner, S M, Cooper, M S, and Smith, S J, 'Glutamate induces calcium waves in cultured astrocytes: long-range glial signaling', *Science*, 1990, 247, pp470–73

23  Pereira, A, and Furlan, F A, 'Astrocytes and human cognition: modeling information integration and modulation of neuronal activity,' *Progress in Neurobiology*, 2010, vol.32 (3). pp405–20

24  Ibid.

25  Koob, A, *The Root of Thought: Unlocking Glia – The Brain Cell That Will Help Us Sharpen Our Wits, Heal Injury, and Treat Brain Disease,'* Pearson FT Press, NJ, p200

26  Koob, A, 'The Root of Thought: What Do Glial Cells Do?', *Scientific American*, 27 October 27, 2009

27  Galilei, Galileo, *Dialogue Concerning The Two World Systems*, University of California Press, Berkeley, CA, 1953, p397

28  Shanon, Benny, *The Antipodes of the Mind*, Oxford University Press, Oxford (UK), 2010, frontispiece

# Bibliography

Armstrong, K, *The Spiral Staircase*, Harper Perennial, 2004

Baron-Cohen, Simon, *Autism and Asperger Syndrome*, Oxford University Press, Oxford (UK), 2008

Bogdashina, O, *Sensory Perceptual Issues in Autism and Asperger's Syndrome: Different Sensory Experiences, Different Perceptual Worlds*, Jessica Kingsley, London, 2003

Delcato, C, *The Ultimate Stranger: The Autistic Child*, Academic Therapy Publications, Noveto, CA, 1974

Eliade, Mircea, *Shamanism: Archaic Techniques of Ecstasy*, Penguin Arkana, London, 1989

Evans, M, *A Ray of Darkness*, John Calder, London, 1978

Fleischmann, A, and Fleischmann, C, *Carly's Voice: Breaking through Autism*, Touchstone, New York, 2012

Geschwind, N, and Galaburda, A M, *Cerebral Lateralization: Biological Mechanisms, Associations and Pathology*. MIT Press, Cambridge, MA, 1987

Gottesman, I I, *Schizophrenia Genesis*, W H Freeman & Co., New York, 1991

Grandin, T, *The Autistic Brain: Exploring the Strength of a Different Kind of Mind*, Rider Books, London, 2014

Green, C, and McCreery, C, *Apparitions*, Hamish Hamilton, London, 1975

Grinspoon, L, and Bakalar, S, *Psychedelic Drugs Reconsidered*, Basic Books, New York, 1981

Hallowell, M J, *Invizikids: The Curious Enigma of 'Imaginary' Childhood Friends*, Heart of Albion Press, Marlborough, Wiltshire, 2007

Hameroff, S R, and Penrose, R, *Orchestrated Reduction of Quantum Coherence in Brain Micro-tubules: A Model for Consciousness*, MIT Press, Cambridge, MA,1996

Huxley, A, *The Doors of Perception*, Chatto & Windus, London, 1954; Random House, 2010

Koob, A, *The Root of Thought: Unlocking Glia – The Brain Cell That Will Help Us Sharpen Our Wits, Heal Injury, and Treat Brain Disease,'* Pearson FT Press, New Jersey, 2009

La Tourelle, M, *The Gift of Alzheimer's*, Watkins, London, 2015

Monroe, R R, *Creative Brainstorms: The Relationship between Madness and Genius*, Ardent Media, London, 1992

Moorjani, Anita, *Dying To Be Me*, Hay House, London, 2012

Ouspensky, P D, *Tertum Organum*, Alfred Knopf, New York, 1981

Peake, A, *Is There Life After Death?: The Extraordinary Science of What Happens When We Die*, Arcturus, London, 2006

– *The Daemon: A Guide to Your Extraordinary Secret Self*, Arcturus, London, 2008

– *The Infinite Mindfield*, Watkins, London, 2013

– *The Labyrinth of Time*, Arcturus, London, 2010

– *The Out-of-Body Experience*, Watkins, London, 2011

Penfield, W, *Mystery of Mind: A Critical Study of Consciousness and the Human Brain*, Princeton University Press, Princeton, NJ, 1975

Ramachandran, V S, and Blakeslee, S, *Phantoms in the Brain: Human Nature and the Architecture of the Mind*, Fourth Estate, London, 1998

Sacks, O, *Migraine*, Picador, London, 1993

– *The Man Who Mistook His Wife for a Hat*, Picador, London, 1985

Shanon, Benny, *The Antipodes of the Mind*, Oxford University Press, Oxford (UK), 2010

Stillman, W, *The Autism Prophesies*, New Page Books, New Jersey, 2010

Strassman, R, *DMT: The Spirit Molecule*, Inner Traditions, Rochester (Vermont), 2001

Treffert, D, *Extraordinary People*, Black Swan, London, 1990

Williams, D, *Autism: An Inside-Out Approach: An Innovative Look at the Mechanics of 'Autism' and its Developmental Cousins*, Jessica Kingsley, London, 1996

– *Autism and Sensing: The Unlost Instinct*, Jessica Kingsley, London, 1998

– *Like Colour to the Blind: Soul Searching and Soul Finding*, Jessica Kingsley, London, 1999

– *Nobody Nowhere: The Remarkable Autobiography of an Autistic Girl* (revised edn), Jessica Kingsley, London, 1998

– *Somebody Somewhere*, Doubleday, New York, 1994

Wheeler, J A, and Ford, K, *Geons, Black Holes, and Quantum Foam*, W W Norton & Co., New York, 1998

-aura.com/content/e27891/e27265/e26585/e49268/e49335/index_en.html', Lancet, 1961, 1:15.net/infoparent.html-children-and-youth/basics/symptoms/con-20029260.com/family/childszsym.htm-epidemic/

# Index